Tro

Troublemakers

The Struggle for Environmental Justice in Scotland

Kevin Dunion

Edinburgh University Press

© Kevin Dunion, 2003

Edinburgh University Press Ltd
22 George Square, Edinburgh

Typeset in Minion by
Pioneer Associates, Perthshire, and
printed and bound in Great Britain by
CPI, UK

A CIP Record for this book is available from the British Library

ISBN 0 7486 1781 7 (paperback)

Contents

For Gary, Steven and Shelley

Preface

THIS BOOK has been percolating throughout my eleven years with Friends of the Earth and I have benefited enormously from speaking to the many community activists with whom we have worked during that time. I would like to thank especially Ann Colman, Joan Higginson, Rosie Kane, Cathy McCormack, Stewart McKenna, Gus MacArthur and Ian Lewis.

I also had the privilege of discussing issues of sustainable development and environmental justice with many colleagues in Friends of the Earth International. In particular I would like to thank Joachim Spangenberg, Martin Rocholl and Daniel Mittler from Germany; Bobby Peek in South Africa; Karin Nansen in Uruguay; Leslie Fields, USA; Teo Wams, John Hontelez and the much-missed Manus van Brakel from the Netherlands.

Inspiration and valuable insights have come from Wolfgang Sachs, Juan Martinez Alier, Mathis Wackernagel, Maria Adebowale and Sunita Narain. Bob Bullard crossed the Atlantic at our invitation and immediately connected Scotland with the environmental justice movement.

My colleagues at Friends of the Earth Scotland have been immensely supportive. Siobhan Samson is the archetypal troublemaker and went from being a local activist to a key member of staff. Eurig Scandrett and Tara O' Leary have pushed notes of helpful references, and critical comments, in my direction. Dan Barlow and Lang Banks have enthusiastically searched out statistics, press clippings and photographs. Kirstie Shirra organised the access to information survey of public bodies. Hazel Petherick turned torrents of words into text.

Many people in Scotland have allowed me to talk to them

about the issues in this book, and some even took the time to comment on early drafts. I am grateful in particular to Dr Margaret Hannah, Chris Norman, and Professor Jeremy Rowan-Robinson.

Professor John Fairley of Strathclyde University encouraged me to get thoughts on to paper, and the Board of Friends of the Earth Scotland enthusiastically backed the concept and the book. Dr Mark Huxham, in particular, provided detailed comments, while Fred Edwards and Lesley Clare have been unflagging in support.

A colleague, who asked how the book was getting on, said that she envied me being able to sit in a garden scribbling down thoughts. If only it was like that. So my heartfelt thanks to Linda, who has had to put up with a laptop being the focus of life this year.

Kevin Dunion
December 2002

Introduction – Trailing across Dirty Scotland

IF I ASKED you to imagine going for a walk in Scotland, it is fair to assume that in your mind's eye there will immediately be pictures of rugged Highland scenery, or of Argyllshire trails which picturesquely skirt lochs, and wander through forests. It is the very image of Scotland – natural and contemplative, wildness, if not wild land. But as we all should know by now, it is an artificial landscape, showing the lasting effects of human exploitation. Even back in the eighteenth century when Johnson and Boswell made their much-retraced journey, Johnson noted that 'A tree might be a show in Scotland as a horse in Venice.'[1]

Yet though denuded hills are evidence of deforestation and overgrazing, they still have a pleasing aesthetic, as many writers and tourists have appreciated. This is demarcated countryside, unspoilt, protected by wildlife and landscape designations and promoted as our natural heritage. This suggests that there other parts of Scotland which are spoilt, lacking (or, rather, little deserving) protection and exploited beyond recognition.

Imagining a walk in that environment means breaking a new route over well-worn ground, opening up the Dirty Scotland Trail. Set off from the west, from somewhere on the Ayrshire coast, maybe from Largs, with an ice cream from the world-famous Nardini's. A surreal place to start, looking down at a beach which does not exist. Largs beach is not designated by the government in Scotland as a bathing beach, so those people you see in the summer splashing about are a figment of your imagination. By not designating it, the beach does not have to

1

meet European bathing water quality standards, which is just as well, as the coastline of Ayrshire, affected by sewage discharge and effluent coming down the river from farms, fails to meet the necessary standards.

As a destination, for pleasing symmetry, we could head to the opposite coast, to Leven in Fife, where I used to go on my holidays as a child. There is a promenade, a caravan site and great bird life – the area is now protected under European legislation. But that long stretch of sand with the ugly big power station at the end is not a recognised bathing beach either.

Moving inland, the countryside around here is actually rather pretty, even in the coalfields of Scotland, which makes the opencast mines pockmarking Ayrshire and South Lanarkshire so intrusive. Yellow vehicles are heard beeping in reverse down in the excavations. With the right timing, you'll get to hear the detonations as blasting rips up the coal. We don't do deep mining in Scotland anymore.

One of the fabled placenames around here is Tillietudlem. It has such an *Alice in Wonderland* resonance, that the local authority has to keep replacing the village nameplate as tourists purloin it as a souvenir. Michael Russell, the man said to be responsible for persuading the Council that the 'rickle of a dozen or so houses on the edge of a hill'[2] deserved to be marked by roadside signs, went on to become a member of the Scottish Parliament. Before he did so, he meandered around Scotland, musing on our condition.

His views on industrial Lanarkshire are frank: 'There is something dirty about Lanarkshire roads. Even the country lanes have a sort of grimy edge to them . . . It takes no leap of imagination to surmise that beneath these fields lies the detritus of the industrial revolution, decayed and collapsed but lurking just below the soil like the ruins of a pre-nuclear holocaust civilisation.'[3]

There is plenty of evidence of that, and it's not always hidden. By heading north we encounter the chromium-contaminated land of Rutherglen and Cambuslang, where people woke up one morning to find signs on their parks saying, 'Contaminated land – Keep out.' Soil-remediation work is promised when the next big motorway project cuts through these communities. The M74 extension, a five-mile stretch of road, 50 feet above the ground, will be, at £250 million, the most expensive ever built in Scotland. Perched on concrete stilts, pile-driven into contaminated land, it will bulldoze its way through areas where maybe half the households have no access to a car.

Included among them are some of the 700,000 homes in Scotland that are too expensive for the families to keep warm. Inadequate heating systems are drained of energy by poor insulation, ill-fitting windows and doors which suck out the warmth. Curtains at the windows do a better job retaining the heat than the walls do. Mould climbs up wallpaper.

There is much to detain a quizzical visitor to Glasgow. On a rainy afternoon time can be whiled away trying to understand the traffic-management plans for the city. These seem to indicate that, even after traffic-reduction measures have been implemented, traffic volumes will rise faster over the next twenty years than if no measures were put in place.

But we have got to head up towards Airdrie, and into the countryside around Greengairs. When Edwin Muir, the celebrated Scottish poet, came here in the 1930s, he said, 'It was as if in this region nature no longer breathed, or gave out at most the chill dank mineral breath of coal and iron.'[4]

Even now, if you have only a day to spend looking for evidence of environmental injustice in Scotland this is the place to come. You can't miss it. The landfill sites, the opencast mines, the derelict land. Not long ago, a road from Greengairs, which parents used to get kids to school, collapsed when one of the mining companies got greedy and excavated right underneath it. Hang around and you might get to experience the smell of lorry loads of rotting fish being dumped, or see a cargo of pigs' heads unexpectedly turning up on the weighbridge. This is wild west country – there is probably a greater concentration in this area of companies that have been prosecuted for environmental crimes than in any other part of Scotland.

Others, who have carried a notebook on their travels through here, have remarked on the industrial landscape of the central Lowlands. 'It is a grey and littered countryside that heavy industry has blasted, and all the more depressing now that industry has been "rationalised" leaving a litter of abandoned works, grass-grown bings and yards, rusty iron and battered notice-boards behind.'[5] This is not a recent commentary but, like Muir's, a view from the 1930s – Scotland as seen by George Blake. In the following year Blake wrote *The Shipbuilders*, which 'explored the social and psychological impact of industrial decline and depression'.[6]

The legacy of the industrial revolution is long lasting and the process of development and decline is cyclical. Cross into West Lothian, and look over to Bathgate. There are the grass-grown monuments to past industrial glories. West Lothian's shale bings are pink pyramids which mark George 'Paraffin' Young's pioneering extraction of oil from shale and coal, which eventually led to Scots being involved in oil production across the globe. The shale works were followed by an ill-fated car and truck plant, and then optimism flared and guttered with the fortunes of globalised sunrise micro-electronic industry.

However, it would be a mistake to characterise central Scotland as some kind of sacrifice zone. That may have been how it was treated in the past, and some would still approach development on that basis. Yet the surrounding countryside has a surprising amount of biodiversity. In East Ayrshire the moorlands are important sites for protected species such as hen harriers. The opencast companies there have been at the forefront of trying to stop the land being designated as a site of special scientific interest. People walking up on the higher watersheds will be among merlin, peregrine, curlew and short-eared owl. Nature adapts itself to, and colonises, even industrial landscapes. The endemic orchid Young's helleborine is to be found only on bings and mineral spoil heaps.

Up by Bo'ness is Avon Gorge, a site of special scientific interest which borders rolling farmland, within which are the remnants of the second-century Roman Antonine wall. Beyond rises the impressive twentieth-century industrial architecture of the Grangemouth petrochemical complex. The transnational companies on site, such as Zeneca and BP, are at the forefront of globalisation. In the 1990s there were plans to tear up the fields and cut through the Roman wall to create a huge toxic-waste dump, after earlier plans for an incinerator were opposed. The community around here thought it had fought off the dump, but there is talk of a new application.

Over the Forth by Kincardine Bridge, the road to take goes past Longannet Power Station. It is now entirely dependent on opencast and imported coal after the catastrophic flooding in 2002 of the last deep mine which used to directly feed it. Not far from here is historic Culross, where Sir George Carnock sunk two mine shafts, one emerging on an artificial island in the Forth, which allowed ships to be loaded directly. It too closed after being inundated by flood water, but that happened way back in 1625.

On towards Rosyth, where the naval dockyard is rumoured to be earmarked as the final resting place of nuclear-powered submarines. There is a history of ship breaking in these parts – along by Inverkeithing sections of the foreshore were made radioactive by the fluorescent paints from ships' dials.

Further along the coast is Burntisland and the Alcan aluminium works. After eighty-five years of operation the company closed in November 2002, with the loss of nearly 400 jobs. It specialised in aluminium-based chemicals, which were used in toothpastes and fire retardants. In Scotland, where almost everything else is discarded, aluminium cans are one of the few materials that are successfully collected for recycling. It is not well known, however, that when the aluminium industry feared that the effects of can recycling and the making of light-weight materials would affect their business, Alcoa's head, Paul O'Neill managed to persuade the US government to permit an aluminium cartel, which kept prices artificially high. O'Neill became US Secretary of the Treasury.[7]

Anyway that's an economic and geographical digression, as we are not going in that direction. Detour instead north up the

M90 motorway, against the flow of the commuters who daily pour over the Forth Bridge into the congested streets of Edinburgh. A park-and-ride scheme has been established by Inverkeithing. Frustratingly, though, the queues for the bridge often tail so far back as to block the access to the slip road for the park and ride.

Approaching the Halbeath interchange, a common species of Scottish fauna – the white elephant – can be found. It's the factory built for the Korean giant Hyundai to its specification, close to a motorway (although far from public transport), with sophisticated, and expensive, water-treatment facilities. It cost £2.4 billion, more than five times the cost of the Scottish Parliament building, but the Asian crisis meant the company never occupied the site. Eventually Motorola said it would take it over, which is why its sign adorns the contours of the expensively landscaped mounds, hiding the site from view. But the US giant has decided to pull out of Scotland as well.

Turning east again, past Cowdenbeath and Lochgelly, is another of Scotland's 'what shall we do with it?' holes in the ground. At one time the former Westfield opencast mine's excavations gouged down to 215 metres, the kind of depth that deep mines would have been worked, even in the relatively recent past. The local people were promised that the site would be rehabilitated but they were less than impressed when the scheme involved annually importing 500,000 tonnes of waste from across Scotland. Fife only produces 200,000 tonnes of its own. The plans were for a state of the art materials recovery plant which envisioned high levels of recycling. But the planning application also left open the prospect of landfilling, if the market did not appear for the recovered materials. The company's assurances were received sceptically by the local people, among whom trust was in short supply.

Skirting past Glenrothes New Town, it is noteworthy that you can get trains to two stations that carry its name. However, neither are in the town itself, which was built with little thought for public transport. I once put my kids on a train to Glenrothes, intending them to go to Markinch, but they ended up in the other Glenrothes station, which is really Thornton.

The trail crosses to Methil, if only because it is immortalised in the Proclaimers' anthem for the lost economy of Scotland, 'Bathgate no more, Methil no more...' Once the busiest coal port in Scotland, the docks cling on to oil-rig work for the North Sea. The chimney of Methil power station marks our journey's end, as we step down on to Leven's ghost beach.

This is an imaginary journey – it is a journey of images. But what can it tell us of Scotland? It confronts us with the dilemma of current development. There is the evidence of the branch economy closures, while we are still determined to find a niche in a globalised economy. There is nostalgia for our great industrial heyday, for which we continue to pick up the bill, due to our inheritance of pollution and contamination. The route travels over and past what are euphemistically named brownfield sites, which everyone agrees we should develop before ruining more green field. But what about the communities living nearby who face a succession of polluting, ugly activities?

To know what it really tells us about living along the Dirty Scotland Trail we would need to listen to the people who live there. They want jobs but do not necessarily want that to be at the expense of their lived environment. Even though their bits of countryside may not have national significance, local green space and access to nature matters to people. Just because this part of Scotland is used to pollution and industrial activity does not mean that the people who live there are unconcerned about emissions, noise and traffic movements. In fact, they have greater experience than most of operational standards promised and not met. They want environmental rights to be upheld, and they want the cumulative impact of polluting activities to be taken into account by decision-takers. Decisions are taken for them but which do not sufficiently reflect or consider their experiences and preferences.

This book is borne from the experiences of some of those people in Scotland, who are taking the trouble to make their claim of environmental justice heard.

Notes

1. Johnson, *A Journey to the Western Islands of Scotland*, p. 9.
2. Russell, *In Waiting*, p. 72.
3. Ibid. p. 71.
4. Ibid. p. 71.
5. Blake, *The Heart of Scotland*, p. 44.
6. Keay and Keay, *Collins Encyclopaedia of Scotland*, p. 86.
7. Stiglitz, *Globalization and its Discontents*, p. 172. O'Neill resigned from the US Treasury in December 2002.

1

Environmental Justice – Rights, Decency and Fairness

O N A BRIGHT blustery February day in 2002, Scotland's First Minister travelled back to Edinburgh, having spent the morning meeting with some people who had told him what it was like to live next to opencast mines and landfill sites.

Gathered waiting for him were Scotland's decision-takers from public agencies, local authorities, businesses and environment groups. On such occasions they had been used to hearing political leaders praise their efforts in bringing about an overall improvement in Scotland's air and water quality. Even when there had been ministerial exhortations for a greater investment in cutting waste and emissions, these had been couched in emollient rather than critical language, emphasising the tempting prospect of saving money as well as, incidentally, safeguarding the environment.

What they heard this time was different. Jack McConnell had already surprised political commentators by deciding to make his first policy speech on environmental issues. Even more unexpectedly he took the opportunity to sanction the concept of environmental justice, with words that had the audience shifting in its seats:

Too often the environment is dismissed as the concern of those who are not confronted with bread and butter issues. But the reality is the people who have the most urgent environmental concerns in Scotland are those who cope daily with the consequences of a poor quality of life, and live in a rotten environment, close to industrial pollution, plagued by vehicle emissions, streets filled by litter and walls covered in graffiti. This is true for Scotland and also true elsewhere in the world. These are circumstances which would not be acceptable to better off communities in our society, and those who have to endure such environments in which to bring up a family, or grow old themselves are being denied environmental justice.[1]

The implications of this message were uncomfortable for some of those present, suggesting that not only had they failed to focus on the lived environment of Scotland's urban communities but also that their decisions over the years may even have exacerbated the conditions confronted by the poor in those communities.

Environmental justice would be an entirely new concept for most of the audience, leaving them wondering how it had secured such prominence. After all, there appears to be little academic research into environmental justice in Scotland. We still urgently need to examine data, to establish whether or not, in certain geographical locations and for a range of activities, poorer people are disproportionately exposed to pollutants. Perhaps more studies will look at the health consequences, if any, of such exposures. More importantly, we need to consider the cumulative impact with other aspects of a poor quality of life. (In so doing, it should become clear that the process and nature of research is in itself an environmental justice issue. Who carries it out, for what purpose, and whether or not it is framed by reference to the concerns of those who are the subject of research affect the results and the acceptance of those results.)

Even without this data, however, I suggest that environmental injustice exists in Scotland. To recognise its occurrence needs a definition, applicable to our circumstances. It is easier to define where injustice exists and requires to be rectified than to suggest a circumstance where justice prevails. In so doing we have to encompass the many circumstances where grievances are experienced. In Scotland we have to address a variety of deficiencies, not just the most grotesque. If we confine the environmental justice agenda to dealing with only those who are wilfully exposed to pollution, or denied their rights to the point of actual harm, then we ignore or excuse actions (or more often failures to act) that many ordinary people experience as unfair or unreasonable and that undermine their quality of life.

It is important to recognise that environmental justice is not just about the illegality of actions. Some legal groups rightly stress the need to secure better provision for afflicted communities to be able to secure redress. However, the concept goes beyond legalistic confines, to encompass a sense of fairness. We are well used now in Scotland to a concept of social justice which lies at the heart of the Scottish Executive's programme for Scotland. This has entered into the lexicon of modern-day politics without much concern for establishing a rigorous definition or scope of the term. However, at a United Kingdom level, the Commission on Social Justice, in articulating what it felt were the principles of social justice, recommended that 'we must recognise that although not all inequalities are unjust, unjust inequalities should be reduced and where possible eliminated'.[2] Clearly by this they did not mean inequalities which arose out of breaches of legislation but those which offend societal norms and expectations of fairness. So too with environmental justice.

Injustice will be experienced not just as the result of a deliberate or malevolent decision but also as the consequence of a careless or unwitting approach to policies. It will be experienced as a result of a single exposure to illegal pollution or as the cumulative impact of many individually legal, but undesirable, activities. The notion of justice will encompass demands for new rights but also the insistence that existing rights are enforced. It will expect action from authorities yet also challenge patronage.

So, from the perspective of present-day Scotland I propose the following definition: people perceive environmental injustice when authorities fail to afford or uphold rights; where people are unable adequately to participate in the decision-making processes which affect them and where means of redress are inaccessible. In particular, environmental injustice is experienced as a result of practices or policies which, intentionally or unintentionally, disparately impact on the living conditions of people in low-income groups.

My purpose is to write as someone who has been a protagonist not just an observer in campaigns for environmental justice. I sympathise with those who are classified as troublemakers, not because their fears or attitudes are always justified but because they are confronted by a system which has created a culture to cope with and often exclude their protestations. Deficiencies in the professional preoccupation with sound science, cost–benefit analysis and property rights are compounded by a sometimes intimidatingly legalistic approach to resolving disputes and by the exercise of patronage as to what is in the public interest.

For some time I have believed that it is mistaken that Scottish politicians, particularly those purporting to be on the Left, should adopt a muscularly dismissive approach to environmentalism, to the detriment of those whose interests they so often claim to naturally represent. It was almost a badge of being real man or woman of the people to depict environmentalism in the manner of the Labour cabinet minister Tony Crosland, who once said, 'the conservationist lobby... is hostile to growth and indifferent to the needs of ordinary people. It has manifestly a class bias and reflects a set of middle and upper class value judgments.'[3]

It still suits some politicians to depict a crude division between their rugged real-life pragmatism rooted in providing for the immediate economic needs of the disadvantaged with the dreamy idealism of those who are preoccupied with the legacy for future generations. Environmentalists are regularly caricatured as tree huggers, as if they were sentimentally more concerned with nature than people. It is an accusation that comes from left and right and from both urban and rural sources. 'The right wing settles into a long dirty campaign against environmentalism' feigning 'an ironic certainty that strong environmental warnings are only apocalyptic fearmongering or worse a neobolshevik tree-hugging hysteria'.[4]

Others suggest that somehow environmentalists have the middle-class luxury of concerning themselves with protecting nature while ordinary people have simply got to make ends meet. A fishermen's leader from the Shetland Islands has characterised it as 'the school educated fishermen against the university educated tree huggers'.[5] A *Daily Mail* journalist deployed this stale allusion when describing the community activists who enrolled in Scotland's first ever course on environmental justice, saying, 'they are widely parodied for their woolly jumpers and their occasional public display of affection for trees'.[6] A lazy ignorance lies behind the snickering reference. Yet even a mainstream conservation leader such as Robert Napier, the Chief Executive of WWF, has been known to protest, 'we are not a bunch of tree-hugging environmentalists' to prove their hard-headedness.[7]

Let us get this one out of the way once and for all. Far from being middle class, the real tree huggers were not even school educated. Nature was not a playground but was the bread and butter of their livelihoods. They stood in the way of those who saw the environment as irrelevant or as a source of cheap raw materials to be plundered. Stop thinking of Afghan-coated hippies embracing trees as played out in a recent TV advertising campaign for an internet provider. Think instead of ordinary village women in northern India, wondering what they could do to stop commercial loggers and sports-goods manufacturers from felling the trees which grew on the Himalayan mountain slopes. They knew that the loss of trees made the floods which afflicted them much worse. The women were outraged that the forest, which they regarded as a common resource essential to their livelihoods, providing fodder for animals, fuelwood for cooking, timber for their dwellings, and fruits for their diet, was being turned into private property and auctioned off. Government officials pursued a tree-planting programme under which the felled oaks were replaced by pine, which did not substitute for the loss of a complex forest. Getting nowhere with arguing and pleading, the women banded together to defy the loggers, by encircling the trunks with their arms and daring them to cut through their legs if they wanted to get at the trees. They were at times beaten up or threatened with rape. They became the direct-action Chipko (meaning tree huggers) movement. As Indian commentators have pointed out 'notwithstanding its public image as an environmental movement Chipko is best viewed as a peasant movement'.[8]

Those were the tree huggers – local women transformed into troublemakers, risking arrest and assault, from a recognition that their environment, livelihoods and quality of life were inextricably linked. Having been to the Himalayas to witness the effects of deforestation and the local resistance to it, I recognise the women's campaign also as part of the environmental justice movement. A poor and marginalised people were confronted by the implementation of decisions which were made without their voice being heard, where the profits were secured by wealthy outsiders and the environmental and social consequences were felt by locals. It is all far removed in geography and complexity from the crass metaphor employed by anti-environmental commentators.

However, contributing to the misapprehension that the environment has little to do with the lived reality of the majority of our population is the conflation of groups, which may have very different agendas and approaches, under a broad umbrella term of 'conservationist'. As ample literature shows, this is inadequate and misleading. Conservationists, environmentalists and ecologists have quite different values, although they share some common issues.

Yet when Scotland's environment is brought to mind it is still predominantly written and spoken about as natural heritage, located within a rural experience. John Muir, although spending his early boyhood being thrashed in Dunbar for wandering off into the neighbouring fields and woods, is synonymous with the great outdoors and wilderness in America. My children's great-grandfather was gamekeeper to the family of Gavin

Maxwell, whose account of rural life and anthropomorphic engagement with an otter has beguiled readers in Scotland and far beyond. There has always been a fascination with those who took themselves off to the remote peripheries of Scotland. Books such as *Island Farm* and *Island Years*, by Frank Fraser Darling, the influential ecologist, were popular as much for the account of an outlandish way of bringing up a family on isolated Tanera, as for the natural history observations of the seals which he was ostensibly there to study.

The focus of most conservation organisations has been on the consequences of political decisions and developments which affect protected areas or species; wrangles over forest monocultures; fights over tourist developments which intrude into the landscape; and rights of access to the countryside. This is reflected in the political and policy attention given in recent years to countryside issues in the Scottish Parliament – principally, land ownership and reform, national parks, rural development conflicts, such as the Cairngorms funicular, expansion of salmon farming and so on.

While this may allow urban politicians to dismiss the environment as a rural concern, their rural counterparts characterise conservationists as townies indulging the weekending urbanite's desire for a wilderness playground, and so hindering development and resource-use decisions which should be left to country dwellers. They complain, 'People in London would rather give up fish than have seals killed. They would sacrifice Scottish fishermen before the seal pup.'[9] The people versus the environment agenda is prominent in these disputes. After all when the Harris superquarry was rejected by Scottish ministers in 2001, pro-quarry journalist John MacLeod acerbicly concluded, 'Jobs are scarce here but the Scottish Executive has sent a stark message to other possible investors in Harris, the Western isles and throughout Scotland that flora and fauna are more important than people and jobs.'[10]

It is a simplistic zero sum equation, in that it is suggested that nature can only be protected to the detriment of development opportunities, which conservation groups reject. None have a vision of Scotland's landscapes as an empty land, devoid of people. Working to protect, interpret and enjoy the land also provides employment. Developments vary in impact. Exclusive rights to choose to despoil cannot be demanded where there is national and indeed international significance to the biodiversity and landscapes concerned. Of course there will be disputes – even among environmental groups, as the siting of wind farms shows. A balance has to be struck, but for a long time in Scotland the balance has in fact been heavily weighted in favour of development – too often inappropriate and short-lived at that.

The rural perspective is complicated by economic development agencies and tourist boards that want to attract those very town dwellers on the basis of environmental assets. The Cairngorms funicular can only survive if sufficient coach loads of otherwise urban couch potatoes are separated long enough from their TV nature programmes to actually take a trip up to the Highlands. Here, they can totter from craft shop to tearoom, including one up the only Arctic mountain range in Scotland, without ever being exposed to the weather or the outdoors.

But for preference these will be tourists from abroad or at least south of the border that spend time and money staying in hotels and B&Bs. There is little nostalgia for the old days when the youth of the industrial cities escaped the shipyards and mills by getting out into the hills for a brew-up.

Oddly, just as the urban society is becoming ever more white collar rather than flat cap, its depiction of itself has become even more grim and insular, almost wilfully confined. Iconic Scottish authors such as Neil Gunn and Lewis Grassic Gibbon, who were rooted in and mythologised agricultural and fishing communities in the north of Scotland, have been progressively succeeded by William McIlvanney, James Kelman and Irvine Welsh, who, to a degree, mythologise urban life. Increasingly, the impression grows of a divided nation, where people have an urban or rural identification and allegiance. We can still buy into each other's experience, real or imagined, out of dewy romanticism or gawping curiosity. There is no end of dramas,

documentaries and contrived reality TV programmes to bolster stereotypes or conform the otherness between town and
country.

This is all predicated on the pigeonholing of the environment in a Scottish context, which may be convenient but fails
to encompass the complexity of the modern environmental
agenda.

I was struck in a recent book on Scotland's environment by
Alastair McIntosh by the account of his upbringing in Lewis. It
is a rural idyll in the mould of Maxwell and Darling, 'where
cows were hand-milked, where looms driven by foot filled the
air with their clackety-clack and the atmosphere was perfumed
with the dusky reek of peat fires'.[11] Childhood was in a house
with no running water, except that running off the roof into
a rain barrel. Growing up was learning to fish and having
your own boat – intimately aware of the wildlife, yet not senti-
mental about it. With a few anachronisms (like the arrival of
the BBC, the solitary TV station, in the 1960s) it could have
been written almost at anytime in the last 100 years. Without
wishing to be at all critical, it typifies a notion of closeness to
the environment as nature, and a rural culture, which is beyond
the experience of most Lowland Scots. His childhood is foreign
to mine, yet he is probably my exact contemporary.

My preoccupation with issues affecting what may be called
dirty Scotland is informed by a different lived experience. I
grew up in central Scotland, in Alloa. Unlike Alastair, I cannot
trace my roots back into the days following the Highland
clearances. I have no personal claim of affiliation to a rural, far
less Highland, part of Scotland from which we were displaced
by clearance or economic necessity. Yet there is no doubt that
the convergence of family demographics, which caused me to
be born here, were entirely economic. From my father's side, it
was migration from Donegal to become miners and colliers.
On my mother's side, my great-grandfather had arrived at
the turn of the century, as did so many others from the Tuscan
mountain communities around Barga, becoming one of the
4,000 or so Italian-born residents of Scotland.[12] They were

seeking a better life as restaurateurs, bus operators and shop-keepers (all of which my Bertolini grandparents did simultane-ously). I went to a Roman Catholic school, our green blazers confirming our otherness. There, I was surrounded by the off-spring of families who had taken similar decisions to move – among the Italian, Irish, Polish and Czech names there was a smattering of Scots. Whatever our backgrounds, we chil-dren lived in the present, with no nostalgia for a lost land or way of life. And our present was unreservedly the bustle of eco-nomic activity – the mines; the distillery; the brewery; the glassworks; the ever-present sound of the shunting railway wagons down at the engineering works on the Forth. The smells were not of Alastair's 'dusky reek' but of hops and malt, of diesel and coal smoke. I spoke to few men during the day except for a curious few, like my uncles who had been invalid-ed by their injuries in the mines or had their hands crushed by factory machinery. If our presence in Alloa was conditioned by economic circumstances, so for many was the departure. Classmates would disappear as their families emigrated for a better life to Australia or Canada, especially with the benefit of the £10 assisted-places scheme.

We had no aristocratic landowners to look up to. Yet we were acutely aware of patronage – sports facilities and parks were the gift of the various entrepreneurs, or reserved for their employees' use.

The Council provided our houses of course – wind and watertight with front and back garden but unremittingly cold with the only heat from the single fire in the living room. The place was unashamedly working-class Scotland, with the icons of our industrial heyday prominent in sight, sound and smell. Nature, if it was evident, was municipally permitted such as the oaks in the public parks, or the rhododendrons in the pleasure gardens; water voles were found in the stream border-ing the cricket ground. Or else it intruded in the unkempt crab-apple trees of derelict sites, or the bramble bushes that twined along the bottom of the rubbish dump that was our habitual playground. Nearby though were the Ochils, and once you got beyond the smell of the piggery in the middle of Tilliecoultry, you could be up in the hills.

We had an affinity by class and occupation as much as by nationality or geography. The Aberfan disaster had a profound effect, the suffocating slagheap enveloping the classrooms of the primary school, killing children my own age in a recognisably similar mining community. As I collected my classmates' play-piece money to send down to Wales, even then I was aware of the growling anger of miners who knew that it should never have been allowed to happen. The loss of those 116 children and 28 adults in 1966 could be seen as one of the most traumatic British episodes of environmental injustice. Mining had littered the landscape with disused often unstable spoil heaps – in Wales at that time there were over 8,000 hectares of disused spoil heaps alone. As one historian has concluded: 'industrial and mining areas were characterised by the sight, sound and smell of environmental pressure'.[13]

I make no claim to having endured environmental injustice. What I do recognise, however, is the mentality which particularly persists in central Scotland that nature and environmental protection have no relevance to people's way of life. Those who would wish to improve and safeguard the lived environment in and around towns are marginalised by the kind of language which suggests that this is an agenda that is only of interest to those who have the financial security to pass up chances for work. This attitude lets down and leaves unrepresented many people in working-class communities in Scotland who have a blighted daily existence as a result of decisions on land use, pollution control and the built environment, which combine to give an unacceptably poor quality of life. In so doing there is the familiar portrayal of developments as an issue of 'jobs versus the environment', and a cavalier attitude is adopted towards natural assets, which may not be of national significance but are locally valued. This is typified by the local councillor who when challenged at a public inquiry as to the impact of a development on local biodiversity, exclaimed, 'Biodiversity? We're a Council, no' a zoo.'

There is a fundamental difference between conservationism and environmentalism. The preoccupations of conservationism, it has been said, are wilderness protection, efficient use of renewable resources, maintenance of soil quality and protection of habitats. By contrast environmentalism's focus is on human settlement, especially air and water pollution, population, energy use, resource depletion, occupational health, hazardous-waste management and recycling. This is an agenda that caters for the majority, at least in northern nations, who live in urban areas and also provides a better fit with the priorities of progressive politics.[14]

But it does not guarantee a progressive agenda. Within environmentalism there is also a broad and indeed even antagonistic spectrum of technocentrists and ecocentrists. Technocentrists believe that, if well managed and regulated, economic growth and resource exploitation can continue indefinitely. In the business world they tend to advocate voluntary implementation of new techniques rather than regulation. Within public authorities, technocentrists stress that environmental management should be founded on scientific and technological expertise.

Ecocentrists, even leaving aside the deep environmentalists, are generally mistrustful of techno-fixes to environmental problems, and challenge the dependence on elite expertise (even environmentalist elites) in favour of a strongly participative approach to decision-making and protection for minority interests.

Some environmentalists, it has to be said, have been insensitive to the socio-economic variability of environmental degradation. They may advocate environmental protection measures that exacerbate a poor quality of life for historically socially excluded sections of communities. There can therefore be a mismatch between the preoccupations of what has been called the green sustainability agenda and the brown environmental health agenda. Sustainability may be more concerned with the impact of environmental damage on future generations, and thus emphasise the overuse of resources, the need to curb atmospheric emissions, and the loss of land and habitats to urban development. Environmental health agendas tend to be dominated by immediate impacts on current generations, often especially those in low-income groups, and require improved environmental services to reduce exposure to localised pollutants, poor water and waste provision.[15] Without proper thought, present-day efforts to mitigate even the environmental concerns of the poor can displace the effects of pollution to future generations. At the same time, attempts to safeguard resources in the interests of future generations, through for example ecotaxation, can impact upon the poor. (As when the Conservative government proposed to impose VAT on domestic fuel and purported that it was an environmental measure, securing the support of some environmentalists, and outraging those concerned with fuel poverty.)

Marrying ecocentrism and environmental justice is an explicitly human focused agenda, which tends towards the anthropocentric values of ecosocialism, which is described as committed to 'realising the potential of social humanity within an ecological context'.[16]

These fundamental value distinctions and more subtle nuances are sometimes obscured. In Scotland, conservation, recreation and environmental groups have a tendency not to dwell on what philosophically distinguishes them but pragmatically form networks and common cause on topical issues of concern. However, Friends of the Earth Scotland would regard itself as part of a social movement, in a way that most others in umbrella networks such as Scottish Environment Link would not. Academics have identified 'three types of green social movements: the green parties, the more radical environmental organisations such as Friends of the Earth International and green direct action groups such as Earth First' in contrast to others, of which 'the most obvious examples are conservation groups such as WWF, the RSPB and the National Trust. These do not engage in protest, do not challenge the system and are not generally committed to the green collective identity based upon the interdependence of ecological rationality, social equality and grassroots democracy.'[17]

The environmental justice agenda, as advocated here, does encompass a challenge to authority. It is part of an international demand for sustainable development. It requires more than just a rational use of resources but instead expects national and global equity. It demands a voice for those who are most affected by the decisions which impact on their lived environments. Without such values it is easy to see how what can be loosely called environmental agendas can be conflictual.

We can, and should, ensure that the poor are not disadvantaged by environmental policies. Environmental and social justice researchers have drawn up guidelines for green, and socially just, environmental policies, stating that 'a general improvement in the environment will bring disproportionate benefits to the poor and disadvantaged' but cautioning, however, that 'the poor should not be required to pay for cleaning up the environmental mess caused mainly by the overconsumption of the rich'.[18] The challenge then is to press ahead with an agenda that will transform our impact on the environment and not only avoid negatively impacting on the poor but serve to improve their circumstances.

Instead, then, of regarding the environment as either a middle-class preoccupation irrelevant to ordinary people, or an arena for the competing priorities of environmental elites, we would do well to heed the judgement of US author Tom Athanasiou. He observed, 'Environmentalism is changing. It has already shed much of its middle class veneer and if it is to succeed it must lose a great deal more. The social issues, justice first among them, figure large in its future.'[19]

We cannot be satisfied that current approaches reflect this. Look at UK transport policies. The judgement is that 40 per cent of benefits go to the richest 20 per cent of households. Only 12 per cent of the benefits go to the bottom fifth of households.[20]

Equally, however, we should guard against the affluent anti-environmentalist using the social justice agenda to shelter behind the poor. We are all familiar with the well-heeled drivers, who delight in a 4-litre 12 mpg performance but baulk at having to pay the true cost of their social and environmental impact. They feign to protest against fuel duty increases on the grounds that those who can just about afford to drive a clapped-out banger might be forced off the roads. (The 35 per cent of Scots, largely the poorest, who have no access to a car, and for whom the real cost of transport is rising faster than for car users, are of no concern as they do not benefit from the solidarity of car drivers.)

Environmental justice combines the brown and green agendas and provides the basis for an agreed set of priorities, environmental and social. In this way we can resist the attempts to drive a wedge between those who have a common concern for equity whether within this generation or between generations. It has been said that 'the failure to raise and seriously address issues of environmental justice is far more of a threat to suitable political decision making than any genuine disagreements about how just decisions ought to be made'.[21]

In many respects, Friends of the Earth Scotland typifies an adjustment in the focus of the green movement, precipitated by shifts in analysis and impact of personal agendas. Certainly over at least the last decade the focus has been on, what I earlier described, as dirty Scotland. We have battled against leaking landfills and faulty incinerators, exposed gross soil contamination and resisted opencast mines and quarries. These are to be found not just in the predominantly urban central belt but also in the settlements of rural and Highland Scotland. There is little in our work now which is the conservationist agenda – previous issues such as resisting the culling of seals or whales, damage to peat bogs or conifer afforestation have gone from our agenda and we are not engaged with scrutinising biodiversity programmes or site designations. It is not because these are unimportant. It is simply that ours is an environmentalist agenda, harnessing environmental health and social justice to the sustainability issues of living within our environmental space. There are technocentric aspects to it – commenting on the competing claims of technologies to handle waste for instance or to mitigate emissions of CO_2 and other climate-change gasses.

However, predominantly it is an ecocentrist approach, challenging the autocratic and often lax implementation of environmental regulation by authorities and by insisting that people have a voice in decision-taking and are equipped to be effective in making their voice heard. Friends of the Earth Scotland has an explicit environmental justice agenda, for instance demanding improvements to the built fabric of Scotland's homes to end fuel poverty for 700,000 households who spend more than 10 per cent of their income on energy. Furthermore, 17 per cent of Scotland's homes have a poor energy rating of between 0 and 3 (on a scale up to 10, the most energy efficient); 60 per cent of those living in such homes have an income of less than £200 per week. Yet a family in a house with a rating of 0 will have fuel bills 330 per cent higher than a family living in a house with an energy rating of 7. This desperate attempt to keep warm blights lives through ill-health and drains the meagre financial resources of low-income households. It also undeservedly requires such families to consume excessively fossil fuels and emit climate-change gasses.

On many parts of this agenda, to bring about change requires activism. It is naive to believe that improvements are achieved simply by bringing matters to the attention of authorities who then extend regulatory control or cohort technologies and financial resources to fill a gap in market provision. Solving problems around a table is part of the equation, but getting to the table in the first place is a different matter. We need campaigners to press those in authority, or with resources, to do something they would otherwise not do, or would do insufficiently. In particular we need to ensure that those who feel powerless or excluded are effective in bringing their concerns to bear on decision-takers. This is why Friends of the Earth Scotland developed, with Queen Margaret University College in Edinburgh, Britain's first ever Certificate in Environmental Justice. This equips activists from communities, which by their own assessment are being confronted with environmental injustice, to understand environmental and planning law, to access information and to mobilise effectively for change. At the heart of this work is a recognition of seeking to redress power relationships. This is distinctively different from environmentalists in public authorities and private enterprise and often also from more mainstream conservationist voluntary organisations.

This is a progressive agenda, dealing with issues that should matter to people who share my background. Yet mainstream left politicians are just as likely as the free marketeers to resent interference in development, which is based on concerns over pollution or resource use. They routinely believe in the capacity of technology to tackle the former and in the inexhaustibility of the latter. As the former Scottish communist turned ecologist Malcolm MacEwen notes: 'I saw the Earth much as it was seen by the Victorian capitalists and by Marx and Engels: as a cornucopia, a source of endless wealth waiting to be developed by human labour using science and technology.'[22]

The application of human labour to the extraction, processing, manufacturing, transporting and marketing of resources has provided not endless wealth for some communities, but a stunted notion of a quality of life. Environmental injustice arises from a combination of historically unsustainable development with a modern-day belligerent insistence on planning and economic development projects that trade off environmental quality for the sake of jobs. Such developments – opencast mining, road building, or edge of town retail developments – often produce little real benefit for the economically excluded, who, nevertheless, are expected to put up with yet another intrusion into their neighbourhood, which would not be welcomed in more affluent parts of the nation.

The first time I ever publicly used the term 'environmental justice' was in support of the community of Greengairs in North Lanarkshire. In 1996 we learned that 160 tonnes of contaminated soil laced with polychlorinated biphenyls (PCBs) were being driven up by lorry from Hertfordshire in England to be dumped into a huge landfill site owned at that time by Shanks and McEwan. Shanks was the United Kingdom's second biggest waste company and would in 1998 announce pre-tax profits of £25 million on a turnover of £177 million. As the financial pages noted, 'holes in the ground such as those owned by Shanks in south east England, in Scotland and Belgium have great potential if they have planning consents for waste disposal'.[23]

One of the biggest holes in the ground, which they owned, was situated next to the community of Greengairs. Greengairs is not going to feature on a tourist postcard: it is a typical west of Scotland mining community. It doesn't offer much – council houses sit next to a solitary pub and a few local shops. But what it does have to offer is a huge hole in the ground caused by the excavation of opencast coal over the years and into this void waste from all over Scotland is deposited. One day it could be asbestos, which has been removed from 1950s office buildings and schools, the next day it could be hundreds of tonnes of dead fish, which have been brought from the salmon cages on the west coast of Scotland. In July 2002 the decomposing 30- feet long, 8-ton carcass of a sperm whale, which had washed up on the banks of the River Forth, was transported for dumping into the capacious Greengairs' landfill.

For years local people had been complaining about the operation of the site. It was the usual things – infestation of flies; appalling smells; foul liquids leaching out. It was bad enough being Scotland's dumping ground, but how on earth could it be justified to bring contaminated soil 400 miles over the border? The answer was quite simple – it was deemed too toxic to dump in England. There the Environment Agency had tightened the controls over the dumping of toxic waste in landfills by altering the site licences, setting a limit of 50 parts per million (ppm) for PCB contamination. However, in Scotland the Scottish Environment Protection Agency (SEPA) had not got round to reviewing the site licences and so a legal loophole existed permitting at Greengairs PCB contamination up to a level of 10,000 ppm. With scope to exploit levels 200 times greater than in England it was no wonder that, commercially, the best practicable option was to truck it north. The other option, of course, would have been to take the soil to a special

Greengairs – villagers block lorries carrying waste to Shanks landfill site.
Lang Banks

waste incinerator in Wales (also owned by the company) but
Shanks & McEwan had pitched its price for its landfill below
the cost of incineration. Nevertheless, it was still set to profit
handsomely from the anomaly. The normal price for dumping
special waste in the Greengairs facility was around £100 per
tonne; it was said that Shanks was to be paid almost £1,000
per tonne for the PCB contaminated soil.[24] SEPA's oversight
was valuable to Shanks.

The local community's anger was not helped when they
discovered that the Managing Director of Shanks, Ken Morin,
was actually a member of the Scottish Environment Protection
Agency's Board for the west of Scotland. A Scottish tabloid
newspaper uncompromisingly emblazoned their front page with
the message 'Poison soil boss is green watchdog – Hypocrite
paid to protect the environment.'[25]

Raymond Francis, of the local Greengairs Action Group,
which had campaigned for tougher action against the landfill

companies, said, 'anyone can see there must be a conflict of interest'.[26]

SEPA, however, expressed surprise and distaste that anyone should think that the decision to permit PCB dumping had been influenced by his presence, pointing out that, 'If Greengairs came up at a Board meeting then Ken Morin would declare his interests and leave the room.'[27] Shanks also saw no contradiction that a regulator should have on its Board representatives of those companies which it was charged to regulate, 'It would be a very strange state of affairs if various industries were not represented in these kind of advisory roles.'[28] (The current SEPA area boards do have members from a variety of industries, including chemical, nuclear and oil.)

The PCB dumping was normal business for the company and perfectly legal so far as SEPA was concerned. Testing the decision in court was out of the question, even if any wrongdoing was taking place. In Greengairs, and pretty much every working-class community in Scotland, nobody has got the money or the connections to risk taking an interim interdict to challenge such things. Anyway the point was not that it was illegal, it was just wrong, so far as the community were concerned. So they did what people do all around the world and got out on to the streets and blockaded the Shanks site. The story made a big splash in a Sunday newspaper. Under the headline 'People Power' were pictures of kids on their bikes wearing gas masks and carrying placards emblazoned with the warning 'Toxic time bomb'. Their mothers and fathers were pictured stopping lorries and remonstrating with the drivers. 'Hundreds of villagers formed a human barricade yesterday in their crusade against dumped chemicals,' the paper reported, adding the following link, which infuriates business and government agencies, 'the chemicals have been linked with cancer and birth deformities in children and animals'.[29]

The story was taken up by the Glasgow *Evening Times*, which, echoing the power of popular protest, ran a headline warning 'Don't mess with the people'. Pointing out that it was a peaceful protest, with no arrests, it then developed the theme of environmental justice saying that 'nobody wants a waste dump next to their homes. Shanks and McEwan has learned that you can't just force toxic waste upon a community without consultation.'[30]

Eventually the company defused the situation by agreeing to pay for an independent assessment of the site by a consultant of the community's choosing. The subsequent report made 28 recommendations to improve operations and relationships (although crucially it strongly recommended that the dumped PCB soil should remain in situ and not be disturbed).[31] The company accepted the findings. SEPA in the meantime decided that the site licence should be amended, although it betrayed the regulator's irritability with local reaction by saying, that it was 'because of the hysteria this seemed to create' that no further dumping would be permitted.[32]

Since then, it should be acknowledged, the company has sought to improve community relations. It is said that it cost £2 million to implement the findings of the independent consultant. In 2002 the renamed Shanks Waste Solutions was approached to accept PCB from a Scottish source at levels of contamination below the revised limit. In this instance the company held public meetings and mailed each household in the village to inform them and hear concerns before accepting the waste.

However, Greengairs typifies many key grievances and fracture points within the debate about environmental justice, especially where the contention is not regarding a failure to uphold the letter of the law but instead encompasses notions of fairness and decency. It would be a mistake to confine the discussion as to whether the community would be exposed to harm from PCBs. That was merely the trigger for action, expressing pent-up frustration with the company and the regulator.

The company view was that it held a valid licence; it was a commercially confidential contract; it had informed the regulator; there was no risk to the community; and it was a one-off event.

The community view was it was exploiting a technical loophole; it was profiteering; the community should have been informed; there was an unnecessary exposure to risk; the regulator had failed in its duty; and it was part of a series of environmentally detrimental decisions.

Table 1.1 Environmental justice – authority versus community views

Authority	Community
Legal	Unfair
Commercial	Profiteering
No real risk	More risk than comparable communities
Case-by-case approach	Cumulative impact
Impartial scrutiny	Cosy relationships
Has to go somewhere	Does not have to go here
Expert opinion	Lived experience

Greengairs can be said to be the launchpad for a conscious campaign for environmental justice in Scotland. It was to there that Jack McConnell later made his visit prior to his seminal speech. However, the approach here has been heavily informed by thinking and events across the Atlantic.

If the environmental justice movement has a birthplace in the United States it is likely to be in Warren County, a poor black area in North Carolina. In 1982, in a precursor to the situation in Greengairs in Scotland, local people were outraged by the decision of the state authorities to dump soils contaminated with PCBs in a landfill site in the town of Afton. The public authorities had accumulated the soil by cleaning up contaminated waste oil, which had been illegally dumped along more than 200 miles of North Carolina roadway. Protests were mounted and attempts were made to stop the lorries rolling into the area. As tensions rose, police arrested protestors.

Warren County wasn't the first local action against polluting activities taking place in somebody's backyard. However, it has been hailed as the first national protest by blacks on a hazardous waste issue. What distinguished this protest from previous actions was that it challenged not only the decision to have a landfill site in Warren County but the siting of hazardous waste in predominantly black communities in the southern states of the USA. It drew interest from organisations that had previously shown little interest in environmental issues but were certainly concerned about notions of racial discrimination. The United Church of Christ's Commission for Racial Justice decried the siting as 'emblematic of widespread official disregard for the environmental health of poor and black communities'.[33] This may have been dismissed as mere inflammation of the situation but was backed by a report by the Commission, which showed that 60 per cent of black and Latino communities were living in areas with at least one uncontrolled toxic-waste site; 40 per cent of toxic-waste sites in the southern states were clustered in only three communities. If this was the case why was it not until Warren County that popular reaction against such dumping became so vocal and confrontational?

The historian Lawrence Stone has picked apart the multicausal threads of upheavals, on the basis that we need to 'unravel the tangled skein of the developing crisis stage by stage'.[34] He distinguished the long-term preconditions, the medium-term precipitants and the short-term triggers when considering what brought about an event.

Warren County may be seen as only the trigger for the campaign against environmental justice in the United States. The precipitant was perhaps the mass protest which had taken place only a few years earlier by local people living around the Love Canal by Niagara Falls. In August 1978 CBS News in the USA first carried the story about the seepage of chemical wastes from a partially completed and abandoned navigation channel into which thousands of drums of toxic chemical waste had been dumped by Hooker chemical company. The canal had been covered up, and the land sold off to establish a model new community. A school and homes were built, but after heavy rains the chemicals that were buried out of sight and out of mind over a quarter of a century earlier began to seep into the school grounds and into people's gardens and basements. Tests by the federal and state authorities showed the presence of 88 chemicals, some in concentrations up to 5,000 times higher than acceptable levels. Homes most affected and those residents most at risk, such as pregnant women and those with children under the age of two, were evacuated. In all, 240 families were moved out. The rest, however, were left in houses of little or no value.

In 1980 demands for action escalated when the US Environmental Protection Agency released a study that found that 11 of 36 residents tested had chromosomal damage. Experts associated these with the potential for cancer, miscarriage and birth defects. The chemical company denounced the findings as preliminary, inconclusive and inadequate but local people were in no doubt that evacuation of the whole community should take place. Under the determined leadership of a local woman, Lois Gibbs, who formed the Love Canal Homeowners' Association, persistent pressure was brought to bear upon the authorities. In a pattern that would be repeated again and again around the world, they believed that there was already evidence of ill-health among the community, despite assurances that the 'at risk' households had been evacuated. They were angry that there was nowhere for them to turn to for advice, support or advocacy. The activists carried out their own community health study. They looked at aerial photographs, geological survey maps and personal photographs and identified old streambeds that could provide a pathway for chemicals to flow out of the canal. The assistance of a cancer research scientist was recruited, who, on the basis of interviews with families living outside of the evacuated area, found increases in miscarriages, stillbirths, nervous breakdowns, hyperactivity, epilepsy and urinary-tract disorders.[35] Eventually President Carter declared an emergency and in October 1980 sanctioned the total evacuation of the community.

The Love Canal incident has all the hallmarks of a local environmental justice dispute: contested scientific data showing the potential for harm and a survey suggesting evidence of real harm; a company which has profited at the expense of unwitting locals and authorities who are unwilling to respond to demands of local activism. To this day there is still controversy over the role played by prominent actors in the dispute and the level of harm experienced, or to which people were at risk. Such was the intensity of the dispute, in 1980 it became not just the biggest environmental story in the country but also the biggest news story in the United States. It has been said that 'One would have had to have been militantly uninterested in the world, uninterested in reading anything, in order to avoid reading something about Love Canal.'[36]

The people in Warren County may not have particularly identified with the white residents in a blue-collar community up by Niagara Falls. However, they would have been aware that among the toxins identified at Love Canal were PCBs, and they would have recognised that only after public agitation was anything done about the problem.

However, the Warren County action was also framed by a precondition and that was the experience and the conviction that as a black community they had been denied civil rights, and had been discriminated against on the basis of race. People began talking of environmental racism.

The five hundred arrests in Warren County, the national interest and the engagement of the black and civil rights movement into environmental issues for the first time did not stop the landfill going ahead but prompted the US government to commission a study on the siting of hazardous waste landfills and their correlation with racial and economic status of surrounding communities. That study showed that three out of four of the off site, commercial hazardous waste landfills in the eight states in the south were located in predominantly African-American communities, even though they made up only 20 per cent of the region's population. The authorities were accused of practising environmental racism, defined by Dr Bob Bullard as 'practices or policies that disparately impact (whether intended or unintended) people of colour and exclude people of colour from decision making boards and commissions'.[37] (Some of the elements of this approach have been incorporated into the definition proposed above of environmental injustice as it applies to Scotland.)

Activists believed that there was evidence of active racism taking place. They pointed to a smoking-gun memo that had been provided by an American consultancy, Cerrell Associates Inc., in 1984 to the California Waste Management Board, which stated:

> All socio economic groupings tend to resent the nearby siting of major facilities, but middle and upper socio economic strata possess better resources to effectuate their opposition. Middle and higher socio economic strata neighbourhoods should not fall within one mile and five mile radius of the proposed site.[38]

Across the USA agitation grew – in 1989 the great Louisiana toxics march stomped its way through cancer alley from Baton Rouge to New Orleans, and African-American children chained themselves to the axles of waste-filled dump trucks in South Chicago, Illinois.

What lay behind the environmental racism movement in the United States was a conviction that 'too often people of colour are disproportionately polluted, whether by toxics emitted from burn stacks or by toxics discharged from pipes or by toxics leaked from landfills. Far more often than other segments of society, communities of colour are affected by manufacturing facilities, sewage treatment plants, incinerators, landfills, and subsistence consumption of contaminated fish and wildlife.'[39]

So what has all this got to do with Scotland? From the perspective of a black minority population facing environmental racism there is little direct comparable experience. Scotland has a small and only relatively recently established minority population. By 1999 1.6 per cent of the Scottish population were from an ethnic minority, of which one-third were from a Pakistani or Bangladeshi ethnic background.[40] Although the commonly held view is that racial tensions are less in Scotland than in England, police recorded 2,242 racist incidents in

Scotland in 1999/2000. Ethnic minority householders were more likely than white householders to have experienced theft of personal property and verbal abuse in a job by someone other than a colleague. Racism exists in Scotland to a greater degree than has commonly and complacently been supposed. At an environmental level, black activists in Glasgow, taking part in a workshop with Bob Bullard, highlighted racist arguments being used in objections to the siting of mosques. They recounted complaints about 'environmental deterioration' when high streets started filling with Asian-owned shops stocked with halal meat and unusual vegetables, and with Urdu signs prominently displayed. Even so there is nothing to suggest that minority populations in Scotland have been the victims of environmental injustice in the way manifested in the United States, not least because patterns of settlement have not led to concentrations of ethnic populations in our cities to any marked extent. On the face of it, there seems little evidence that minority populations are exposed to differential ambient environmental risk.

So why does the US experience resonate? It is because the notion of environmental justice began to be woven into a wider debate, extending beyond race to articulate principles of rights and fairness. These could be applicable to poor populations and indeed any community that was exposed to potentially harmful or polluting activities.

In 1991 1,000 activists gathered for the first People of Colour Environmental Leadership Summit and articulated rights to be accessed by all people. These included liability to be assumed by producers of toxic or hazardous materials; the right of workers to a safe and healthy work environment without being forced to choose between an unsafe livelihood and unemployment; and the ethical, balanced and responsible use of land and natural resources. In particular it demanded the right to participate as equal partners at every level of decision-making, including needs assessment, planning, implementation, enforcement and evaluation.[41]

The scope of this agenda demonstrates that, by the 1990s, the civil rights movement, which had shown little if any interest in environmental issues, was drawing upon principles which had been articulated by mainstream environmental organisations (which, in turn, had shown little if any interest in civil rights and anti-racist action).

Increasingly environmental justice began to be seen to encompass the grievances of low-income households. The acknowledgement of environmental justice as a mainstream issue was given effect by the signing of Executive Order 12898 'Federal actions to address environmental injustice in minority populations and low-income populations' by Bill Clinton in February 1994. This ordered that

> Each federal agency shall make achieving environmental justice part of its mission by identifying and addressing, as appropriate, disproportionately high and adverse human health or environmental affects of its programmes, policies and activities on minority populations and low income populations in the United States.

This is not to say that poor whites were experiencing the same as black households. Research has shown that in some issues race was the only determining factor when looking for any evidence of discrimination or exposure such as for lead exposure where even in poor households twice as many black children showed elevated levels compared to white children from similar low-income families.[42] Nevertheless the movement, both in terms of its principles and in combining with blue-collar activism, embraced the environmental injustice experienced and felt by low-income communities.

A study carried out in Massachusetts in the USA analysed the income-based and racially-based biases to the geographic distribution of seventeen different types of environmentally hazardous sites and industrial facilities. These ranged from power plants to toxic-waste dumps. The study found that communities with median household incomes of less than

$30,000 averaged nearly two and a half times more hazardous waste sites than communities with median household incomes of $40,000 and higher. Communities with median household incomes of less than $30,000 average were exposed to nearly seven times as much chemical pollution from industrial facilities as compared to communities with median household incomes of over $40,000.[43]

A similar split was uncovered in a study carried out in England. Friends of the Earth researchers correlated the Environment Agency's factory emissions data with the government's 'Index of multiple deprivation', applied to all 8,414 local-authority wards in the country. They established that of the 11,400 tonnes of carcinogenic chemicals emitted to the air from large factories in England in 1999, 66 per cent were in the most deprived 10 per cent of wards, 82 per cent were from factories located in the most deprived 20 per cent of local-authority wards. Only 8 per cent were in the least deprived 50 per cent of wards.[44]

The notion that poor people live in poor environments may appear self-evident. However, so far in Scotland similar research has not been carried out, in part due to the inadequacies of the data held by the Scottish Environment Protection Agency, which falls short of that of the Environment Agency in England.

But considering the central belt of Scotland it would seem that, as elsewhere, the most undesirable neighbours, such as chemical plants, opencast mines and toxic dumps, are situated closer to low-income communities.

Environmental injustice concerns in Scotland need not imply a discriminatory procedure that has deliberately and systematically targeted certain communities for the siting of polluting or hazardous activities. More usually differential siting and exposure comes about from a system that fails to appreciate, or acknowledge, the environmental justice implications of local plans and which permits the clustering of opportunistic development applications.

In general, therefore, the notion of environmental justice is bound up with a complex range of failings in the planning, regulatory and commercial functions. In Scotland, environmental injustice will be sensed as a result of a series of failures. Failure to detect and prosecute illegal and polluting activities, failure to provide information to communities exposed to pollution, failure to consult properly with affected communities or failure to act in the interest of communities at risk of, or experiencing, pollution. Environmental justice is compromised by the preparedness to accept the outcomes of perfectly legal planning developments, emission standards and commercial activities, which individually, or in conjunction, provide the perception of injustice or unfairness. Communities are frustrated when their whole story is not appreciated, because it is salami sliced by the various regulatory and decision-taking bodies, which are only interested in a particular aspect of their complaint, with no one, it seems, interested in the big picture. This is aggravated where the community has to cope with the cumulative impact of a number of environmentally degrading activities and perhaps spread over a long period of time.

The lived experience of the community may be one of a polluting factory which has left a legacy of contaminated land; with nearby an opencast mine which after years of dust, blasting and lorry movements is utilised as a landfill dump with smells, flies and fears for public health. Meanwhile the people could be among the fuel poor, living in homes that exhibit past poor construction standards in the public rented sector. Their children may be disproportionately the victims of road accidents, despite the fact that 60 per cent of low-income households do not own a car. Things are being done to them and sometimes being claimed for them without their voice being adequately heard and with the system blind to what they see.

Environmental justice means viewing things through their eyes.

Notes

1. Speech by First Minister Jack McConnell, at ERM Environment Lecture, Edinburgh, February 2002.
2. Commission on Social Justice, *Social Justice: Strategies for National Renewal*, p. 18.
3. Quoted in Smout, *Nature Contested*, p. 166.
4. Athanasiou, *Slow Reckoning: The Ecology of a Divided Planet*, p. 58.
5. Cramb, *Fragile Land: Scotland's Environment*, p. 110.
6. *Daily Mail*, 30 April 2002.
7. *Independent*, 19 April 2002.
8. Gadgil and Guha, *This Fissured Land: An Ecological History of India*, p. 224.
9. Cramb, *Fragile Land: Scotland's Environment*, p. 98.
10. *The Herald*, 4 May 2001.
11. McIntosh, *Soil and Soul*, p. 22.
12. Colpi, *The Italian Factor: The Italian Community in Scotland*, p. 48.
13. Black, *Modern British History*, p. 48.
14. See Paehlke, *Environmentalism and the Future of Progressive Politics*, p. 245.
15. See McGranahan et al., *The Citizen at Risk: From Urban Sanitation to Sustainable Cities*, p. 172.
16. See Dean, 'Green Citizenship', in Cahill and Fitzpatrick (eds), *Environmental Issues and Social Welfare*, pp. 22–37.
17. Barry and Doherty in Cahill and Fitzpatrick (eds), *Environmental Issues and Social Welfare*, p. 123.
18. Boardman et al., *Equity and Environment*, p. 4.
19. Athanasiou, *Slow Reckoning – The Ecology of a Divided Planet*, p. 49.
20. Tony Grayling, 'Travellers Checks', *The Guardian*, 21 May 2002.
21. McGranahan et al., *The Citizen at Risk: From Urban Sanitation to Sustainable Cities*, p. 175.
22. MacEwen, *The Greening of a Red*, p. 285.
23. *The Herald*, 4 June 1998.
24. *Airdrie and Coatbridge Advertiser*, 14 April 1998.
25. *Daily Record*, 27 March 1998.
26. Ibid.
27. Ibid.
28. *The Herald*, 20 March 1998.
29. *Sunday Mail*, 22 March 1998.
30. *Evening Times*, 10 April 1998.
31. 'Environmental assessment, Greengairs landfill, Airdrie' by Leeds Environmental Organisation (Training) Ltd, October 1998.
32. *Daily Express*, 30 April 1998.
33. Foreman, *The Promise and Peril of Environmental Justice*, p. 18.
34. Stone, *The Causes of the English Revolution*, p. 57.

35. These findings were disputed by other scientists, and conclusions are still divided. For an account of all sides see Mazur, *A Hazardous Inquiry*.
36. Szasz, *Ecopopulism*, p. 50.
37. Bullard, 'Residential Segregation and Urban Quality of Life', in B. Bryant (ed.), *Environmental Justice*, p. 77.
38. Ibid. p. 78.
39. Ferris and Hahn-Baker, 'Environmentalists and Environmental Justice Policy', in B. Bryant (ed.), *Environmental Justice*, p. 71.
40. *Equality in Scotland: Ethnic Minorities*, Scottish Executive Central Statistics Unit, 2000.
41. Gibbs, *Dying from Dioxin*, pp. 309–11.
42. Wright, 'Environmental Equity Justice Centres', in B. Bryant (ed.), *Environmental Justice*, p. 58.
43. Faber and Krieg, 'Unequal Exposure to Ecological Hazards: Environmental Injustices in the Commonwealth and Massachusetts'. Report by the Philanthropy and Environmental Justice Research Project, North Eastern University, January 2001.
44. Friends of the Earth Briefing, *Pollution and Poverty: Breaking the Link*, 2001.

2

Causing Trouble – Asking the Emperor's Clothes Question

IT IS NOT that easy to get the picture as seen by local people. The totality of their story is hardly ever told. If they are lucky it may make a local or even national news report. This is more likely, however, if they are prepared to take photogenic action like blockading a site rather than scraping together the resources for a dense, and not always self-evident, legal opinion. Rarely do the frustrations, fears, snubs and patronising attitudes experienced by the community get brought together. We need to appreciate these emotions in order to have an insight into what causes a community to feel so passionately that it has been unfairly treated and that, notwithstanding the actuality of risk or injury suffered, it has been let down by those who were expected to protect it.

The following case study of the David and Goliath fight by a small community against one of the world's biggest companies, as well as the officials of Scotland's capital city, shows how much goes on in the background which both stiffens resolve and reinforces a sense of grievance.

Edinburgh is a great city. It is consistently ranked as one of the most desirable places to stay in the UK. In recent years the establishment of the Scottish Parliament and the strength of the city's financial sector, typified by being the headquarters of major players such as the Bank of Scotland, Royal Bank of Scotland and Standard Life, have boosted house building and office development. Demand has meant that almost any available space in the city centre is being developed. At the same time the boundaries of the city bulge with new office developments. Population is now 460,000 and rising, hugely augmented by commuters, visitors and Festival goers.

All these people and all this activity generate the normal detritus of modern city living. Every week, sometimes twice a week, the city streets are filled with black bags and plastic wheelie bins containing everything that a throw-away society wants to get rid of. This isn't Germany – residents don't have to worry about limiting their waste or separating it out into colour-coded containers for recycling or composting. Everything goes into the capacious bins. Mouldy food, disposable nappies and fast-food containers, ranging from vinegar-soaked chip-wrapping paper to McDonald's polystyrene clam shells and aluminium trays from the Indian and Chinese take-aways. There are tonnes of newspapers, steel beer cans, aluminium drinks cans and plastic bottles from the growing mineral-water market (even though Edinburgh's water is perfectly good to drink). All of this is placed on the kerbside for collection. What isn't then left swilling about the streets by scavenging dogs, seagulls and the occasional fox is collected by the Cleansing Department of the City of Edinburgh Council for disposal. Less than 6 per cent of the household waste is recycled. Where does the rest go? Fortuitously for the residents and tourists of Edinburgh well out of sight and presumably therefore also well out of mind. It used to be that some of it was burnt at an incinerator at Powderhall in the northern part of the city. The grey slab-sided building stood out among the houses, bowling green and children's play park which surrounded it and from which came from time to time complaints about the smoke and the smell. However, to the relief of the residents, incineration of domestic rubbish ceased and the city, like many others in Scotland, packed its waste into railway wagons or lorries to be transported out to landfill sites at or beyond the city boundaries.

In Scotland 16 million tonnes of waste is thrown away every year, 2 million tonnes of which is household/domestic waste. In 1999/2000 only 6.6 per cent of domestic waste was recycled.

Table 2.1 Comparative recycling rates

	(%)	Year
Switzerland	52	1998
Austria	50	2000
Netherlands	46	1998
Germany	48	1996
Norway	40	2000
Sweden	34	1997
USA	31.5	1998
Denmark	31	1996
Canada	29	1997
England & Wales	12	2001
Scotland	6.9	2001

By the end of the 1990s the majority of Edinburgh's domestic refuse was being sent to a landfill site in Dunbar. However, thousands of tonnes continued to be sent in the opposite direction to an old quarry near the village of Kirknewton in neighbouring West Lothian. The community there wasn't happy about the situation of course but it had been going on for years and it was something it would just have to put up with. Then one day, one of them, Stewart McKenna, asked, 'Does this landfill site have planning permission?' With that simple, but fundamental question he became marked out as one of Scotland's foremost local troublemakers.

The question was audacious, downright cheeky, indeed. It was hardly likely that Edinburgh's capital city would be handing over its waste to the arm of one of world's big multinationals, Hansons plc, without having the requisite paperwork. 'Who the hell does this guy think he is?' was the response that most immediately formed in the officials' minds in Edinburgh City Council.

Stewart McKenna wasn't looking for trouble. In fact he was looking for peace and quiet and to get on with raising his family and pursuing, with typical enthusiasm, the various business ideas he had. Every summer, though, family life was a misery as their home was infested with swarms of big black flies, which

Stewart was sure were coming from the nearby landfill site. The rooms of his house were festooned with streamers of flypaper. (By the way, incidence of fly infestation is a recognised environmental indicator. Some years ago the Stockholm Environment Institute came up with household environmental indicators for third-world countries, one of which was to measure the number of flies in the kitchen. Noticeably, and as might be expected, poor households had more than twice as many flies as those in wealthier households, ranging from a high average of 96 in poor parts of Accra to a low average in wealthier homes of São Paulo of 10.[1] In the summer months the McKenna household would register badly on this environmental indicator.) Like the rest of the community, Stewart grumbled and moaned about the operation of the site, the lorry movements, the noise, the smell and the flies. But despite making complaints from time to time, he, and the local community, endured it knowing that it could not go on forever as the site was said to be close to being full. The landfill site was contained in an old quarry, Kaimes quarry. The site had been worked since the beginning of the Second World War. In 1977, planning permission was granted by the City of Edinburgh District Council for the extraction of minerals and stone from Kaimes. At the end of the permission the Council made it clear that it expected the void created by the extraction of the rock to be filled to re-create the former profile of the hill and for the site to be rehabilitated to mimic a more natural landscape.

From the operators' point of view, there was no point making money by creating the hole in the ground, only to lose it by filling it back up again. Therefore they proposed to fill the void with domestic rubbish. So in 1986 the then operators of the site, Kings and Co., proposed that 'over a suitable period of time', they would 'deposit refuse or waste material to a height which does not exceed the level of land adjoining the excavations'. Conveniently for the company, neither it nor the Council sought to define what a suitable period of time was. However, in 1987 it seemed that a couple of years would be necessary. The Council granted an extension of the original

1977 consent to allow rehabilitation of Kaimes quarry and also granted temporary permission for a weighbridge and mess room portacabins to be put onto the site, both of which were to be removed and the site rehabilitated 'to the satisfaction of the Director of Planning on or before the 31st December 1989'. Confusingly, however, in late September 1988 further consent was given for the construction and operation of a containerised waste refuse road/rail transfer facility with permission to operate for ten years. Even so, by 1999, people in the community had the feeling that the site should have been closed, although none of them were experts in planning law and indeed none had really followed the twists and turns of the history of the site to be certain when operations should come to end. They were aware, however, that the site operators had sought to open up new operations at another West Lothian community at Ratho in 1996 and had given evidence that the facility there was desperately required as the operations at Kaimes were expected to be complete in 1998. That application was refused and so the operators turned their attention back to Kaimes. (Interestingly some six years later the Ratho quarry, spared from becoming a landfill, was the subject of a £10 million housing development, which would include a small loch and a park.²)

Instead of casting around for planning permission for a new site and having to deal with the inevitable complaints from a community unused to having a waste management company as a neighbour, wouldn't it be much easier simply to extend its operation at Kaimes? The obvious flaw in this reasoning was that the void was shortly to be filled, but, nevertheless, there was still plenty of space around the site. Instead of a landfill, there could be a land raise, where the waste would be piled up within artificial bunds. Emboldened by its ingenuity the company made an application for an extension to planning permission. Stewart McKenna and others in the community could not believe it. They had put up with the disruption for years and now they were expected to put up with it for years more. Enough was enough. But they had no experience of the planning system, or what material information would be helpful in persuading the local authority and so asked Friends of the Earth Scotland and in particular Siobhan Samson, one of our Community Action Officers, to help them. Siobhan had long been in the front line of opposing waste dumps across Scotland and had been instrumental in helping the Ratho community defeat the proposal there.

The first thing to do was to establish what the original planning permission for the site was and what conditions were attached to it. Then it should be possible to trace any subsequent permissions or requirements on the company, to see whether or not the most recent application could be justified. This should have been a relatively straightforward matter – such information is held by the local authority planning department. But when Stewart McKenna went along in May 1999 to review the Kaimes site file no. 1621, he was puzzled not to be able to turn up, among the mass of documents, anything which appeared to be the planning permission for the site. Nor could he find any plans or drawings to indicate the height to which the material should be infilled. Siobhan Samson doubted whether the Council would ever find the missing documents, so she decided to write directly to Hanson Waste Management, who now operated the Kaimes site, and to ask for a copy of the original planning permission from its files. Con Kerwin, Regional Manager for Hanson in Scotland, replied enclosing a one-page letter from the City of Edinburgh Council dated July 1977 and a one-page annex. This is all that purported to constitute the original planning consent. Stewart and Siobhan sat down with the Hanson documents and the copies from the Edinburgh City Council files and they went through them line by line. They could hardly believe what they were reading. These were not dusty old documents written in arcane legalese. These were straightforward plain English administrative missives. Con Kerwin's letter to Siobhan encouraged her to look at an Appendix Five as justification of the work the company was carrying out. It read, 'within two months from the termination of works for the extraction of stone from the area authorised from this permission all plant, machinery and building shall be removed from this site and the whole site shall be rehabilitated to the satisfaction of the local planning authority'.

His line of thinking seemed to be that as this required the site to be rehabilitated, his operations were permitted to continue until this requirement was fulfilled. Siobhan's reading was different. The planning permission clearly stated that the 'operation and work hereby authorised shall be terminated on or before the 31st December 1987' and then within two months from the termination of works the whole site should have been cleared, cleaned up and rehabilitated and yet here it was that the site was still operating in 1999. The question that formed in her mind was whether the Council should have ever allowed the dumping of waste to go on for any period beyond the two months permitted once the quarry was closed.

Archive documents showed that indeed in 1987 Kings and Co. had applied for an extension to its operations and this was granted but stipulating that 'the operations and works hereby authorised shall be terminated on or before the 31st December 1989'. Yet on 12 December 1989 Edinburgh Council awarded a ten-year waste-disposal contract, despite the fact that the restoration period had only days to run. On the face of it, it would appear that millions of tonnes of rubbish from Edinburgh's capital city had been dumped without permission in the heart of Scotland.

And so the simple but fundamental question was asked: does the site have planning permission? On 4 June 1999 a remarkable response was received, when Paul Devaney, Senior Planning Officer in the Council, wrote back to say that 'it is my opinion that this site does not benefit from a live planning permission'. (That was the last we were to hear from Mr Devaney as the Council decided he should be allocated other responsibilities, such as overseeing the naming of the new streets that Edinburgh's growth was generating.)

Devaney's conclusions threw both the community and the Council into a flurry of activity. Although the admission that planning permission did not exist should have heartened the community in its campaign, it was initially unaware that time was fast running out if it expected the Council to do anything as a result. Under Scottish Planning Law, if an activity that has no planning permission is carried out for ten years and a day without any enforcement action being taken by the authorities, then the activity is deemed to have planning permission and is immune to prosecution or enforcement. If Hanson's could carry on dumping waste until January 2000 the fear was it could carry on indefinitely. The clock was ticking.

Meanwhile up in Edinburgh City Council Chambers, the Devaney letter had caused consternation. On 8 June the Chief Executive met with senior staff from interested departments and it was decided that the position to be adopted was to say that they had taken legal opinion and that Devaney had been mistaken. The Head of Planning, Alan Henderson, wrote to Stewart McKenna saying:

> Further investigations into this matter have now been carried out, legal advice has been sought ... members of the surveying staff of this authority have also been on site to carry out measurements of the levels of the infill and restoration work currently in progress ... this authority is now satisfied that the works now being carried out are in accordance with the schedule of works to rehabilitate the former quarry which were approved in September 1986. The issue of enforcement action does not therefore arise.

It seemed that Edinburgh was about to use three well-worn tactics: first, bluster – telling the troublesome local community that its layperson's interpretation was wrong ('legal advice has been sought') – and, second, technical superiority, that professionals had now assessed the situation. Finally there was always the old standby of delay. Letters were belatedly replied to or indeed not at all. Using Friends of the Earth contacts, the Kirknewton Community Council had secured the services of an Edinburgh law firm that was by now peppering the City Council with letters challenging the legal conclusions and asking for written confirmation of the Council's view that live planning permission did exist. When the Council finally replied it insisted that notwithstanding the wording of the planning permission 'it is clear that the rehabilitation of the site would take a considerable period of time and that this could not be achieved within two months. This Council's interpretation of the condition was that the two month period refers to the removal of all plant, machinery and buildings from the site and not to the subsequent restoration period.' It went on to say, 'when the matter was considered in 1986 the Council did not specify a time limit for the rehabilitation works. The principal concern was that the site should be restored in a satisfactory manner. It is considered that until the works are completed to the satisfaction of the planning authority the condition of the consent (i.e. to rehabilitate) is not fully discharged. The time taken to achieve this is considered to be a "suitable period of time". It is understood that a further period of about a year is likely to complete this site.'

The community's concern that Hanson's was about to slip through the net of enforcement by dint of the ten-year rule was dismissed. 'The question of immunity of operations does not arise as the ten year rule relates to unauthorised works or breaches of conditions. In this case there are no such unauthorised works or breaches. The Council's solicitor was consulted in relation to this site and is of the view that the works which have been carried out are in accordance with the approved schedule of works and as a consequence fulfil the requirements of the relevant condition of the earlier mineral working consent.'

The impression might be wrongly formed that detailed legal engagement with the case had led to a formal opinion being offered by the in-house legal team. On the contrary, there is not a scrap of paper in the public files to support the legal opinion proferred by planning officials and subsequently it was admitted that not once did the Council solicitor put his opinion in writing.

The campaign was not just being fought on the legal front. Adverse publicity was putting pressure on the Council and the company, as the community was also lobbying its MP and its newly elected member of the Scottish Parliament. The Westminster representative was no less than the Right Honourable Robin Cook, at that time the Labour government's Foreign Secretary. He was embroiled in the Balkan crisis but found time not only to fire off letters in support of the community but also to address a packed public meeting organised in Kirknewton village hall. Cook decided to take a walk down to look at the site for himself, accompanied by his new wife Gaynor, Bristow Muldoon, the member of the Scottish Parliament for the area, Stewart McKenna, and myself. At the gates he was confronted by Con Kerwin of Hanson, who waved a letter from his solicitors, which, he claimed, showed that the community's campaign was misguided and that he had adequate planning permission. It read 'Kaimes enjoyed a planning permission for mineral workings granted to your predecessors, Kings & Co. on 1st July 1977. That planning permission imposed a condition requiring rehabilitation to the satisfaction of the planning authorities . . . it is clear that permission exists for the land filling operation and no further consent is required.'

Cook was in no mood to be massaged in this fashion and pointed out that the letter made no reference to the dates for completion of restoration and told a slightly shocked Kerwin that it was 'plain as the nose on his face' that site operations should have now ceased.

Nevertheless it was clear that the community was going to get nowhere by simply engaging in a tit for tat exchange between its solicitors and the Council. Bigger guns were needed but that was going to be expensive, and as usual in this David and Goliath exchange, David had a pocket full of pebbles but no money. However, Friends of the Earth and the community council scraped together the money to commission one of Scotland's leading members at the bar dealing with planning issues, Roy Martin QC. If his legal opinion agreed with the company, and with the local authority, the campaign was finished and the money invested in it was lost.

In fact his opinion was dynamite. Not only did he confirm

that operations were continuing beyond the period for which they had been consented, he was of the opinion that dumping rubbish in this site never had planning permission at all. He argued that it was not sufficient for the Council to permit the use of domestic waste to fill in the former quarry void as part of the process of rehabilitation of the quarry site. He pointed to section 28 (1) of the Town and Country Planning Act (Scotland) 1997, which requires planning permission for the carrying out of any development of land. The expression 'development' is defined by section 26 and includes 'the making of any material change in the use of any ... land'. He argued that the legislation specifically provided that the deposit of refuse or waste materials on land involves a material change of use and therefore it appears to be the case that in principle it amounts to development for which planning permission is required. Planning permission for the quarry itself expired on 31 December 1989 and rehabilitation of the site required to be completed by 28 February 1990, that is, within the two months as specified in the original planning application. His opinion therefore clearly dismissed the interpretation placed on the two-month period by the Council and the company.[3] This opinion holed the Council below the waterline but stubbornly officials tried to hold to the position that any difficulties regarding the Kaimes site were due to administrative oversight rather than fundamental legal issues. After all, Martin's was only a legal opinion and unless the community council took the City Council or the company to court it need not be responded to.

Going to court was risky and expensive. However, local resolve hardened when it was discovered that the very officials with whom the community was in dispute appeared to be encouraging the Council to grant a further valuable contract to Hanson for taking waste. The community felt that councillors were being misled into believing that, having come to an agreement with the company regarding the weighbridge and the temporary accommodation facilities, there were now no outstanding matters to be resolved.

This was provocative. The Council was warned that if it did not take enforcement action against the company then a judicial review of the Council's decision would be taken to the Court of Session in Edinburgh. This was not a decision that the community council or Friends of the Earth could take lightly. The test of whether or not an authority has failed to act properly is a high one. We would have to prove that the Council could have erred in law in its decision. Then there was the matter of cost. If we lost the judicial review we would not only have to pay our own QC's costs but also that of the Council and possibly that of the company. It seemed that the local authority was banking on this scaring off the community. Privately it had taken its own QC's opinion and was startled to find that he agreed with Roy Martin. A second opinion was then commissioned and it unequivocally told the Council that there was no planning permission for the site. Despite that, the Council did not back down and effectively dared the community council and Friends of the Earth to risk everything by going to court. When we called the Council's bluff by initiating court proceedings, it offered a deal at the last minute whereby it would take enforcement action if the petition for judicial review was withdrawn.

This was a humiliating climbdown by the Council, and the Chief Executive was instructed to carry out an inquiry. He commissioned John Anderson of the COSLA Consultancy, whose report was damning.[4]

He found that the preparedness of the Council to believe that no planning permission was required for the thousands of tonnes of municipal waste being dumped in the quarry showed 'a very lax attitude to implementation of planning legislation'.

Regarding the action taken by Stewart McKenna, Friends of the Earth and others, he said, 'I think it is fair to suggest that if the various community organisations had not persisted with their claims and complaints no action would have been taken by the Council and what was probably an unlawful operation could have become lawful because of time bar.'

The complaint of the community groups was not just that

*Stewart McKenna makes headline news in the fight
against Kaimes landfill.*
Lang Banks

the Council had erred in interpreting planning law. It was also
that their concerns were ignored, that letters were not answered
timeously, that answers were on many occasions incomplete.
Effectively they were being fobbed off because of the potential
consequences for the Council's refuse-disposal responsibilities
if Kaimes could not be used. Anderson said, 'I must admit
that I have some sympathy for that point of view.' He points out
that this runs contrary to the Council's own planning enforcement charter, which recognises that the Council relies to a large

extent on members of the public bringing breaches of planning consent to its attention. He was scathing about the way in which the complaints were dealt with by the Council and in particular why 'given the sensitivity of this issue and the fact that the Council had a vested interest in the matter, why no internal legal opinion ever seems to have been produced in writing'. To the embarrassment of the Council's legal officials, he was also frankly dubious about their capacity to provide a robust legal opinion and said, 'I am surprised that planning accepted that legal advice so readily.'

He concluded that 'it seems to me that the community organisations have a right to feel aggrieved' and recommended that some form of ex-gratia payment should be considered in compensation for part of their costs. He also endorsed enforcement action being taken on the company. You would think that would be the end of it – three QCs' opinions and an independent inquiry had shown the community had been right. However, Hanson was not prepared to let the matter rest there. There were millions of pounds at stake, not just from the loss of revenues should the quarry close earlier than had been expected, but also the additional costs of rehabilitating the site, and, above all, the prospect of losing the future land raise. The company decided to appeal against the enforcement notices that would have forced the landfill site to close in October 2000 with a further nine months to carry out final restoration. The company tried to take the high moral ground by claiming that it had given good service to Edinburgh for years, without complaint, and its reputation as a responsible operator was now being damaged.

The local community had long argued that the close relationship between the company and the Council had blinded the local authority to its legal responsibilities to monitor the site and its planning status. After all, Edinburgh Council is the planning authority, the local waste licensing authority and also the client of a company on whose site at Kaimes it had for years depended upon to dispose of Edinburgh's waste. The Council officials were adamant that there was no conflict of interest but somehow Hanson believed that it should be given special consideration. Con Kerwin said, 'what has really saddened me is that given our long standing service to the city it is regrettable that it appears that the Council has paid so little attention to our position'. He gave the impression that running an extremely profitable arm of a multinational company was somehow equivalent to a selfless charitable activity.

The appeal would have to be heard at a public inquiry, delaying a decision and therefore incidentally, prolonging the period over which dumping could take place at Kaimes. The company would have to prove that planning permission did exist and that the Council was therefore wrong to issue an enforcement notice. However, in the company's public relations work it sought to foster the impression that it was a victim of zealous environmental campaigners. Whether or not the issue of planning permission existed was, to the company's mind, merely incidental, given that the site had existed for so long and had operated, it claimed, to a high standard. The company used the trade magazine *The Waste Manager* to press its victimisation claims. An editorial in the March 2000 issue said, 'Friends of the Earth Scotland has gone to great lengths to cause as much trouble for the Hanson site as they possibly can based on what is a planning technicality. Alright it is a pretty big one, no-one is saying that not knowing whether the site has a live planning permission did not cause outcry but it is not Hanson's fault and it does not effect environmental standards at the site.' They tried to portray the Hanson site as a martyr to the cause of waste management, arguing that 'this whole episode is just a convenient stick with which to beat the waste management industry. FoE Scotland picked that stick up and used it because they are anti waste industry . . . the means justify those ends. Causing trouble for Kaimes quarry is just part of the means.'[5]

But taking the offensive to Friends of the Earth was too late for Hanson. The curtain was finally lowered on this drama on 13 February 2001 when a recorded delivery letter was sent to Hanson's solicitors at their fine Georgian offices in Edinburgh's Queen Street. The Scottish Executive's Inquiry Reporter was informing them that he was dismissing their appeals but was varying the terms of the enforcement notices. He instructed that the depositing of domestic refuse and other waste material at Kaimes quarry should cease by 31 May 2001 and that by 30 November 2002 the restoration of the site should have been completed. The site would close almost two years to the day after Stewart McKenna asked the question, 'Does this site have planning permission?'

Commenting on the case in an article in the *Sunday Herald* newspaper, I said 'the people of Kirknewton have been denied environmental justice after being treated in an unacceptable fashion. The treatment of local people as little better than trouble-makers – rather than as citizens with legitimate concerns and rights to information – is prevalent.'

The community at Kaimes overcame official and commercial opposition to successfully demonstrate that it had been the victim of environmental injustice. But in many other cases strenuous efforts have been made to silence or marginalise those whom authorities regard as troublemakers.

Notes

1. McGranahan et al., *The Citizen at Risk: From Urban Sanitation to Sustainable Cities*, p. 76.
2. *Edinburgh Evening News*, 13 May 2002.
3. Opinion of Senior Counsel for Kirknewton Community Council Landfill Subcommittee, 17 July 1999.
4. Report for Chief Executive of the City of Edinburgh Council, 'Investigation into Planning Consents and other issues relating to operations at Kaimes Quarry, Kirknewton.' COSLA Consultancy, March 2000.
5. *The Waste Manager*, March 2000.

3

Silencing Trouble

FOR ALL THE fine talk by government about civic participation or by big companies regarding stakeholder engagement, the reality is that decision-takers still remain intensely suspicious of anybody who forcibly expresses an opinion, and they circle the wagons when confronted by objections. They seem to operate on a presumption that the vast majority of the public are complacent, content, or couldn't care less about matters that are best left to professional decision-takers. So, if a small minority of people not only stir themselves to get involved but actually start asking awkward questions or adopt sceptical, even hostile, positions, then this is often regarded as unrepresentative and an indication of a failing on the part of the individuals concerned rather than the system.

Officially there is a straight-faced commitment to listening to people's concerns. Occasionally, however, the guard can drop. A harassed planning official in the Western Isles Council was asked to analyse the voluminous objections to the proposed superquarry in Harris. At that time the officers were sympathetic to the proposals and were irritated at the number of objections coming from far and wide, which threatened to jeopardise approval of the development. The Council official's report, clearly intended purely for internal consumption, was leaked, not least because it contained the noteworthy observation that one of the objections came from as far as Thailand and the official conjectured that the individual was probably there on a sex holiday, as borne out by the shaky handwriting in the letter of objection! However privately disparaging, it is rare to find somebody in authority daft enough to put such observations down on paper.

Others are not so reticent in dismissing what they collectively refer to as the 'green ink brigade'. *The Times* columnist Anthony Howard once said that 'subjects guaranteed to get the crack pot brigade going are water quality, opinion polls and anything to do with the railways . . . The moment you see green or mauve ink your heart sinks, you can tell they are mad. I don't answer them, it is a waste of time. They only write back.'[1]

Not replying is one of the favoured approaches to dealing with troublesome campaigners. Many other methods have been used to cope with activism. Indeed, a whole industry based around PR consultancy, seminars and management books has been spawned in response to the threat posed by campaigners.

One such guide offers gentle advice recommending that companies should examine their own record on the environment, workers or animal rights, hazardous-waste emissions or ethical behaviour and then draw up a list of activists' groups, which may target the company as a result. Having done so, the author of the guide suggests, 'building relationships with less hostile groups first may lead to valuable information on other activists particularly the more hostile ones'.[2]

However, the author warns companies against really underhand tactics, which may rebound, citing the case study of a New Zealand company, Timberlands West Coast Ltd, which had sent 'moles to conservation group meetings, had threatened protesters with legal action, had created a community front group, had got local residents to sign letters to the press drafted by the company's advisors and had exaggerated the number of local people employed in the logging enterprise'.[3]

It is intended as a salutary tale, the underlying presumption being that most companies would not seriously contemplate such maverick, roughhouse tactics. But when the stakes are high, many companies utilise these and similar techniques that are clearly intended to undermine opposition. The notion that companies are sitting ducks, ambushed by resourceful campaigners who refuse to play by the Marquis of Queensberry rules, only exists in the PR spin of companies themselves.

Over the years a pattern of engagement with the public and campaigning organisations has emerged. We have not yet seen the kinds of public notices on display in the Philippines, which warn 'Do Not Listen to Agitators and Troublemakers'.[4] But the attitude is pretty much the same. Reflexively, companies' response to campaigners demands for information or improvements has usually been 'What has it got to do with you?' This bullish response is still all too evident, but bruising campaigns have persuaded a number of companies to acknowledge public concerns, and issue reassurance that something was being done about putting their house in order. This was not to accede to a notion of public accountability. At best there was a managerial focus on pollution mitigation and performance improvement but still determined by affordability, legal compliance and professional relationships with regulators. The public, including local people, were still excluded from the scrutiny of company performance and simply expected to trust that senior executives were being responsible. The chemical industries in particular found that this line was simply not being swallowed by a sceptical public, who continued to be concerned at episodes of gross pollution and emissions, and so they shifted to a new position of 'don't trust us, track us' (indeed this was a slogan adopted by Dow Chemical). This meant putting into the public domain voluminous data on emissions and signing up to voluntary agreements to cut pollution and to regular reporting. But this is still a passive form of accountability and so campaigning organisations are moving to a position of 'prove it', where the company in question has got to demonstrate that no harm is coming from its activities and that it is setting, and meeting, tough standards to improve its activities. This is not just in respect of local pollution at the point of manufacture. It also encompasses the environmental impact of the extraction of the raw materials used by the company (leading to demands for producer responsibility and chain of supply information), the human rights of the communities in which the company is operating or the employment practices of contractors and subcontractors, particularly with regard to child labour. Even where a company provides such information or constructs corporate policy it is still often challenged or exposed, much to the irritation of companies who seem to believe that producing such material should insulate them from criticism. Lord Holme the Liberal peer and Director of Rio Tinto Zinc has complained that 'the main utility of accountability and reporting is to improve performance. It is not to provide a conveyor belt of juicy issues for campaigning NGOs, or to feed the blame culture of the media'.[5]

Companies do not make such investments just to improve performance – they are also intended to secure a public acceptance that the company is above reproach. The hope is that if subsequent criticism is to be levelled anywhere, it will either be directed at competitors who have not changed their working practices, or turned back on campaigners who have not acknowledged the changes being made. Finding the right person to express these sentiments is important, which is why a recent phenomenon has been the recruitment of former NGO leaders to better paid commercial ranks. In 1993 Monsanto recruited Carol Tucker Foreman, former Executive Director of the Consumer Federation of America as a lobbyist to dissuade Congress from requiring the labelling of milk from cows injected with bovine growth hormone.[6] It is no coincidence that Monsanto should repeat the tactic in the UK by hiring Ann Foster directly from her post as Director of the Scottish Consumers Council. Similar captures of NGO leaders were made in Europe. There has been an almost embarrassed reticence to draw attention to this development. However, when Peter Melchett left Greenpeace to pursue a variety of interests, which included being retained by Burson-Marstaller, the worlds largest PR firm, the journalist George Monbiot waded in. He observed that the majority of Britain's most prominent greens have been hired by companies whose practices they once contested and warned 'Environmentalism, like almost everything else, is in danger of being swallowed by the corporate leviathan.'[7] This drew a furious response from Des Wilson, former Director of Friends of the Earth in London, once on the executive payroll for the British Airports Authority, and who was included in Monbiot's list of defectors. He not only defended the importance of having greens on the inside but dismissed grassroots activists saying that he and others 'have decided they have a better chance of promoting change by working with business and industry, instead of engaging in the kind of invariably useless confrontational activity enjoyed by the punk end of the movement'.[8] This is the same Des Wilson who once wrote a guide to citizen action, expressing the view that big business depended upon negative attitudes and the belief of individuals that they are powerless. He argued that companies failed to understand that the antidote to apathy is anger and then tub-thumpingly got into his stride, proclaiming 'Throughout Britain people are getting angry. Instead of succumbing to apathy or feeling powerless they are getting together with others and fighting back. You can be one of these people.'[9] Clearly the punks have taken his advice too literally.

There has always been this dilemma, of transforming a progressive agenda with radical long-term goals into pragmatic and implementable action. There is an argument to make that as long as companies exist and affect real people lives in real time, then it is desirable that those impacts should be substantially mitigated and environmental measures accelerated by the presence of powerful in-house advocates. I want to see companies improving their performance and when appointing senior staff, securing the necessary expertise to do so.

What the Monbiot–Wilson spat reveals is not the venality of the ex-NGO leaders in accepting a role within the system or inside industry. Certainly, in some cases, they would be naive for believing that it was only their professional skills for which they were being recruited, and must be aware of how their presence is seen as either an endorsement of their company or a rejection of other ways of pressing for change.

But more substantially, they become part of the problem,

not part of the solution, if they characterise industry as having accepted its responsibility by seeking to overcome technical and managerial deficiencies. This ignores or denies the political and social context for much of today's resentment and resistance. As Monbiot observes, 'There is a long-standing split, growing wider by the day, between people who believe that the principal solutions lie in enhanced democracy and those who believe they lie in enhanced technology (leaving existing social structures intact while improving production processes and conserving resources).'[10] This is a restatement of the tensions between the technocentrist versus ecocentrist approach within environmentalism identified earlier and which seems now to form a generational fracture within the environmental movement. No longer is it about being asked to pronounce on the desirability of lean burn engines over catalysts. Now the question being posed is whether a corporate world (however technically efficient) within the constraints of maximising shareholder return and serving a globalised market is compatible with the values of sustainable development. It is an issue to consider later.

Returning, however, to the deliberate recruitment of NGO activists, it is worth finishing on a lighter if salutary note. The UK Atomic Energy Authority, which operates the Dounreay nuclear plant in Caithness, seemed to believe that, at a modest scale, it had scored a point against its critics when it announced that it had appointed, as a public relations officer, a former employee of Friends of the Earth Scotland. He solemnly repeated the Wilson soundbite of believing that he could do more good working within the company than by being outside as a campaigner. However, the company had not bothered to establish that he had never been employed but had merely been a volunteer for a brief period following a somewhat chequered past. As he ill-advisedly told a journalist, this had at one point included being a children's comic entertainer. This revelation allowed the tabloid press to run with the memorable headline 'Clown in charge at Dounreay'.

Companies in the firing line because of their impact on the

environment may utilise their financial, technical, political and PR resources to assuage, corral or crush public opposition. Campaigners are therefore confronted by a variety of some-times conflicting countercharges by companies.

A common tactic of course is straightforward denigration as demonstrated by Des Wilson, although the targets are just as likely to be sober-suited shareholders, as much as direct-action punks. Take, for example, the annual general meeting of British Petroleum (BP) in April 2002. BP is a company that prides itself as an open, engaged even reformed multinational, which claims to take the environment seriously and invites stakeholder dialogue. Yet when shareholders in the company at its AGM raised concerns about human rights issues and environmental destruction the company chairman rebutted not only the criti-cisms but upbraided the shareholders for having the temerity to voice them, saying 'this AGM on an annual basis is not going to be allowed to become a pantomime for the discussion of political issues that we in the Board and you, most of the shareholders, are not concerned with'.[11]

He may have been rattled of course by the fact that investors representing 11 per cent of the company's shares voted against his Board of Directors. They did so in favour of a rebel resolu-tion calling for the company to adopt a more transparent environmental policy, in respect of its operations in environmen-tally or culturally sensitive areas. This is a globalised company and issues from across the globe should be raised at its AGM, however geographically remote that event may appear to be from its operations. The rebel shareholders on this occasion were thinking particularly of the likely prospecting for oil in the Arctic National Wildlife Refuge. In future we can expect the same concerns over the planned $3.3 billion, 1780km Azer-baijan–Georgia–Turkey pipeline.

Closer to home, BP was at the centre of controversy when it began drilling operations in the so-called Atlantic Frontier, west of the Shetland Islands. This is also the kind of pristine environment that environmental campaigners believe should not be exploited if claims of moving beyond petroleum are to be taken seriously. The company sought to deploy another common tactic, not of denigration but of co-option. Friends of the Earth environmental activists in Shetland were angered by the company's refusal to listen to local concerns. After the company had belatedly consulted with them the group wrote politely to thank the company for the meeting. BP took advantage of their politeness. A full-colour leaflet, 'A New Frontier for Britain', was inserted into every BP forecourt garage in the UK explaining the Atlantic Frontier developments. It claimed that the process of community consultation had been praised by Friends of the Earth (Shetland). A vigorous protest secured an undertaking that the leaflet would be withdrawn and not reprinted but the damage had already been done.

Sometimes there is not a friendly or unwitting local group around when you want one, in which case why not create your own? Business recognises that it is vulnerable to attack even from relatively small NGOs. Trust in big business has become so eroded that the public seem unwilling to accept public relations assurances, or company scientific data and are inclined to side with critics. When the company mobilises its resources against such criticism the image of the bullying multinational crushing grassroots protest is an unsavoury one. (Look at the Pyrrhic victory of McDonald's over the McLibel defendants.)

This has caused frustration among those who decry the loss of respect for traditional leadership and expertise within government and industry. The anti-environmental justice academic Christopher Foreman recommends that trust be recovered by the establishment of support groups to get facts and rational information to communities regarding health risks and to discuss priorities and trade-offs. Companies are increasingly tempted therefore to bankroll their own crypto civic society groups whether in the science community or at the level of a local support group.

Biotechnology companies, taken aback at the level of hostility directed towards them in the furore over genetically modified (GM) foods and crops, established CropGen with the stated mission to 'make the case for GM crops by helping to achieve a greater measure of realism and better balance in the UK public debate about crop biotechnology'. The public face of CropGen is a panel of scientists who advocate the potential benefits of GM technology on the basis, they say, that such advantages have not been aired in public debate (notwithstanding the full-page adverts taken out by companies like Monsanto). The website states that CropGen is 'ultimately funded by industry' but gives no details of the sponsoring companies or the level of funding they provide.

By contrast with deploying high-profile individuals or experts, companies recognise the importance of the support of ordinary folk. Mobilising a public movement is a well-worn approach. Burson-Marsteller came up with the idea of the National Smokers Alliance to lobby for smokers' rights, bankrolled by their client Philip Morris Tobacco Company. Another of their clients, Monsanto, benefited from the support of the Maryland Citizens Consumer Council, a front organisation whose key representatives were Burson-Marsteller employees.[12] So pervasive are these artificial grassroots groups that they have been dubbed 'astroturf movements' in recognition of their synthetic base. Astroturf groups form part of a 'grassroots programme that involves the instant manufacturing of public support for a point of view on which either uninformed activists are recruited or means of deception are used to recruit them'.[13]

Such tactics apply at the local level. Confronted with the might of Friends of the Earth (turnover £500,000 per annum), Redland Aggregates Limited, soon to be part of of the Lafarge group (worldwide sales £7,600 million annually), hired Barkers Communications to do something to redress the balance. Barkers is no novice outfit, boasting that its establishment in 1812 makes it the United Kingdom's first ever advertising agency. Now it is part of Barkers Norman Broadbent, with a turnover in 2001 of £132 million. It counts among its non-executive directors Rt Hon. John Redwood, a failed candidate for the leadership of the Conservative Party in the UK and who famously was filmed vacuously pretending to sing the Welsh national anthem while Secretary of State for Wales.

Barkers is well connected to Scottish public life, however, counting the Scottish Executive, the Scottish Qualifications Authority and Glasgow City Council among its clients. No mention, however, of Redland among its present-day commercial clients.

The public inquiry into Redland's proposal for a 600 million tonne superquarry on the Isle of Harris had been a public relations disaster for Redland – it had dragged on for months and far from serving as a platform to articulate the benefits of the quarry it had highlighted issues which alarmed local people. Daily life would be punctuated by noise, dust and blasting. Explosions would rip the face away from Roineabhal mountain, and crushers would turn the white anorthosite into the basic aggregate for road building, or roof tiles. Huge ships, bigger than anything ever seen coming into the islands, would manoeuvre among the small fishing boats. The company offered the prospect of jobs but surprisingly few for local people, given the scale of the operation. Against this was the potential for ecological and economic damage to the shellfish and fish-farming resources of the Minch. Redland was paying the price for presuming that what mattered was solely the clash of experts within the confines of the public local inquiry room in the Seaforth Hotel in Stornoway. Its legal team had deployed its skills in cross-examination to marginalise those local people who wished to give evidence against the quarry, depicting them as being self-interested, irrelevant or obsessive. Redland had failed to invest in its relationship with the community, as was literally demonstrated when only grudgingly could it be persuaded to agree to pay into a community fund based upon a few pence for each tonne removed. As the inquiry drew to a close in May 1995, a referendum carried out on the island showed that local opinion had dramatically shifted against the company with 68 per cent of residents opposed to the development (on an 83 per cent turnout in a secret ballot).

The company needed to demonstrate that it had greater local support. Fortuitously then, in 1996, within months of the disastrous referendum, a local pro-quarry group was formed – the

Coastal Quarry Local Supporters Network (CQLSN). This was just what the company needed – ordinary local people who could be relied upon to vilify the mainland-based NGOs as outsiders interfering in matters that should, in their eyes, be left to the locals. (A stance that overlooks the gross presence of a Leicestershire-based multinational, soon to be swallowed up by an even bigger Paris-based global corporate giant, with the express intent of serving markets lying entirely outside of Scotland.) As a bonus this group included the journalist John MacLeod, who used his newspaper column to pour bile on 'the environmentalists, the clergy, the real live Red Indian, the seaweed spa merchant, the corncrake nuts, and the whole host of non-resident aliens who descended on Harris and reduced the public inquiry to a three-ring circus'.[14] With the exception of a few days the inquiry in fact took place in Stornoway with local people having to make the 100-mile round trip from Harris to hear what was being played out. John MacLeod was not one of them and so would not have heard week after week the technical evidence on everything from blasting over pressure to landscape impact.

Nevertheless, this did not stop this small band of residents placing adverts and circulating a glossy brochure to households on Harris, which purported to be findings of fact arising from the inquiry. 'Findings of fact' is a technical expression, being the conclusions of a Reporter in a public inquiry. What was circulated was the group's self-opinionated (or externally prompted) wished-for conclusions. Local credulity could be stretched only so far. There was no way that the well-informed carefully crafted press statements and mailshots had not benefited from a little outside help. Indeed a lot of help. The grassroots group, it transpired, could turn to Redland to pay for the mailshot, and in fact Redland was more than happy to meet other expenses. The question of whether Barkers had initiated the mailshot as part of its public-relations strategy was left unanswered. Luckily too the group could turn for help to the Edinburgh firm Burness, which describes itself as one of Scotland most prestigious commercial law firms and which happens also to be

Redland's solicitors. The Redland account was lucrative and throughout the long public inquiry a partner in the firm, Martin Sales, had sat alongside Redland's QC. The firm describe him as 'having in-depth knowledge of the minerals industry and how to overcome the difficulties it faces in obtaining planning permissions, with particular experience of giving specialist advice on planning inquiries into major developments in areas of environmental sensitivity'.

Certainly the firm seemed happy to provide specialist advice (presumably at Redland's expense) for the Coastal Quarry Local Supporters Network, which included drawing up the group's constitution and even its unwieldy name.[15]

The role played by Redland and its advisers was too much for one of the coastal quarry supporters, Catherine MacDonald, the former local councillor, who objected that the 'CQLSN's findings of fact document sent out recently had Barkers' name at the top of it. They used my name and attributed comments to me without even asking my permission to do so. I also feel that other letters which they say have come from the CQLSN have in fact been written by Redland's consultants.'[16]

Redland's ingenuity is matched by other companies, which are increasingly proactive in their responses to criticisms and campaigns. These can be soft initiatives, like chemical and oil companies funding local environmental improvements such as tree planting or native flower seeding. Or educational: the giant packaging company Tetra Pak found itself in the firing line as the traditional bottling of milk and doorstep delivery in Scotland gave way to the supermarket-bought cartons. The replacement of an indigenous, reusable and recyclable material with an imported one-trip product was portrayed in schools' materials, sponsored by the company, as good for the environment. This was on the basis that the milk carton burnt well and therefore helped domestic-waste incinerators to operate more efficiently. (Hardly a compelling argument at the best of times but particularly not in Scotland, where little domestic waste is burnt.)

Sometimes companies can straightforwardly buy off any

criticism. In the West Lothian town of Winchburgh adverse views on the local landfill site were muted as company money poured into the Auldcathie Trust, which paid for community improvements, including repairs to the roof of the local parish church. (Not quite as altruistic as it appears, as the money came from landfill tax, which the company would otherwise have had to pay directly to the Treasury.) What local people did not know was that the company had made no financial provision to restore the dumpsite. So when the local authority had the temerity to issue an enforcement notice because of major breaches of planning control, the operator simply drove his vehicles off the site and abandoned it. Millions of tonnes of exposed waste were left rotting.

Companies have long been vulnerable to accusations that they are profiting at the expense of people's health and the environment. They are seen as tainted; NGOs have public trust. So, clumsily, PR companies are trying to spin the line that NGOs are manufacturing conflict to boost their membership and donations. It is a line which reputable scientists seem happy to peddle. Professor Anthony Trewavas has been an outspoken advocate of the desirability of GM crops and a belittler of environmental concerns regarding agriculture whether it is GM crops, pesticide use or the desirability of organic farming. He has claimed that 'To maintain the status of officers in such [environmentalist] groups, and to maintain the group itself, requires campaigns constructed over increasingly trivial issues . . . whose sole purpose is to raise unwarranted anxieties in the minds of the consumer.'[17] (Despite his insistence on hard evidence for claims of wrongdoing by agri-business, it is unlikely that his view of NGOs is derived from peer-reviewed social-science research.)

If all else fails companies can resort to legal action. Often this can be risible. The high-profile 'Stop Esso' campaign targeted the US giant corporation because of its continued role in the Global Climate Coalition and efforts to undermine the Kyoto Protocol on global warming emissions. The company decided to take action against Greenpeace, claiming that its reputation had been damaged by the use of a campaign logo that, it said, was the logo of Esso doctored to resemble the symbols of the Nazi SS. It called for damages of $80,000 dollars and a further $80,000 per day if the offending material continued to be used. As Stephen Tindale of Greenpeace said, 'we simply replaced two letters in Esso's logo with the internationally recognised symbol for the US dollar. We find it ironic that the richest corporation in the world can't recognise the dollar sign and confuses it with a Nazi symbol.'[18]

Table 3.1 Silencing trouble – company responses to campaigns

Problem	Response
Public mistrust of company	1. Fund independent panel of scientists 2. Employ ex-NGO leaders 3. Promote dialogue events
Big business seen to be bullying NGOs; noticeable lack of popular support	1. Fund a local grassroots support group 2. Establish a national support organisation
Company accused of damaging environment	1. Sponsor local environmental activities around site 2. Enter into alliance with national conservation NGO
Claims of profiteering at risk to the environment and health of people	1. Allege NGOs are scaremongering to raise funds and recruit members 2. Insist no evidence of harm 3. Call for more research
Proposals for legislation/ regulation	1. Warn of loss of jobs 2. Adopt voluntary code of conduct 3. Argue that legislation will fail to achieve desired outcomes
Local people opposing development	1. Portray as emotional obsessive, 'Not in my backyard' attitude 2. Set up liaison group 3. Offer community fund 4. Buy out those most affected

It is a shock for local activists to encounter such tactics, which have often been developed to take on seasoned campaigners. Many of the people involved in environmental justice campaigns stumbled into activism. Rosie Kane, who fought against the extension of the M74 motorway, tells of how she had been aghast to hear that the road would carve its way through Govanhill, where she lived, and so she travelled into the centre of Glasgow to speak to someone in authority. She turned up at the headquarters of the then Strathclyde Regional Council, unaware that it was a major proponent of the scheme. 'That's when I became a roads protestor,' she says, 'because Charlie Gordon [the leader of the Council] sent a security guard down to see me and he said, "Are you a motorway protestor?" and I said, "Well, I'm a protestor and if that road's a motorway then I suppose I am." So he phoned the police.'

She was disillusioned by the Council consultation on the proposed development. 'There was a massive model of the motorway but no houses on it, no people. We wanted to find out which houses were going to be knocked down and realised that many of them had been left unrepaired and people were saying anything to "get out of this house". So we realised the connectedness – if they helped us to oppose the motorway, we would have to help them in a campaign for repairs and better housing.'

She has a clear appreciation of what is involved in addressing environmental injustice:

I'm a working-class woman and I understand the difficulties in the community and I understand poverty. Unless you empower the poorest people in society then these motorways are gonnae keep getting built through the areas of little or no resistance, and the resistance is zero because of poverty.

Rosie Kane and three others set up 'Residents Against the M74', going door to door to the households along the whole five-mile route of the proposed motorway. She realised quickly that press coverage was essential and targeted the Glasgow

Rosie Kane, M74 road protestor – 'resistance is zero because of poverty.'
George Wilkie/Photonews Scotland

Chamber of Commerce which was a prominent advocate of the road. 'I ran in and chained myself to their reception.' The response played into the protestors' hands. 'Luck was on our side because we got locked in. The police thought that the press were also protestors, so they locked us all in and we were stuck inside for two hours with a live TV camera and a live radio broadcast and it was fantastic.'

She articulates what environmental justice is about when she says, 'Everybody is looking closer at what happens in their community and now I hear people talking about their environment, talking about their local traffic systems about how they are choking, about their ill-health and about how their kids can't play on the streets anymore. There are no pedestrians anymore and so there is crime in the community as a result. People are making these links.'

Another first-time roads campaigner was Joan Higginson. She says that when she got involved in the campaign to stop the

Joan Higginson, A701 roads protestor – 'I didn't know how the system worked.'
Colin Hattersley

A701, 'I had never been involved in anything like this. I didn't know how the system worked. I was very naive.' Although not a seasoned campaigner she was not frightened of local politicians – her father, a former miner who was injured in an accident, had been a local councillor. From the outset Midlothian Council had been determined to get approval for the road. A favourite tactic of advertising the planning application over Christmas had been used in the hope that it would attract little attention or response, but over 400 objections were officially lodged.

Like Rosie Kane, she knew that she had to gather support and so decided to target those along the route who had objected to the road. She was amazed at how many people were opposed. Over 100 walked the route in protest. The Council was less than happy at facing opposition. Relationships with the objectors deteriorated. The Council instructed library staff to refuse to accept leaflets outlining the local objectors' case. The police were called when the protestors attended a planning committee meeting. 'The application came before the planning committee where it was passed within three minutes, without any debate. We were outraged. However, matters really came to a head when the scheme was given the go-ahead by Sarah Boyack (the then Scottish Planning Minister) after she had privately met with two Midlothian councillors.' The public inquiry, which the group presumed must result from the controversy and the huge level of objections, was not to be permitted.

What justification there was for the road was not going to be tested. Whatever persuaded the Minister was not made available to local people. Under the rules previously established by the then Scottish Office on private finance initiative (PFI) schemes the Council had to prepare an outline business case. This had to include a full appraisal of alternative projects designed to achieve the project's objectives. Friends of the Earth did not believe that the public-transport alternatives or the upgrading of the existing road had been properly considered, so asked to see the outline business case. The Council refused this on the grounds that it contained commercially sensitive information. When challenged it insisted it did not contain any environmental information. We argued that the whole document could not be withheld as the rules on access to environmental information meant that the commercially sensitive elements could be excised but the remainder released. The Council asserted, however, that this would be prohibitively expensive and would leave little of the original text.

Now this is particularly worrying as the trajectory of policy in the UK and including Scotland is to use private finance initiative or public–private partnership (PPP) for major schools refurbishment programmes or hospital construction schemes. These investments will shape the infrastructure of education, health, use of land, and traffic movements in the area, for the forthcoming thirty years as the PPP guarantees a revenue stream, for the private companies involved for that period. They also mobilise substantial financial resources with some £4 billion being made in PFI payments in the UK by the public sector in the financial year 2002/2003.

Without the public inquiry protestors were denied the opportunity to argue that the road was not value for money, that the existing road, if upgraded, could carry the traffic necessary and that the route of the proposed new road was unstable.

Dramatically they were proved right when a huge crater appeared on the proposed route. Old limestone workings, which honeycombed the ground, had collapsed. Finally the Council admitted that due to a lack of funds it would invest in upgrading the existing road.

People become objectors because we have an adversarial planning system, which gives people up to twenty-eight days to object. If they feel strongly enough to seek out others who share their concerns, they become campaigners. Campaigners will do and say things that make those in authority uncomfortable. But this is the whole point. Local politicians and company executives would prefer if people stayed within the confines of a system that is heavily weighted in their favour. The assumption they make is that the system is neutral – as we shall see later, it is not. There is an imbalance of power between those in authority and those who are affected by their decisions. There is a wholly disproportionate access to financial resources and expertise.

Disputes may arise over an issue that the decision-taker feels is a marginal detail or an unreasonable fear. People's knowledge of the failings in the system are given no space in the decision-making process, which breaks issues down into scientific and regulatory technicalities, as if best practice will always be followed and standards will be met. A community's lived experience is discounted in favour of professional expertise.

Industry consultant Denise Deegan indicates some insight into how this feels noting, 'when employees go home, the local community is still there, living day and night with the organisation in its presence', coping with 'the unsightliness of a factory, smells, noise emissions, contamination of water and the potential for explosions and fires'.[19]

She is wrong to say, however, that it is fear that unites a community. Rather, it is the sense of injustice that it should have to put up with what others are unwilling to. It is not right that because a community has one polluting industry, it should be allowed to attract others. Or that it should have to put up with the detritus of an affluent society. Or that standards could be higher but industry has successfully lobbied to avoid regulation. It is not right that information that could reasonably be made available to those affected is withheld or is simply not even collected.

Sometimes it is asserted that troublemakers have forfeited the right to be listened to, as they have chosen to expose themselves to the environmental conditions of which they now complain. Living next to Paterson's of Greenoakhill landfill site, young mothers complained that their children were driven indoors by the appalling smell and that the litter from the site blighted the landscape, with one mother saying that her kids thought that plastic bags grew on trees given the number caught in the branches around the site. As emblems of our throwaway, non-biodegradable, someone-else's-problem society they have even entered into our literary landscape. The Scottish novelist Alan Warner opens one of his books with a musing on what he calls the 'ghost bags ... snared on the top barbed-wire of the roadside fences – vibrating, thrumming wild in prevailing westerlies, non degradable ends ragged'[20] and wonders where they have come from. Perhaps the ghost bags have come bouncing across the field from shops in the next village, or sailed a hundred miles from the nearest city; maybe they escaped from roadside skip bins, or were uprooted by a reversing bulldozer on a council landfill site.

Many of these families had moved into the area in recent years. By contrast the site (which covers an area equivalent to 660 football pitches) had been operating for fifty years. This provoked one indignant individual to write splutteringly to a national newspaper: 'I think that the people who bought houses that were known to be close to a landfill site are the "dumpties". They bought their homes knowing that Paterson's was there and had been there for decades. Their houses encroach on the landfill site – it is not the landfill site encroaching on their homes. No one is forcing the "outraged public" to live where they do. There are plenty of sites for homes but very few sites for essential landfill. If you want a radical solution, I think that all housing within a two-mile radius of this site should be razed to the ground and just let the landfill site get on with doing the very necessary job it does.'[21]

The fact that the letter writer was exposed later as the boss of a skip-hire and haulage company that used the site devalues his views, but others share them. One senior public health figure told me: 'Paterson's housing attracts less well off families (because they are cheaper), who are prepared to put up with the smell, wind-blown garbage, and lorry movements. They are trading a nice house off against the environment.'

No they are not; they have moved to start or bring up their young families in what they want to be a nice house and a nice environment. Research has shown that there is a strong association between well-being, housing quality and environmental surroundings. Movers use perceived air quality as a proxy indicator in determining whether they live in a good environment.[22]

In this particular case experts have even declared that troublemakers' complaints do not deserve to be acknowledged. In the eyes (or nose) of Professor George Fleming of Envirocentre, the community had nothing to complain about in the first place, claiming that he has never detected a foul odour whenever he has visited the site. Professor Fleming is retained by Paterson's to monitor the site.

The public's faith is coloured by knowledge of regulatory failings and hollowness of previous assurances. In this particular case, people living next to Paterson's site suspected that it might be accepting loads that were not permitted under the terms of its licence. Yet obtaining evidence of this would be difficult to come by. Every load has to be accompanied by a waste-transfer note, on which the carrier stipulates what is being brought on to the site; this has to conform to the site licence and the notes are checked by SEPA. However, these notes are not available for public inspection.

To test the stringency of the system, a BBC *Frontline Scotland* investigative documentary programme arranged for a lorry to present itself at the gates. The waste-transfer note plainly stated that the load contained soil contaminated with lindane, a poisonous powder used in weedkiller and insecticide (although in fact this was not the case). Yet the load was accepted without query or challenge.[23]

It may all just be mere paperwork, but getting the regulatory checks right is what is required to convince sceptical residents. When these very residents point out deficiencies then they mean trouble.

In Ayrshire Hugh Frew could not believe it when hundreds of tonnes of waste began to be shipped from Northern Ireland to be dumped in the Straid Farm landfill site near his village of Lendalfoot in Ayrshire. The Irish local authorities had made it clear that it was cheaper to ship the waste to Scotland rather than open up facilities closer to home, making a mockery, it seemed, of Scotland's national waste strategy, which aimed to reduce the amount of domestic waste going to landfill sites. Lorries were pounding along the narrow country roads, with debris sailing out of the back to litter roadside verges and hedgerows. To add insult to injury, the lorry movements on to the site were happening outside the sites permitted daytime hours. The licence had the flexibility that 'should there be a wish to work outside the operating hours, on any one occasion, a written request shall be submitted to SEPA and written approval obtained prior to opening any such extended hours'. Yet lorries had been seen entering and leaving the site early in the morning and on Sundays, and SEPA admitted that the operator had supplied no prior written request. Nevertheless, permission was subsequently supplied.

Hugh then posed the Emperor's clothes question – are you

sure this transfer of waste is legal? He had noticed that the lorries all had Northern Irish numberplates, and although the landfill site was entitled to accept waste originating from within the UK, only registered haulage contractors were entitled to transport the waste. Tyrone Waste Recycling Company was registered with the Environment and Heritage Service Northern Ireland, but this was invalid in Great Britain. If the company wanted to operate in Scotland it would have to register either with SEPA or the EA in England. They had not. SEPA blustered in response that the company was advised of the need to register as soon as SEPA was aware of the situation but refused to say when it had belatedly told the company. Was it as soon as it had seen the Tyrone lorries roll off the ferry or, more likely, was it when SEPA received our letter and realised to its embarrassment that there had been an oversight? It is any-body's guess but it should not be. The failing had raised the prospect that SEPA has no provision for checking the register of authorised carriers before it issues such certificates. Or, unfortunately, it had mistakenly assumed that the Northern Irish registration was valid for Scotland, failing to appreciate the very laws it was meant to uphold.

For the regulators this was a mere technicality. However, the US campaigner Saul Alinsky would have approved of the skirmish as one of his rules for radicals was 'make the enemy live up to their own book of rules'.[24] The language may be a bit lurid, but the advice is right. People have campaigned for rules. Whatever has been achieved has been a struggle, inevitably compromised by powerful contrary voices and with generous lead in times to allow authorities and industry to put their house in order.

Causing trouble may offend political and professional eti-quette but it is necessary in the dynamic of change. Social strictures can act as the precursor to legal norms. The concept of civil regulation has been suggested whereby campaigns against companies like Nestlé, Nike, Shell and Monsanto provide societal constraints on their business even if legal intervention was not possible. They have to consider the degree to which their reputation could be damaged by civil action and whether it would affect their business performance.[25]

Campaigning tactics that have been used change over time – for example boycotts, shareholder proxy voting and demonstrations. Some commentators have decried a formulaic approach to campaigning, which sometimes inappropriately tries to draw upon other successful campaigns which have created a 'drama of conflict, sometimes including civil disobedience, that compelled distant bystanders to take sides'.[26] Part of the blame is attached to the desire or need to capture the media's eye so that 'frustrated causes find themselves escalating the terms of theatricality to the level of bizarre stunts or ersatz versions of civil disobedience'.[27]

If this is so, it is because campaigners fear that politicians are often more interested in public perception and reputation than in seriously addressing the concerns soberly raised by objectors. It is also a product of feeling on the outside with no voice over substantive decisions. At an international level it was interesting to note the different forms of civil society engagement at the G8 summits in Gothenburg and Genoa, and the world trade talks in Seattle. Peaceful street demonstrations were overshadowed by vandalism, and petty taunting of the authorities, which, unfortunately, was often met by a truncheon and trigger-happy response from the police. By contrast the World Summit in Johannesburg, despite disillusionment, passed off peacefully even though thousands were present. This is because protestors there had access to lobby negotiators, could speak to the press, hold meetings to develop alternative agendas, and critique national and international positions.

Civil disobedience is relatively sparingly used and sometimes legitimated by society. According to the celebrated moral philosopher John Rawls, 'a community's sense of justice is more likely to be revealed in the fact that the majority cannot bring itself to take the steps necessary to suppress the minority and to punish acts of civil disobedience as the law allows'.[28] Sometimes in the UK this happens. A jury in January 2001 acquitted an anti-nuclear protestor who admitted that she intended to damage HMS *Vengeance* while the submarine was docked in Barrow-in-Furness. The Norwich jury in the case against twenty-eight activists accused of destroying a crop of genetically modified maize acquitted them in April 2000, after hearing Greenpeace lawyers argue that the actions were justified by lawful excuse. In many other instances, however, civil disobedience has led to conviction.

In most instances in Scotland local grievances are aired by local people who do not think of themselves as campaigners. However, rather than just shaking their heads and saying 'but that's not right', they do something about it. They may dare to dissent from official explanations, insist that their experience is at odds with assurances or complain that they are being ignored or kept in ignorance. The point is that they do not regard themselves as troublemakers.

Notes

1. *Press Gazette*, 18 January 2002.
2. Deegan, *Managing Activism*, p. 67.
3. Ibid. pp. 30–1.
4. Klein, *No Logo*, p. 212.
5. *The Guardian*, 7 August 2002.
6. Stauber and Rampton, *Toxic Sludge is Good For You!*, p. 69.
7. *The Guardian*, 15 January 2002.
8. Ibid. 16 January 2002.
9. Wilson, *Citizen Action*, p. 5.
10. *The Guardian*, 15 January 2002.
11. *The Independent*, 19 April 2002.
12. Stauber and Rampton, *Toxic Sludge is Good For You!*, p. 59.
13. Ibid. p. 79.
14. *The Herald*, 25 March 2002.
15. McIntosh, *Soil and Soul*, p. 258.
16. Ibid. p. 258.
17. *Sunday Herald*, 6 October 2002.
18. *The Guardian*, 25 June 2002.
19. Deegan, *Managing Activism*, p. 108.
20. Warner, *The Man Who Walks*, p. 1.
21. *The Herald*, 30 January 2002.
22. Kahlmeier et al., 'Perceived environmental housing quality and well-being of movers', *Journal of Epidemiology and Community Health*,

October 2001, vol. 55 no. 10, p. 712.

23. BBC *Frontline Scotland*, 'The Dirty Business', 24 April 2001.
24. Alinsky, *Rules for Radicals*, p. 128.
25. See Zadek, *The Civil Corporation*.
26. Greider, *Who Will Tell the People*, p. 206.
27. Ibid. p. 205.
28. Rawls, *A Theory of Justice*, p. 339.

4

Cowboys and Sheriffs

SECURING ENVIRONMENTAL JUSTICE goes well beyond simply rounding up those who break the rules. However, there is no doubt that access to justice, in the narrow legalistic sense of being able to secure redress against those who breach legislation intended to protect people's health and the environment, is a core requirement of environmental justice. From the perspective of working with communities who have to put up with potentially polluting companies, the requirements for an effective framework of legal protection can perhaps be framed along the following lines:

- Is there in place legislation that provides sufficient protection of the environment, health and the capacity to enjoy normal life?
- Are there systems in place to detect breaches of this law?
- Where the law is broken, is there a preparedness by the authorities to prosecute those responsible?
- When cases come before the courts, are the prosecutions normally successful – that is, leading to a fine, imprisonment or other penalties?
- Is the sentence sufficient to penalise the offender and to deter others?

Environmental justice concerns also require us to question whether the flouting of regulatory requirements disproportionately happens in the vicinity of certain sections of the population.

In Scotland, modern environmental protection legislation developed along largely similar lines to England. As the effects

83

of the industrial revolution caused large-scale pollution, measures were carried into effect to mitigate or prevent it. So the primary legislation in response to industrial pollution was aimed at chemical processes with the passage of the 1863 Alkali Act and the establishment at the same time of HM Alkali Inspectorate. Subsequent major pieces of legislation were the 1906 Alkali etc. Works Regulation Act, the 'etc.' encompassing the wide number of other polluting processes that required regulation. However, it was not until 1971 that this was reflected in the name of the regulatory body, which became HM Industrial Pollution Inspectorate (HMIPI). The London smog of December 1952 focused attention on air pollution from more diffuse sources leading to the Clean Air Acts 1956 and 1968.

In 1974 two statutes were passed which were intended to form a bulwark against polluters by protecting the workplace and the surrounding environment. The Health and Safety at Work etc. Act provided safeguards to those who were most likely to be affected by exposure to pollution – the workers. The Control of Pollution Act recognised that a broad regulatory approach was required to deal with sources of pollution and nuisance which could disturb the local community and the environment in which people lived, whether it came from effluent discharge to water courses or unacceptable levels of noise.

In 1990 the Environmental Protection Act came into force and in 1995 this was reflected in the establishment of the Scottish Environment Protection Agency (SEPA). This is a public body, with a Board appointed by the Scottish ministers, to regulate potential pollution of water, air and land and the storage, transportation and disposal of controlled waste. It employs almost 800 staff and carries out around 15,000 inspections every year. When it was brought into being it was widely welcomed as bringing under one roof the responsibilities of a variety of previous public bodies such as the River Purification Boards, dealing with water pollution; HMIPI, dealing largely with facilities with the capacity to pollute air and water; and the air pollution departments of Scotland's local authorities, which dealt with things like paint sprayers, incinerators and so on. In particular it was hoped that SEPA would improve the rate of prosecution of polluters by having the capacity to carry out more inspections, and by improving in-house legal expertise to ensure that evidence was collected which would stand up in court.

A robust regulator is essential if legislation is to have any practical effect. In Scotland it is virtually impossible for a local community to bring about the prosecution of an offending company. Even in the case of the Kaimes quarry the legal action was being taken against the local authority, not against the company. The basis for the action was that of seeking a judicial review of the local authority's unreasonable decision not to take enforcement action against the company for breaching planning law. As Reid has noted, 'In the absence of legal title deriving from some direct consequences for individual health or property rights it has not been possible for individuals to take action to enforce environmental laws.'[1] For all practical purposes, then, people are entirely dependent on public authorities pursuing the prosecution of polluters. Usually for environmental offences this means the Scottish Environment Protection Agency (SEPA).

Aspirations were misplaced that the shake-up of existing systems, which had brought SEPA into being, would somehow bring about radical changes in approach. Optimistically some had advocated that the new agency should have the powers similar to its counterpart in England, the Environment Agency. It not only has the authority to bring about prosecutions but also, when successful, is able to recover its expenses as offenders are subject to costs in addition to fines. In Scotland the weight of over 400 years of legal tradition quashed hopes of a similar approach being taken here. SEPA is not allowed to take its own prosecutions but, in a tradition going back to 1587, relies upon the Lord Advocate as the public prosecutor. In effect that means that SEPA officials have to report breaches of the law to Procurators Fiscal, who have then to decide whether to initiate proceedings against the offender.

For years, prior to SEPA's establishment, there had been concern that this system meant that Fiscals were insufficiently exercised by offences couched in scientific or technical terms such as exceeding the permitted discharge of suspended solids into water or emissions which are measured in parts per million.

The level of successful prosecutions for environmental polluting offences still continues to cause concern in Scotland. Matters came to a head in 1999/2000 when 65 per cent of the cases taken by SEPA to the Procurator Fiscal for the west of Scotland were returned marked for no proceedings.[2] This is an exceptionally high figure but even so nearly a third of all cases taken that year to Fiscals across Scotland by SEPA led to no action. By comparison for all crimes Procurators Fiscal decline to take action only in around 13 per cent of the cases reported to them.[3]

Why is there such a great disparity? Nobody knows – the Fiscals are not obliged to divulge reasons for not proceeding with a case. It is their decision whether it is in the public interest, or whether the evidence is sufficient to secure a prosecution. The conclusion is that somehow environmental misdemeanours are a distraction from pursuing real wrongdoing. One legal commentator suggests the problem lies in 'persuading the busy prosecuting authorities to devote their energies to cases which may be seen as marginal to their main work'.[4] A distinction has been drawn between conventional crimes, such as murders, rapes, burglaries, and regulatory offences which 'cannot be regarded as "criminal" in any meaningful sense but merely infractions of a technical nature, somewhat akin to an "off-side goal" in football'.[5]

It has been hinted in the past that the level of evidence supplied was insufficient to guarantee conviction due to a difference of perspective between the SEPA staff and Fiscals. The legal officers' criteria of obtaining evidence, establishing burden of proof and technical competence may not have matched the field officers concern with the 'obduracy of the offender or the record of the firm in complying with legislative requirements'.[6] There is no doubt that the agency staff have become aware of the importance of taking, what are in their mind, solid cases to court. Consequently nothing like every pollution incident will be reported to the Fiscal. Indeed in Scotland from 1999 to 2000 there were 2,306 pollution incidents recorded by SEPA which resulted in 84 cases being reported to the Procurator Fiscal.[7] (It surely is not unreasonable to assume that there are many more pollution incidents which have either gone undetected or unrecorded by the agency.)

Getting the Procurator Fiscal to take the case is one thing, securing a successful prosecution is another. Of the 47 cases that were actually heard in 1999/2000, fines resulted in 36 of the cases. In other words 33.5 per cent of those prosecuted were found not guilty or let off with an admonishment.[8]

Starting with the thousands who have committed acts of pollution against Scotland's environment, we are left with a hardy band of a few dozen who actually end up going through the system and are unlucky enough (from their point of view) to be sentenced. Do they then stand, in fear and trembling, in the dock wondering what the Sheriff will do to them?

Not likely. The maximum fine that can be levied for a pollution incident is £20,000 (although if the case is taken on indictment, which hardly ever happens, there is no limit). Unlike England, there are no sentencing guidelines for Sheriffs, as one of the fundamental principles of the Scottish legal system is that the trial judge must decide upon the appropriate sentence in each case and the responsibility is entirely his or hers.

The average fine per successful prosecution in Scotland in 2001/2 was well under £2,500.[9] These ranged from a £100 fine on a caravan park owner for allowing sewage effluent to get into a tributary to the record £18,000 imposed upon GM Mining Limited, which operates the Drumshangie opencast coal site at Greengairs, for breaching an emergency prohibition order. This was the only fine greater than £5,000, however, and 10 fines were less than £1,000.

Inevitably comparisons are made with England and, however much SEPA finds these to be invidious or unfair, they do give rise to a sense of disgruntlement. In 2000–1 the Environment

Agency took 700 prosecutions directly (no need, as mentioned, to involve and persuade another authority to do so). These prosecutions resulted in 669 successful outcomes, giving rise to total fines of over £2.5 million and costs of £1.5 million awarded to the agency. The average company fine was £8,532. In addition there were 6 custodial sentences.[10]

Table 4.1 Pollution prosecutions in Scotland (1998–2002) – fines in excess of £5,000

Company	Offence	Year	Fine
GM Mining, Greengairs	Slurry waste water escaped to land	2001–2	£18,000
GM Mining, Greengairs	Water pollution (5 offences)	1999–2000	£16,000
Highland Council, Fort William	Diesel oil to controlled water	1999–2000	£15,000
Seed Crushers (Scotland) Ltd, Arbroath	Offensive odours	1998–9	£15,200
BP Fuels Marketing Ltd, Galashiels	Gas oil discharged to river	2000–1	£15,000
East of Scotland Water Authority and Clachan Construction, Drymen	Sewage effluent to controlled water	1998–9	£10,500
Millgrist and Fireclay Ltd, Falkirk	Trade effluent to controlled water	1998–9	£10,000
Caird Environmental Ltd, Opencast Coal Site, Hartlouphill	Trade effluent to controlled water (4 offences) and mineral solids to controlled water (2 offences)	1998–9	£8,000
Shanks Northern Ltd, Greengairs	Odour conditions at landfill site	2000–1	£7,000

One early case study we examined, when looking at environmental justice issues, seemed to characterise the disparity. Caberboard was a company based at Cowie, near Stirling, making chipboard – a process that involves using substances such as formaldehyde in the glues binding the wood particles together. It was a serial environmental polluter, which was regularly reported to the Fiscal and was more than familiar with the inside of the Sheriff Court. By 1994 it had 9 guilty verdicts returned against it; yet this profitable company could easily swat aside fines that averaged just £350 per offence. By comparison, two years previously, Eggar UK a chipboard manufacturer found itself in court for comparable water pollution offences, but it had committed these just over the border. It was fined £20,000 with a further £9,500 in costs.[11]

At every turn the Scottish system seems to have its deficiencies. There can be no doubt that many pollution incidents go either unreported or undetected. Communities, individuals and the natural environment are exposed to far higher levels of pollution and degradation than is evident in the official records. Fires to dispose of rubbish are lit on wasteland, emitting black acrid fumes, but by the time they are reported to the authorities the culprits have gone. Frequently householders may not even know what their rights are and to whom they should turn. Fly tipping is on the increase, with discarded items being dumped in lay-bys and on road verges in an attempt to avoid having to pay the landfill tax on loads taken to licensed waste disposal facilities. Even at landfill sites, lorry movements outside the permitted working hours take place, sometimes with the suspicion that unpermitted loads of waste are being accepted and covered up. Breaches of regulation may be carried out clandestinely but sometimes brazenly in the confident knowledge that action by the authorities is unlikely to happen. One resident phoned an opencast operator, as he watched the lights of trucks moving coal long after the permitted operational hours. The company's employee assured him that no breaches of conditions were talking place and that operations had ceased at the stipulated time. 'In which case you better get down here quick,' said the exasperated householder, 'because somebody's nicking your coal.'

Of course, some companies are caught in the act, and cases do come before the courts but it is staggering the level of local concern that often needs to be manifest to bring about some action. One of the larger fines imposed in Scotland was on an oil seed rape processing plant in Arbroath on the east coast of Scotland. Oil seed rape has become something of a visual motif of the impact of changes in agricultural policy in Scotland over the years. Swathes of the countryside, which may have previously grown traditional crops of barley, are now given over to blocks of oil seed rape, which in full bloom paints our landscape in primary yellow. A processing plant was built in Arbroath where Seed Crushers (Scotland) set up operation with a government grant of almost £0.8 million in 1995. Within a year, local people were complaining of the smells coming from the site. The company's authorisation required there to be no detectable odours beyond the boundaries of the plant. However, a consultant's study concluded that odours from the process were likely to be detectable at more than 500 metres. As SEPA moved to take action, the company fought back, initiating an appeal to the (then) Scottish Office saying that if the consultant's report, on the composition of emissions from the process and its abatement, were made public it would breach commercial confidentiality. As the appeal and other legal challenges dragged their way through the system, local people continued to be assailed by noxious smells. Complaints reached 200 per week. Still the company stalled, saying that it was not reasonable that SEPA's officers should make a decision on whether odours were offensive but instead an objective test should be established. This legal challenge was rejected in court and the way was paved for prosecution. Eventually the company was found guilty on five charges and a fine totalling £15,000 was imposed on it. Even so the company had operated for over two years in breach of its authorisation and avoiding therefore having to invest in improvements to its biofilter and vapour scrubber and other costly measures to block sources of emissions. In that time over 4,000 complaints by householders had been made to the Scottish Environment Protection Agency.[12]

It is difficult, for those who have not experienced it, to convey just how intrusive and appalling it is living, day after day, month after month with a noisome neighbour. The whole quality of life is affected: doors and windows have to be kept closed, people scurry along the street to get away from the smell as quickly as possible and it becomes the primary topic of conversation. Psychologists have noted, 'Foul odour is a uniquely intrusive stimulus, capable of spoiling the enjoyment of home and the use of one's property as well as curtailing the use of public amenities. While odours may or may not indicate exposure to hazard, there is the sense that, if one can smell the facility, one is breathing contaminated air.'[13] It is intolerable, yet may not even result in legal action.

Imagine what it was like living next to the Shanks landfill site at Greengairs when a thousand tonnes of fish waste was delivered to the site. The smell was immediate as truckloads of waste passed the homes of villagers. And it stank for over three weeks with people phoning SEPA to complain that the waste lay on the surface inadequately covered. The site licence required 15cm of cover to be applied to the working surfaces at the end of each day, yet a SEPA investigation found that in some areas of the landfill there was insufficient depth of cover and sometimes none at all. Shanks tried to explain away the incident, blaming the weather and the age of the waste. It is precisely that kind of 'it is not our fault' response by multinational companies that convinces people that environmental injustice exists. None of the rich directors of the company would have to tolerate the kinds of smells emanating from a thousand tonnes of rotting fish, coming from salmon farms, the high-priced products of which the Greengairs villagers were unlikely to ever buy. And why should they be subject to the vagaries of weather and the conditions of the waste? If the site cannot guarantee to operate properly, whatever the weather conditions and whatever waste types it takes on, then in the views of the villagers it is not fit to operate at all. In this particular case, SEPA served an enforcement notice on the company requiring it to improve its management practices.[14]

Even when a company is taken to court and pleads guilty the result can be frustrating. The Scottish opencast coal company GM Mining, which operates Drumshangie opencast site, was discovered to have allowed silt to discharge from the site settlement ponds so that a trout stream was being polluted with water containing suspended solids measurable in several hundred parts per million, compared with a consent condition of thirty parts per million. When the case came to court, SEPA wasn't informed of the trial date and only the Procurator Fiscal represented the prosecution. GM Mining pleaded guilty to the offence but told the Sheriff it wasn't its fault, saying that it had inherited the site with inadequate and unsuitable settlement ponds, which had been the cause of the incident. As a result the company was let off with an admonishment. SEPA officers who had investigated this case and prepared it for prosecution were infuriated. In their opinion, a substantial fine should have been levied as they believed that the ponds had been constructed by GM Mining itself but in the absence of this direct knowledge the Procurator Fiscal was unable to do anything to counteract the mitigating plea by the company.[15] (GM Mining was subsequently found guilty of five other offences of water pollution and breaching prohibition orders, leading to record Scottish fines.)

Some companies do attract stringent penalties. Kettle Produce, which operates on farms in the north-east of Fife, is well known throughout Scotland for growing and packaging vegetables and salad crops. No one could believe that growing so much garnish could cause so much grief, when in March 1995 it came to public attention for poisoning over 600 people in local villages.

The company drew water from its own borehole but hooked up to a local stream when it experienced supply problems. Almost immediately residents in the nearby village of Freuchie began to suffer gastro-intestinal illness. By the following week the Director of Public Health for the county had to warn local

Greengairs landfill – residents overwhelmed by smells, including those from 1,000 tonnes of rotting fish.
FoE Scotland

people to boil water and the local authority water services attempted to flush out the mains water supply. Eventually it was discovered that there was gross contamination of the mains and high nitrate levels were present. When prosecuted it turned out that not only had Kettle Produce linked the stream to the main water supply but also was abstracting water downstream of a discharge from a sewage works. As a result 633 of the 1,100 population of Freuchie reported abdominal pains and five cases were sufficiently severe to require hospital treatment. One four-year-old girl fell critically ill after suffering acute kidney failure. Convicted at court, Kettle Produce was fined £60,000.[16] Whether or not the fine is appropriate is a matter for debate but it is important to note that this was not a case taken under environmental legislation or by the Scottish Environment Protection Agency. The police and the local health authority made the report and the company was prosecuted under the Health and Safety at Work Act.

So, by and large, if a company is prosecuted under environmental legislation it can expect to get off relatively lightly. As a result, environmental protection authorities fear that companies are treating prosecution as an acceptable risk.

Table 4.2 Multiple appearances in court (1998–2002)

Company	Appearances in Court	Total Fines
North of Scotland Water Authority	7	£22,350
GM Mining	3	£34,000
Snowie Ltd	3	£9,000
Aardvark Opencast	3	£4,300
Caird Environmental Ltd	2	£10,500

A number of repeat offenders seem to suggest that the courts hold no fears for a company for whom pollution is a byproduct of business as usual. In Scotland the waste contractor Transorganics makes its money by getting rid of waste. One of the cheap and profitable ways of doing this is to spread on land what are called exempt wastes, which include blood and guts from abattoirs, distillery wastes, paper wastes and septic-tank sludges. Very little regulation beyond prior notification of the environment protection agencies is required. This means we have insufficient knowledge of how much of this gunk is being applied to land. But it can give rise to odour, river pollution and we are left wondering what happens to the pathogens and potentially toxic elements contained in the wastes.

In October 1997 the Avon water near Hamilton was foaming as a pollutant poured into it – blood and guts had been injected into fields but ran off the heavy clay soils and into a stream. Transorganics was eventually taken to court and fined £1,500. This was no unlucky event. The company had two previous convictions in Scotland since 1995, and SEPA was at the time investigating two further pollution incidents by Transorganics, to decide whether to recommend prosecution. A month prior to the Avon water pollution SEPA had issued a warning letter regarding a similar run-off incident affecting the North Calder

Water in Lanarkshire. And in England the company had also caused several pollution incidents leading to five prosecutions by the former National Rivers Authority and two in 1998 by the Environment Agency. In one incident over four kilometres of a river in Devon was turned red by abattoir waste.[17]

Prosecutors in England have secured much higher fines for polluting rivers with abattoir wastes. Magistrates in Grantham fined a company £12,000 with £950 costs for polluting the East Glen River in Lincolnshire.[18] The guilty party was Shanks Waste Solutions, the operators of the Greengairs site. There is big money to be made from waste disposal, which should mean that companies are heavily penalised for pollution incidents – it is inexcusable to have leaking pipes or poor professional site monitoring failing to prevent run off.

Yet even in England, where ostensibly the situation is better, with a higher level of prosecution and fines, the feeling is that these are still not sufficiently effective in deterring companies. The chairman of the Environment Agency complained that the 'current scale of penalties levied by the courts makes pollution an acceptable risk. Fines will need to substantially increased for businesses to understand the environment's true value.'[19] In 1999 the Sentencing Advisory Panel, set up by the Home Office, looked at the track record for environmental offences and came up with three recommendations to punish offenders. First, it wanted courts to take full account of companies' ability to pay when setting the level of fines. Second, to impose fines which have a real economic impact on large firms and, third, to make greater use of compensation orders.

It clearly indicated that, when sentencing, the company's culpability should be taken into account. If the offence resulted from a deliberate policy, or was known to be a likely consequence, this should be weighed when setting the level of fines. The court should look into aggravating factors. Is there evidence of mismanagement? Has the company been warned by employees that it was likely to be breaching the law? Did it adopt a cavalier attitude towards environmental risks? Has it been dismissive or obstructive in its attitude towards the regulators and is the breach part of a pattern rather than simply an isolated failing?

It recommended that custodial sentences should be considered where the offences involved noxious, widespread or pervasive pollutants and were caused by deliberate breach of the law or were driven by financial motives. For corporate offenders, fines should reflect the means of the company concerned.

The Environment Agency has also adopted an approach of naming and shaming companies, and issues an annual league table of companies prosecuted most frequently for environmental offences.

In Scotland the situation is very different. It is left entirely to Sheriffs to decide the appropriate level of fine. They may feel that putting at risk a valuable salmon river in the Highlands or the Borders is worthy of a greater penalty than subjecting a community to weeks of misery from noxious smells and fly infestation. They may feel that repeated offences are simply an occupational byproduct from an otherwise responsible firm. They may wonder what all the fuss is about regarding suspended solids or incidents of air pollution measured in parts per million. Environmental transgressions may be thought of as victimless offences, when there is no observable impact such as fish floating belly up or elevated levels of hospital admissions.

As we have seen, where Sheriffs observe an unmistakably real danger to the public then the fines can be substantial. BP was fined £1 million in January 2002 for two incidents at its petrochemical complex in Grangemouth, when a fire broke out after pipes ruptured. (We should again note that the prosecution was brought under the Health and Safety at Work Act.) As a site of major chemical hazard and as a blue-chip multinational company it can be argued that the sentence at Falkirk Sheriff Court applied a penalty that reflected the company's ability to pay and the threat that it posed to the community.

However, the same court also dealt with Zeneca, another major Grangemouth petrochemical company, which had allowed thousands of cubic metres of red, highly acidic effluent to escape into the public sewers, disabling the sewage works and entering the River Carron. Untreated sewage from 100,000 people flowed into the river for a week until the sewage works were repaired. Prosecuted under Integrated Pollution Control environmental legislation, the fine for this world-class company was the princely sum of £500.[20]

There is little to suggest that the courts are getting tougher with polluters in Scotland or that the Fiscals are responding to the concerns of communities and the regulators by taking more prosecutions to court. If anything it is getting worse. Between 1998 and 2002 the number of successful prosecutions hardly varied from year to year, at between 37 to 38. The average fine over the period was £2,354. That is for all pollution offences, whether water, land, or air. Yet back in 1994/95 prior to the establishment of SEPA, the River Purification Board in Scotland secured 35 successful prosecutions for water pollution offences alone at an average fine of of £2,715.

Table 4.3 Pollution prosecutions and fines in Scotland (1998–2002)

Year	1998–9	1999–2000	2000–1	2001–2
Number of Successful Prosecutions	38	38	37	37
Total fines	£93,310	£81,325	£87,050	£83,600
Average Fine	£2,666	£2,140	£2,353	£2,259

The low levels of prosecution and sentences that rarely approach the maximum available suggest that environmental breaches are not regarded as of great consequence by the courts. This should disturb us. After all, much of the legislation has been hard fought for. It is likely to have come as a consequence of many communities, and the environment generally, having suffered, owing to inadequate measures being available to the authorities to stem the pollution until the legislation was secured. Most environmentalists, and the communities with which we work, still see legislation as the most effective way of requiring a change of practice by polluters. It establishes rights, and makes provision for enforcement (whatever the deficiencies), in a way that codes of practice or other voluntary measures cannot do.

An illustration of the efficacy of regulation is provided by what happened to clinical waste incineration in Scotland. Under the arcane legal procedures of the United Kingdom, hospitals enjoyed Crown immunity from prosecution. As a result the hospital incinerators, which disposed of clinical waste, operated outside the purview of air pollution legislation. Such incinerators had to be able to reach temperatures that were sufficiently high to dispose of whatever may come down from the wards and laboratories. Into the furnace went wilted daffodils from patients' bedside tables; swabs and soiled bandages; body parts from the theatres; and even cancer-treating cytotoxic drugs which require temperatures of 1,000 degrees Celsius to render harmless. Yet complaints were regularly voiced by local residents who experienced black plumes coming from the chimney stacks – evidence of poor combustion and low temperatures. In Greenock residents said that their cars were being stripped of paintwork by the emissions coming from Inverclyde Royal Hospital. Immunity was withdrawn from hospitals, which were brought under the umbrella of air pollution legislation. By 1995 when they were required to meet minimum standards most hospital incinerators had closed and clinical waste was being sent to external facilities that could meet the necessary temperatures.

There is no doubt in my mind that legislation is still the most effective and necessary way of securing environmental justice against gross pollution and poor industrial practice. Business of course sees it differently. It is forever complaining about the unnecessary costs and bureaucratic imposition of new laws. It characterises these as a heavy handed, one-size-fits-all approach to pollution control and doubts whether any environmental benefit will be secured. In response, we should note that it has always been so. When mill owners gave evidence to the Royal Commission on River Pollution in 1870 they defended the status quo (even where it caused gross pollution) as 'any material change would involve such outlay and destruction of existing property as to be practically confiscating it, on measures which might after all fail to secure the purification of water after use'.[21] Nowadays, when I hear industrialists similarly complaining about environmental laws, I am reminded of the US environmentalist Paul Hawken, who dismissed such squealing with the question, 'which came first, the laws or the breaching of societal standards which called them forth?'[22]

The other reason we should be concerned is that it is quite clear in Scotland that when cases are reported to the Fiscals by SEPA it is usually an action of last resort and will reflect the agency's view as to the seriousness, wilfulness and obduracy of the company or body against which action is being taken. For a third of such cases not to get to court means that something is wrong in the system.

If legislation is insufficiently enforced, then not only does it fail to deter the perpetrators of pollution, but does much to discourage the preventers of pollution. When SEPA officers see cases not taken up, or fines which do nothing to reflect the costs in bringing cases to court (bearing in mind that they cannot recover costs) then a culture change begins to seep into the organisation. Instead of prosecuting, a virtue is made of a pragmatic approach of working with polluters to achieve mitigation. Of course it is right that the regulator should, on the basis of inspections and reports, recommend measures to companies for improved good practice, nor should trivial failings be subject to court proceeding. Prosecution is not about persecution.

Communities, however, are not always persuaded that SEPA is a body of frustrated enforcers who have to fall back on persuasion and encouragement. We are aware that from the inception of regulatory bodies there was never any zeal to adopt an attitude of zero tolerance towards polluters (in the way that the Environment Agency is now recommending to company boards). The first ever Chief Inspector appointed under the Alkali Act said, 'it is better to allow some to escape occasionally than to bring in a system of suspicion and to disturb the whole trade by a constant and irritating suspicion'.[23]

SEPA, it seems, has rationalised the lower levels of prosecution by adopting a stance which seems to suggest that not only is prosecution the last resort but that somehow it represents a failing on its own part. It would wish to have established a working relationship with the company which would have prevented pollution or caused it to voluntarily accept the need for mitigation measures before a court enforced the law. Enforcement officers often do not see themselves as policing industry but rather as seeking compliance. This they pursue in different ways, one of which is as educator/adviser, believing offences are committed through ignorance rather than deliberately.[24]

But for communities who have experienced pollution, there is a perpetual suspicion that companies will offend again and will be particularly sanguine about doing so if they feel they can escape detection and, even if detected, avoid prosecution. SEPA's stance of co-operation not coercion can estrange the community. Local people, who wish that the pollution did not exist at all, are expected to accept that compromises have to be made if it is thought unlikely that the polluter can be brought to court. Furthermore they may come to believe that some environmental protection officials have a closer working relationship with the polluter than with the polluted. Although this will be strenuously denied, academic writers have suggested, 'Collusion may well grow between regulator and regulated, since regulators will wish to preserve harmonious working relationships with the firms with whom they are working and with whom they may find a future career.'[25] I have not seen evidence of individual officials keeping open the prospect of future jobs. But there can appear to be a white-collar camaraderie, which takes a different view of corporate anti-social behaviour compared to that committed by other sections of society.

A postscript to the Kaimes quarry case was that belatedly the company claimed to have found a badger's sett in the artificial bund which bordered the site and which the company was obliged to remove and landscape. A local officer from Scottish Natural Heritage inspected the site to establish the limits of

Cowboys and Sheriffs

disturbance that would be required to protect the badger. But usefully for the company he observed that in his view removing the bund would not significantly improve the landscape. So he recommended that the Council should 'under-enforce' the planning requirements. This ignored the intense campaign and court action to get the planning conditions upheld in the first place. Quite simply he had not made himself familiar with the case or sought the opinion of the community. Not surprisingly local reaction was of fury at this cosy exchange between professionals.

SEPA's enforcement policy is that it will not ignore any knowingly criminal, or negligent act by any person which damages or threatens the environment or which flouts the law. However, this is tempered by an approach that requires enforcement action to be proportional to the risks posed to the environment and the seriousness of the offence. In the eyes of the regulator then, even if the community complaint is technically justified, it is often regarded as being blown out of all proportion. So we are invited to contrast the pragmatic approach of the authority, which works on the assumption that minor breaches of consent or operation can be remedied, and the fundamentalist approach of the community, which seizes upon these failings to bring about a greater end, such as the cessation of operations by the polluter.

Near Motherwell an animal rendering plant operated by William Forrest and Sons (Paisley) Ltd had caused complaints for years, due to what one local complainant called the 'objectionable stench', which it emitted from time to time. As far back as 1997 SEPA proposed to vary the condition of the plants authorisation, to control odour at or beyond the boundary of the site. It was a condition not dissimilar to that imposed on Seedcrushers in Arbroath. The company appealed the decision. In 1999 the appeal was sisted (that is suspended) until the outcome of a court action in England by the UK Renderers Association, of which Forrest is a member. However, the legal proceedings down south dragged on and still the foul odour assailed the community around Newarthill. In a two-month period from 1 November 2001, over 100 complaints from residents were recorded by SEPA. Eventually a date was set for a public

101

inquiry to be held in November 2002. But, after the community had taken legal advice, prepared its case, organised technical documents and so on, the company dropped its appeal. It had come to an agreement with SEPA. The regulator had agreed that it would not be a breach of its odour conditions if the company could show that it took all reasonable steps and exercised due diligence to prevent the release of offensive odours. The company is confident that the investment it is making in the plant such as filters, oxidisers, air-locks and a management system will be able to demonstrate due diligence.

Forrest is owned by Argents By-Product (on whose behalf John Gummer the former Conservative Environment Minister used to call me on occasion, to let me know of the investment it was making). Argent says it wishes to operate in a cooperative and collaborative manner in its moral obligation to protect or at least minimise the inconvenience that is caused from time to time.[26] The problem for the community is that it has had no say in whether the new authorisation is acceptable. It simply has to put up with odours, which the company and SEPA judge to be unavoidable. How will local people be able to gauge what is emanating from the site despite due diligence and what is due to some failing in the plants operation? More to the point is how SEPA will establish this distinction, assuming that it will still respond to complaints in the future.

From a community point of view, the very presence of a company may have been built on an assurance that local misgivings about pollution were misplaced. Furthermore, the community will be aware that case companies are provided with considerable leeway. They are not required to have zero emissions but are permitted to discharge wastes to water or air, within agreed limits. Where, then, breaches or operational failings occur, communities feel that their reasonable fears have been vindicated, and that, unlike other breakdowns in finance or administration systems, the consequences are exported outside of the company.

Pollution should not be seen as a right, which some bureaucrat then tries to limit. It has to be regarded as a privileged

World Summit 2002, Johannesburg – rights for people, rules for big business.
Kevin Dunion

concession made by society. Our preference would be no pollution – the concession should be to permit the least that it is necessary to pursue the business activities. The capacity of the environment to absorb the pollution and human health to withstand its impacts should not be seen as an upper limit, to

103

be filled up. We have the right to a clean, healthy environment and so businesses should be expected to operate within the constraints we have permitted. We do not need to prove harm but unacceptable impact on quality of life. Sometimes that will mean the business cannot operate at all, or not in the locations it would prefer.

A banner which was waved outside the World Summit stated simply, 'Rights for people; rules for business'. That is how it should be.

Notes

1. Reid, *Green's Guide to Environmental Law in Scotland*, p. 3.
2. Environmental Data Services, *The ENDS Report*, November 2000.
3. SEPA, 'Environmental Prosecutions in Scotland', Report to Board, November 2000.
4. Reid, *Green's Guide to Environmental Law in Scotland*, p. 6.
5. Rowan-Robinson et al., *Crime and Regulation*, p. 206.
6. Ibid. p. 222.
7. SEPA, *Annual Report*, 1999/2000.
8. SEPA, 'Environmental Prosecutions in Scotland', Report to Board, November 2000.
9. Ibid.
10. Environmental Data Services, *The ENDS Report*, October 2001.
11. Matthews, *Watered Down*, pp. 14–15.
12. Environmental Data Services, *The ENDS Report*, July 1998.
13. Edelstein, 'Contamination: The Invisible Built Environment', in R. Bechtel and A. Churchman (eds), *Handbook of Environmental Psychology*, p. 564.
14. Environmental Data Services, *The ENDS Report*, September 1999.
15. Ibid. May 1999.
16. Ibid. January 1996.
17. Ibid. November 1998.
18. Ibid. June 2002.
19. Ibid. October 2001.
20. Ibid. October 1998.
21. Clapp, *An Environmental History of Britain*, p. 81.
22. Hawken, *The Ecology of Commerce*, p. 120.
23. Clapp, *An Environmental History of Britain*, p. 35.
24. Rowan-Robinson et al., *Crime and Regulation*, p. 207.
25. Weale, *The New Politics of Pollution*, p. 46.

5

Whose Environment, Whose Risk?

PEOPLE LIVING IN a degraded environment, with poor air quality, on top of contaminated land or next to a polluting industry are naturally concerned whether they are being affected by exposure to risk. This is particularly true when the exposure is illegal, above accepted limits, or only recently discovered. Communities question whether it is right to be exposed to such risks. An environmental justice agenda would address not just whether such risks are being borne by poorer sections of our society but whether they need be encountered at all. The approach of authorities and critics of environmental justice is to question whether there is any evidence of people coming to real harm as a result of this proximity. Thus the onus is being placed on communities to prove that they have been affected.

Pollution can harm people insidiously. At high levels, lead is extremely toxic and can bring about dramatic symptoms such as paralysis, fits and result, ultimately, in death. However, at low levels lead is a slow-acting poison that accumulates in the blood and inhibits the development of the brain, particularly in babies. Prolonged exposure to very low levels has been shown to lower intelligence and to alter the behaviour of children. One of Friends of the Earth's early campaigns was over the incidence of lead in drinking water in Scotland. We fought and won a complaint to the European Court that grants should be reinstated by the Scottish Office to help householders with the cost of removing lead piping.

It is an issue that has returned to the public health agenda as the limits for lead in drinking water have been substantially tightened (reducing from 50 parts per billion, to 25 in 2003 and

10 by 2013). Perhaps as many as 400,000 Scottish homes will exceed this new limit. Similarly 1 in 5 Scottish public buildings may also fail to meet the new standard.[1] Disgracefully, the problem has been made markedly worse by the illegal activities of tradespeople and contractors who have continued to use lead solder in plumbing even though this was outlawed in 1988. So widespread is the practice, with as many as 30 per cent of new homes affected,[2] that a whole new generation of children has been exposed to harm. Authorities advise that families can take measures to reduce their exposure for example by using only the kitchen cold tap for drinking water and running this for one minute before drinking, or by supervising children so that they do not swallow when brushing their teeth. Societally, however, we have decided that these risks should be removed not just mitigated. We have inherited clean-up costs, which may have been lessened if earlier action had been taken. The bill has significantly increased, as our view as to the adequacy of safety thresholds has altered in the light of research and changing acceptability of risk. Unnecessarily, the costs have been made worse by the illegal action of businesses against which action has still to be taken.

Living in a poor environment in particular can affect your health. Air pollution alone is thought to be responsible for up over 20,000 premature deaths in the UK, caused in part by minute particles in car exhausts triggering asthmatic and bronchial attacks. It is likely that such people are from poorer backgrounds. Research in England shows that higher levels of poor air quality are often to be found in the most deprived areas of cities.[3]

Building a body of evidence about the effects of living in a polluted environment should not be about providing evidence of bodies. Ill-health is not only gauged by mortality or physical manifestations. Air pollution, for instance, is also associated with mental health problems. Individuals living in more polluted areas experience more negative moods and they also showed more adverse reactions to negative life events. An increase in psychiatric emergencies has also been established on days when pollution was higher.[4] Air-quality limits have now been set which require local authorities to identify hotspots and take action to reduce the incidence of pollution.

We have not waited for parents to sue a public authority over their children's asthma. Nor to seek redress from their local plumber, for exposure of their child as an infant, on the basis of subsequent poor school results, or intelligence tests. We have taken the view that such individual cause and effect tests are unreasonable and a precautionary approach to the risk should be taken, however costly.

This is because we know how difficult it is to prove cause and effect, even where workplace exposure is at levels which are unlikely ever to be experienced by surrounding communities. Take asbestos. The history of the fight for compensation for workers suffering lung cancer and mesothelioma from exposure will be familiar to many. It has created a jaundiced view of the authorities' willingness to accept popular insistence that health is at risk.

In Scotland asbestos manufacture got under way in the 1870s. It is now thought that asbestos related diseases account for 400 deaths annually. Researchers estimate that by 2025 some 20,000 Scots will have died through exposure to asbestos.[5] The experience of these victims is not one of science urgently studying risk, coming to conclusions that there is a causal effect through exposure and harm, so leading to industry acting to safeguard its workforce. Instead there was a prolonged gap between the concerns of workers and their representatives being raised and the eventual scientific acceptance of anecdotal, intuitive and localised health studies regarding the health impacts of exposure to asbestos.

The dangers of the use of asbestos have been known for over a century. Life insurance companies, which operate a financial precautionary principle (refusing to accept risks on the balance of probability rather than scientific certainty) stopped selling policies to asbestos workers in the USA and Canada at the end of the First World War. However, up until the 1960s asbestosis was little mentioned even in papers dealing with occupational disease. This may have been because manufacturing was limited in Scotland (as opposed to the use of asbestos materials) or because there were more pressing occupational health issues to preoccupy researchers and medical staff. It was also possible that the deaths, which even by that time were occurring, were not attributed to asbestos and therefore there was an under-estimate of the effects of exposure. It has even been suggested that the risks and the associated health impacts and premature mortality were accepted as being a trade off against the societal benefits of the use of asbestos as a fire retardant. Was the chronic condition of the workers a price to be paid to forestall catastrophic incidents among the general public? Whatever, it is clear that the scientific expertise and peer-reviewed consensus as to harm took many years to catch up with the lived experi-ence and popular knowledge among workers and their families of the effects of using asbestos.

The response of the industry to the risk has been self-interested, obstructive and grudging. Johnson and McIvor have documented the history of the asbestos tragedy in Scotland. They say that even accepting the incomplete knowledge, contemporary attitudes towards workers' risk and the other priorities for the medical and regulatory authorities, 'there remains a strong case – indeed an irrefutable one in our opinion – to be made against both industry and the regulators for neglect and inaction on the asbestos issue from the mid 1920s'.[6] They conclude that 'the asbestos producers and the primary users of the products in Scotland – invariably and quite calculatingly placed profit before workers' health, neglected basic safety precautions, failed to educate and develop a safety conscious workforce and intensified the workloads to levels that seriously jeopardised workers' health and well being. Moreover even where there was recognition that inhaling dust was unhealthy – there was a widely held view that there was an acceptable level of morbidity and even mortality.'[7]

The major manufacturer in Scotland and indeed in the UK was Turner and Newall. In a manner that is all too evident from the activities of companies everywhere, it was found to have opposed government dust control and medical schemes and thereafter failed to implement them. The company paid only token amounts of money for industrial injuries and deaths and sought to suppress research linking asbestos and cancer, giving the government inaccurate data about disease among its shipyard workers.[8]

Since then there has been nothing short of a scandal in the way that claims from workers have not been settled. There is a clear implication that those who may be liable are waiting for the workers to die. In particular insurers have argued that victims who had worked for more than one employer had to prove which company was responsible for the source of their disease, before liability would be accepted. Over 500 Scottish workers claims were held up waiting for a ruling on this defence which was finally rejected in a landmark House of Lords ruling in 2002, opening the way to up to £8 billion in claims from victims.[9]

The American scientist William Baarsachers is concerned that the public have taken what he regards as almost entirely an occupational health issue and come to the general conclusion that asbestos causes cancer in the belief that there is no safe dose, fearing that a single fibre can trigger disease. He sees this as one of many factoids, 'untruths which are repeated so often that they begin to take on the aura of truth'. The consequence of the extrapolation of the asbestos problem into the arena of public health is that 'extensive legislation has now made asbestos into an expensive burden on the public purse and a liability for many property owners'.[10]

But we have taken the same approach to exposure to asbestos fibres as we have taken with lead and particulates in the air. Societally we have concluded that it is a sufficient risk to justify removal. The cost is particularly burdensome because of the continued manufacture and use of the material long after concerns had been raised. Even with the prospect of big compensation claims by workers, it is not the case that the polluter pays. Tenants and property owners are also footing the bill as, in the UK, the Control of Asbestos at Work Regulations

2002 mean that as many as 1.5 million workplaces with asbestos in them will have to be assessed.

However, we do not respond to every potential risk of harm by paying for its removal. Asbestos manufacture is just one historical source of pollution in Scotland. There are many others. By the beginning of the twentieth century the Scottish economy was still dominated by iron and steel, coal mining, shipbuilding, heavy engineering and textiles. On top of that were gas works, distilleries, chemical works and tanneries, all of which have passed down to us to a greater or lesser degree a history of contamination.

It is as well to bear in mind at this point that the 1990 Environmental Protection Act promised to establish registers of land that have been put to contaminative uses. These registers, to be drawn up by local authorities, were expected to be in place by 1993. However, implementation was delayed as those with property interests argued that the stigma of potential liability would make land unsaleable and depreciate site values. Ten years on we are still waiting to have publicly available compilations of the state of contamination of Scotland's land.

Local authorities have to trace the industrial history of their areas. Take Falkirk, for example. It is examining records going back to the eighteenth century when the town itself was noted as a major market for leather goods. The industrial revolution saw the establishment of the Carron Iron Company, the Imperial Chemical Industry's dye works opened after the First World War, and then British Petroleum took over the Scottish Oils Plant at Grangemouth with the North Sea oil fields coming on stream. This industrial legacy has bequeathed to modern-day inhabitants of Falkirk district. Some 1,500 sites are thought to be at risk of contamination and have now to be investigated to see whether they pose a pollution risk.[11]

This list, of course, may not be complete and knowledge of the scale of pollution may be obscured by the passage of time. Some of the contamination may be attributed to the inadequacies of contemporary regulation, where pollution was either accepted as the necessary byproduct of economic development or the risks were genuinely not appreciated. However, there are instances where the scale and longevity of these operations are such that we can say that ordinary working people in Scotland have been deliberately, systematically and in some cases illegally exposed to risk. Over a long period the response of the authorities has often been inadequate, negligent or complacent.

The oft-repeated mantra of Scottish Enterprise is that Scotland should aspire to have world-class industries. Well, once we did. One of our foremost businesses was J. & J. White, which in 1820 began the manufacture of chrome salts and would later become the largest producer of chrome in the world. It made the fortune of the White family not only financially but in terms of reputation and status. John Campbell White, who took over the firm in 1884 on the death of his father, used his wealth to build the Christian Institute in Glasgow, which housed the YMCA, the Sabbath School Union, the Bible Training Institute and the Foundry Boys Religious Society, all of which enjoyed White as a benefactor. In return for his philanthropic and religious work he was created a peer, becoming Baron Overtoun and made a freeman of the Royal Burgh of Rutherglen in 1905.

Lord Overtoun is not much remembered today except that a park in his name still remains in Rutherglen. However, a more famous Scot clashed with him in 1899, when the Labour leader Keir Hardie accused him of scandalous conditions in his Rutherglen works. Hardie detailed the results of medical examinations carried out on workers, which had found that the cartilage of noses had been destroyed and that ulcerous 'chrome holes' covered their arms. Grudgingly some improvements were made to comply with the minimum required under the Factories Act. It is perhaps not surprising therefore that a company that was founded on a disregard for its workers should exhibit little concern for the community in which it was located. Over 441 acres were required for the extensive Rutherglen works and a further 12 acres had been set aside to accommodate the spills and wastes it generated, but this was not enough for the company which for years dumped wastes across the south of Glasgow.

In 1991 these chromium wastes began to turn up across Cambuslang, Carmylie, Rutherglen, Toryglen and Eastfield. Council officials investigated and found elevated levels of chromium in the soil. Badly affected public areas were fenced off and signs were erected on parks with the warning, 'Keep out, contaminated land.' The Public Health Department of Greater Glasgow Health Board was asked to establish whether exposure to the chromium waste had caused elevated levels of cancer in the communities, as chromium in the workplace is associated with increased risks of lung cancer and possibly nasal cancer. The research reassuringly concluded that a review of routine mortality in cancer incidence data concerning the major known occupational risks associated with hexavalent chromium provided no evidence of adverse effects on the health of people living in areas of proven and suspected contamination. Furthermore, the levels of exposure, which had been recorded, posed no significant risk to human health. As a precautionary measure, it was recommended that exposure to chromium in airborne dust should be avoided and that children should not play in areas involving direct exposure to the hexavalent chromium.[12]

The failure to fully include the local population in designing and carrying out the initial health report created tensions between the authorities and the community activists. It seemed to them that the authorities, which were meant to regulate industry, had no idea of the scale of illegal dumping. In response an official action group called Cambuslang, Carmylie and Rutherglen against Pollution, with the unforgettable acronym CCRAP, was formed.

When a public meeting was held, it became apparent that there was extensive local knowledge of the contamination. Local activists found a former driver for the factory (which had latterly been called British Chrome and Chemicals Limited) and he in turn helped to track down other drivers to begin to put together a list of possibly contaminated sites. They remembered dumping the material that banked up the terraces around Rutherglen Glencairn Football Club and memories came back of depositing soils that formed the basis of the Duke's Road Park and the Burnhill Football ground. A report documenting the communities' experience called 'How safe is safe?' was published. Without the effort of the local activists and their links with the community, the extent of contamination was unlikely ever to have been discovered.

When these sites were investigated, extremely high levels of chromium contamination were established. Measurements were taken for both total chromium and hexavalent chromium. It is important to distinguish between chromium III, which occurs naturally in the environment and is an essential nutrient, and chromium VI, which is produced by industrial processes. According to the fact sheet issued in 2001 by the Agency for Toxic Substances and Disease Registry of the US Department of Health and Human Services, 'breathing high levels of chromium VI can cause irritation to the nose such as runny nose, nosebleeds and ulcers and holes in the nasal septum'.

It warns that 'Ingesting large amounts of Chromium VI can cause stomach upsets and ulcers, convulsions, kidney and liver damage and even death,' and adds that 'Skin contact with certain Chromium VI compounds can cause skin ulcers. Some people are extremely sensitive to Chromium VI or Chromium III. Allergic reactions consisting of severe redness and swelling of the skin have been noted.'[13]

In Scotland at the time of the investigation the threshold level measurement for total chromium in the soil was 1,000 milligrams per kilogramme (mg/kg) and for hexavalent chromium (CrVI) it was 25mg/kg. There is no action level. So not surprisingly local people were appalled to find that the illegal waste deposits at the Duke's Road playing fields measured 9,500mg/kg for total chromium and 1,230mg/kg for Chromium VI. The figures were even higher at the Rutherglen Glencairn Football Club, with total chromium measuring 26,150mg/kg and 4,450 for the hexavalent chromium.

The British standards were massively exceeded and by international comparison these limits are not onerous. Health Canada has established more detailed guideline limits for chromium contamination. It recommends that for residential/park-land areas the limits for total chromium should be not be more than 220mg/kg and for hexavalent chromium only 8mg/kg.[14]

Furthermore, in all of this it is interesting that there seems to be no suggestion that legal action against the company should be taken. The Glasgow operations closed down in 1968 and its business moved to Cumbria in England. City Council officials travelled to the company's laboratories there for training in how to measure chromium levels. However, the rule of law in Scotland is one of caveat emptor, let the buyer beware. The case of Clydebank District Council versus Monaville Estates Limited 1982 established that where any accumulation or deposit is a nuisance or injurious or dangerous to health, it has to be cleaned up by the owners of the land, even though they may not have been responsible for the contamination in the first place.

The chromium deposits were eventually the subject of detailed study, principally as a result of a Spanish Ph.D. student carrying out thesis work on the correlation between exposure to chromium and public health. Two studies, on congenital anomalies and leukaemia, were published in the *Journal of Public Health Medicine*.[15] Previous research had shown an excess in leukaemia in Cambuslang, for which there is no accepted explanation. Similarly, Glasgow also has a relatively high reported incidence of congenital anomalies compared with other UK and European cities, again for which no explanation has been found. The Spanish-led research looked at a ten-kilometre circle centred on the most polluted area, subdivided into ten concentric rings, each one kilometre in width. The assumption was that the closer to the most polluted sites, the greater the incidence would be if there were a correlation between chromium pollution and the incidence of leukaemia or birth malformations. In neither case was such a correlation found.

A third study was never published but concerned the incidence of lung cancer. It noted that research in the United States

had ruled out the possibility of an increase in the general population around a New Jersey site similarly contaminated with
chromium. However, it also acknowledged that 'currently there
are no exposure guidelines for the general population since
the US Environmental Protection Agency has withdrawn its
CrVI inhalation values and no safe levels for CrVI in air outside
the occupational setting have been suggested by regulatory
agencies or consensus groups elsewhere'.[16] The Glasgow research
did find a demonstrable decrease in the risk of lung cancer
the further you lived from the areas of concentrated pollution.
However, its analysis of the data showed the correlation
occurred only in men, not in women. This study therefore took
the view that the correlation was not caused by chromium,
but rather by other risk factors such as higher incidence of
smoking or occupational exposures associated with men.

Another team conducting research for Greater Glasgow
Health Board took a different approach. Instead of just utilising
medical records, it sought to compare the self-reported health
of a group of individuals living in an area contaminated by
chromium with a control group of residents in an uncontami-
nated area. The results were published in the *British Medical
Journal* and as far as the authorities were concerned, seemed
to offer satisfactory conclusions. Overall there appeared to be
little difference in the self-reported health in both groups.
However, when the residents in the contaminated area were
asked whether they thought that chromium was harmful to
health 25 per cent of them believed that it was. That group
reported significantly worse health than those who did not
believe chromium to be harmful, registering on average 16
points lower on the quality of life questionnaire dealing with
bodily pain, general health and role limitations due to physical
or emotional problems, social functioning, mental health,
physical functioning and vitality. The researchers concluded
that these noticeably lower scores point to 'the potential
importance of perception and possible anxiety'.[17] They also
noted that those who believed that chromium contamination
affected their health were in a minority. Furthermore, it seemed

that, if given the choice, less than one-third of those living in the polluted areas favoured remediation such as removal or burial of the chromium waste as compared to expenditure on local amenities, housing, education or employment. (This did not stop the authorities spending £40,000 on removing chromium-contaminated soil from the site of the tented village, which was temporarily erected for the reception of dignitaries attending the Champions League final at Hampden Park in Glasgow in 2002.)[18]

What are we to make of this? Here we have a case of gross pollution, carried out by a commercial company over a period of 150 years. Some of this was conducted illegally, yet has led to no prosecutions or recompense from those who had profited. The levels of pollution were greatly in excess of established limits and which a significant part of the population believes has impacted upon their quality of life and health. The health studies, which concluded that there was no excess disease from such exposure, were conducted in a way that did not engage the local population and some were not published until nearly a decade after the discovery. Some were not published at all.

Previous research into significant public health incidents has emphasised the importance of authorities demonstrating that they have responded promptly and also that they include the public in risk assessment and decision-making. In Glasgow's case it appeared, however, that the public authorities were satisfied with a very early study that there was nothing really to be concerned about, even though the researchers were aware that there were community concerns about the findings and the perceived impartiality of the research. The authorities also appeared to blame the continuing perception among 25 per cent of the population that chromium contributes to ill-health to a variety of external influences. (There seems to be a suggestion that the majority were rational in dismissing the chromium as a threat to health and the minority as irrational – a suggestion which is not supported by research on other communities.)[19]

To dismiss a quarter of the population of being ignorant of the scientific facts or dupes of the media and campaigners is sadly typical. There was reassurance to be had that the exposure had not resulted in observable increased incidences of leukaemia, birth malformations or lung cancer. Yet people were entitled to be worried, by a combination of factors. They could remember what had happened to workers, they had found out that the authorities were unaware of the extent of the problem, and suspected an inclination to minimise any suggestion of risk, not least because the authorities bore financial liability for remediation. People could not act to control the situation short of seeking to move away from their friends and neighbours.

The health of the people may still have been affected by the exposure, not in the manner in which occupational exposure afflicts workers but in the commonly experienced diminution of well-being and increase in stress.

Glasgow people could contrast the response here with reactions to chromium contamination elsewhere. On the other side of the Atlantic quite a different community believed it had suffered from chromium contamination. The town of Hinckley in California discovered that its ground water had been polluted with hexavalent chromium by Pacific Gas and Electricity Company (PG&E). The local residents attributed a range of health problems to drinking the contaminated water, and banded together to file a lawsuit against the power utility. The court action caused PG&E to agree to pay £333 million to the 648 plaintiffs. The people of Rutherglen are the unknown complainants of environmental injustice. The people of Hinckley will never be forgotten because Erin Brockovich represented them and it was their fight against big business that became a Hollywood Oscar-winning film.

Yet the very box-office success of that film prompted scientists in the United States to complain that the movie encouraged exactly the wrong way to think about data, by elevating individuals' medical histories to the level of proof and distorting the notion of risk. According to the *New York Times*, 'Scientists, seeing the evidence that so infuriated Erin Brockovich, would be much more cautious – and skeptical.'[20]

It should also be said that scientific studies dispute whether orally ingested CrVI could contribute to ill-health and in particular whether it is a carcinogen when ingested rather than inhaled. Californian scientists have concluded that there is no basis for concluding that orally ingested CrVI is a carcinogen. A similar position is taken in Glasgow, where the Health Board report says, 'once ingested absorption of hexavalent chromium from the gastro intestinal tract is minimal, most being converted by the action of gastric acid to the non absorbable trivalent form. On these grounds we do not think that ingestion of chromium is a significant risk to public health.'[21]

A major problem is that regulatory authorities continue to behave (at best) in the mindset of the industrial society, where risks can be separated, individually measured and assessed. Scientists are carrying out studies to answer questions that they have posed to themselves – the so-called null hypothesis. These may not be the same questions to which the community reasonably wants answers. Why have limits, if they can be massively exceeded and authorities are little concerned about the effects? At what level of contamination would authorities act without waiting to see what the ill-effects had been in the community? What are the limits of interpretation of the epidemiological studies? What happens if the studies are carried out after a timelag so that those who may have been exposed have moved out and those who have been little exposed are included in the study? What about particularly vulnerable populations? What about effects that are not easily recovered from medical records such as skin complaints?

People who have called for a study to be carried out can be disenchanted with the results. This is not just because they differ from their personal convictions but because the manner in which the study is conducted to satisfy sound science may be at odds with what people feel needs to be done.

Communities have certain expectations of such studies, sometimes due to popular epidemiology where they carry out their own assessment of incidence of ill-health and pathways by which it could be caused. However, this is often at odds with the professional approach. Communities may discount people who have only recently arrived in the area but live close to the site of pollution. They may include others such as school teachers or former long-standing residents, who have only recently moved out, on the commonsense grounds that what is being established is whether those who have been most exposed exhibit ill-health or conditions which are not seen to the same degree to those less exposed. A scientific approach will not necessarily adjust for individuals and will include everyone in a geographically defined area. Sometimes though, professional researchers will actually exclude people within affected areas as they seek to weed out 'believers' who may exhibit what has been termed recall bias.

For most communities it would be extremely difficult to demonstrate a causal effect between exposure to pollution and morbidity, especially incidences of cancer or other chronic conditions. The odds are stacked against such a finding – not because there is never any link but because the methodology that is likely to be employed means that a high degree of correlation would be required to be regarded as statistically significant.

In the USA the community of Glen Avon was inundated with millions of gallons of toxic chemicals from a waste dump, which overflowed in torrential rains. These events triggered community concerns about the dump and local incidents of illness were attributed to exposures. An epidemiological study was eventually commissioned, taking in 606 households, providing information on 2,039 inhabitants. The methodology, as normal, split the households into three study groups of high exposure risk, small exposure risk and a control group, which was deemed not exposed. At the press conference to announce the findings state health officials reported that there were no differences in cancer rates, miscarriages, birth defects or deaths in the study groups. However the public statements were not made by the epidemiologist who had carried out the study. He complained 'they presented the results of our study as negative – showing no effect. But this study was inconclusive, not negative and should have been presented to the press and public as being so. We couldn't tell who in the community was really exposed or not exposed – and the numbers were too small for statistical power.'[22]

Mark Huxham has shown the limitations of demonstrating statistically significant results. What if in Scotland, he asks, we decided to test the hypothesis that long-term exposure to electromagnetic fields increases the risk of cancer by just 1 per cent per annum? (So, in this case, a 1 per cent increase against the background level would increase cancers to 2.929 per cent, compared to a background level of 2.9 per cent.) Imagine, improbably, that we were allowed to test on humans by confining some groups to houses under pylons and control groups in villages with no electricity. They would have to be kept apart for at least ten years to allow cancers to develop. Even so, the power of the experiment to secure a 80 per cent chance of detecting a significant difference would need 4,200 groups of over 1,000 people – 4 million people out a population of 5 million.[23]

Often people are being asked to accept the results of research that are difficult to interpret and compare. The public would have to have a fairly sophisticated knowledge of epidemiology and its limitations to be able to interpret findings. In the case of Glen Avon mentioned above they should have been told at the outset that even if 30–40 per cent of the cancers in the community were caused by chemical exposure, the study would not have discovered it. According to the doctor who headed the investigation, 'you'd have to have a tripling or more in the rate of cancer before the study would detect it. The power of the study was not great because the number of people and illnesses we were working with were so small. That's the limitation of the science.'[24]

It is not basic scientific illiteracy that is at issue here. In Scotland there was been long running concern over the performance of a municipal waste incinerator in Dundee. Although now closed and replaced with a more modern (but accidentprone) facility, the potential health consequences of emissions from the old stack were raised following publication of research in France. In this study an association between proximity to a municipal solid waste incinerator in Besançon and clusters of soft-tissue sarcomas and non-Hodgkin's lymphomas was discovered.[25] There were requests for the study to be replicated in Dundee. When the results were published the researchers conclusion was that 'overall we have found no evidence of an association between residential proximity top the Baldovie incinerator and the incidence of non Hodgkin's lymphoma and soft tissue sarcoma'.[26] On the face of it an identical study had come to different conclusions. That is not to say either is wrong; they were just describing what they found (it is not established for instance that dioxin emissions from the French plant are responsible for the clusters there). However, scrutinising the methodology in Dundee reveals some variations from the French research. In particular, the Dundee study used records from when the incinerator first opened. The French study, however, started with records nine years after the start of operations in Besançon, and noted that the incidence of clustering was more pronounced in the years at the end of the study period (1980–95) some twenty years after the incinerator started. The latency period between exposure and diagnosis of cancer could be 15–20 years. As a result the outcomes in Dundee could be diluted by including years in which it would be highly unlikely that any effect from proximity to the incinerator could be seen. Whether or not this has any bearing on the conclusions, it is not something which individuals in a community are likely to spot for themselves.

They certainly will not be able to understand far less comment on research that affects them but is not made available to them. The outcomes of a study which was conducted into the potential health impacts of living next to the controversial Glasgow landfill of Paterson's of Greenoakhill have never been published. A version of the report was submitted to the Greater Glasgow Health Board, which is said to contain about 50 per cent of the data from the original research. Nevertheless a long letter was sent to a national newspaper from the consultant who carried out the study declaring:

This department cleared the Paterson's site of any link to ill-health in 1994, although no report was published of the findings, which were largely epidemiological, at that time. As a result, it was deemed fair to conduct a comprehensive investigation of the site . . . to establish what evidence existed of a potential for ill health as a result of living near the site.

This included epidemiological evidence (more than 130 rounds of analyses), as well as an examination of the consignment and monitoring data (including what is escaping from the site in terms of soil contamination, leachate, and gases). Despite our best efforts to find the evidence we would need to press for revoking its licence on grounds of purported harm to health, we were unable to find such evidence.

Clearly, there are serious issues about the harm done to the environment, the aesthetic aspects of living so near to unattractive sites, and the possibility of remediation of landfill sites. However, having studied these sites extensively, this department is prepared to state that there is no evidence that they are directly harming health.[27]

A summary of the results was presented at a meeting with the local community and the consultant concerned is satisfied that the local people accept the outcome and have focused their attention on deficiencies in the site management. However, in the absence of the full report it is impossible to look at the data and form any conclusions independently regarding the adequacy of the monitoring data provided by the company and by SEPA. The consultant's decision to publish the letter was prompted by what she regarded as scaremongering by politicians and others. It is a commonplace claim.

Drawing upon research around the 1988 Camelford incident (in which the water supply in north Cornwall was contaminated with 20 tonnes of aluminium sulphate), it has been suggested that perceptions of risk to health should be blamed on a cocktail of litigation, community action, self-appointed experts, consumer opinion polls, media attention and accusations of conspiracy.

It is no good accusing people in the local community of hysterical overreaction or scaremongering regarding risks as if the elites in society consistently act dispassionately, and proportionately. The reality is that officialdom can be prone to grandstanding with clumsy attempts at public reassurance or risk eradication. During the Love Canal furore, described in Chapter 1, local residents were consistently accused by those opposed to the environmental justice agenda of a hysterical response to a remote risk. Yet it was the Department of Health that indicated that Love Canal presented a great and imminent peril to the health of the general public and declared the existence of an emergency. It was the public authorities who, when carrying out the remediation work, thought it necessary to have 53 buses with their engines idling on stand by in case of an accident.[28] What on earth were the people supposed to think?

Keep out! Glasgow's contaminated land – who is scaremongering?
FoE Scotland

We should also remember that in Cambuslang and Ruther-glen it was the local authority that dramatically cordoned off the sites of contamination and posted signs saying 'Toxic – keep out'. Having been excluded from the contaminated sites, the local people were then excluded from the process of research and decision-making which was conducted over a protracted period, with conclusions that seemed to be inconsistent with the warnings posted visibly around the community.

A community that has been exposed to pollution deserves to have its concerns listened to and timeously responded to. They should be engaged in any investigation and be helped to understand the limitations, imposed by science or available resources, on the findings that are forthcoming. There should be a willingness on the part of professionals to use community expertise and experience.

The Greater Glasgow Health Board chromium researchers accepted that risk is a social construct and the importance, when evaluating the threat from environmental hazards, of introducing more public participation into both risk assessment and risk decision-making. The benefits of this would be an improved relevance and quality of scientific investigation and, it would be hoped, an enhanced legitimacy and public acceptance of the resulting decisions.

If this is to be done, professionals need to reject the attitude, which is depressingly common, that the public is ignorant of science and irrational over risks. They have also to question whether their use of language and insistence on sound science is as much about establishing a power relationship between themselves and lay people, and maintaining their position with their peers as it is about upholding high professional standards.

The notion of environmental justice is often related to risk. Crucially, it concerns not just the magnitude of any risk, but also the fairness of the exposure to it. Environmental injustice may be committed even if the risk involved is – scientifically speaking – very small. Perhaps there are less risky alternatives, or those who suffer the risk do not benefit from it in any way and have no control over their exposure. This is made worse when there are different perceptions of the degree of risk among those exposed and those regulating.

Decision-makers in industry, politics and planning authorities regard risk as an inevitable feature of technological development. Public attitudes to risks seem to vary depending upon the nature and source of the risk as opposed to just its magnitude. It is thought therefore that involuntary risks (such as exposure to toxins) are less acceptable than voluntary risks (for example smoking, or car driving) even if the voluntary activity involves a greater risk than the involuntary exposure. Other juxtapositions are whether the risk is natural or industrial; familiar or exotic; not memorable or memorable (for example everybody remembers Bhopal or Three Mile Island or Chernobyl); not dreaded or dreaded (such as cancers); chronic or catastrophic; fair or unfair.

All of this of course exasperates many in public authorities and in the scientific community where the common and dismissive view is that 'the degree of concern people have about risks is not based on logical, scientific fact'.[29] The environmental justice debate is often approached, therefore, by those in authorities as an unfortunate or contrived confrontation between at best an anxious, ill-informed public (or, at worst, a politically motivated and scaremongering campaign) and public officials and commercial organisations. These hold themselves to be better informed, indeed often expert, deploying facts to arrive at conclusions and decisions which have to be in the wider interests.

Within this, the scientists are held to be dispassionate, analytical, unbiased, reasoned and considered – all the merits required to conduct sound science. People will be characterised as emotional, subjective, biased, irrational, prescriptive and premature in arriving at their conclusions. 'The assumption of course is that sound science will invoke observing the world in a systematic way, seeing problems, collecting data and testing theories about why the problems are there and rejecting hypothesis which are perceived to be wrong.'[30]

Who would want to argue against something as profoundly

worthy as sound science? For years environmental activists themselves have been ardent advocates of a scientific approach believing that if it was deployed in cost–benefit analysis or environmental assessment in deciding upon whether to permit products, projects or policies, then the environment would be protected.

So in practical terms sound science is required to inform decision-making. However, the assumption that science, as used in contentious environmental cases, is value free needs to be challenged. The question appears to be no longer, 'What does the science tell us?' but 'Who is doing the telling and who paid for it?' A study of research programmes into four commonly used chemicals in America found that of 43 industry-funded studies, only 6 came out with any unfavourable findings; of the 118 studies conducted by those independent of industry, 71 were unfavourable. Jonathon Porritt has said, 'it is hard not to detect the reek of money around such findings.'[31] Others have identified what has been called affiliation bias, with for example toxicologists working for industry seeing chemicals as more benign than do their counterparts in academia and government.[32]

A corrosive flaking of the veneer of irreproachable neutrality has taken place so that less than half the public have confidence in what scientists working in industry have to say about environmental issues (and scientists working for the government don't fare much better).[33]

So while scientists and the decision-takers who depend upon their advice may be dismissive of public concerns and their understanding of science, the public have their own views of experts based upon recent experience of BSE, Foot and Mouth disease and genetically modified organisms (GMOs) as well as more localised scares. They may see scientific research as partial, incomplete, narrowly based, belated, and the scientists themselves as platitudinous, complacent, or arrogant.

Scientists, like lawyers, they believe, can be recruited to justify anything. Whoever saw an environmental assessment carried out by a company that utilising an array of botanists, chemists, geologists and soil scientists did not come to the conclusion that the proposed project could proceed without undue damage to the environment and the surrounding population? The public may doubt whether decision-takers have been provided with all the scientific evidence necessary to come to a conclusion when much of the science is sponsored by companies that have a vested interest in the outcomes. They may be intolerant when finding that research in the non-commercial or anti-commercial areas of public concerns is either scanty or non-existent.

The supposition among companies, scientists and policy-makers seems to be that the public, ignorant about scientific facts and victims of a sensationalist media, unreasonably demands zero risk. Fiona Fox, head of the Science Media Centre, has said there are entrenched misconceptions about science that have to be dispelled if public dialogue on scientific issues is to move forward. She has complained that 'We need to be able to debate issues [such as] genetically modified foods but if the public is expecting a guarantee of 100 per cent safety, how can we have an informed debate?'[34]

Who says that the public demand zero risk? A European research project into public attitudes towards agricultural biotechnologies found that 'Participants did not ask for zero risk or full certainty with respect to the impacts of GMOs and were well aware that the daily activities of ordinary lives are associated with numerous risks and benefits which have to be balanced against one another.'[35]

It was not scientific ignorance which generated concerns about GMOs but fundamental questions over why we need GMOs, and who will benefit from their use. People want to know who decided they should be developed and how. Why are we not given effective choice about whether or not to consume these products? Can controls imposed by regulatory authorities be applied effectively? Have the risks been seriously assessed? We want to be reassured that plans exist for remedial action if unforeseen harmful impacts occur. Will those who developed GMOs be held responsible in case of unforeseen harm and how will they be held to account?

At the height of the furore regarding the application of biotechnology to foodstuffs, the British government backed an Organisation for Economic Co-operation and Development (OECD) conference, held in Edinburgh, to address the issue. A smattering of environment organisations were invited to be present, although the bulk of the audience and the presentations came from those involved in biotechnology research. When one delegate had the temerity to raise her hand and to reflect popular concern regarding the introduction of novel foodstuffs, she was asked by the chairman either to cite the peer-reviewed literature in which these issues had been reflected or else to sit down. Sound science? Perhaps so, but it crystallised the perception that scientists were simply not willing to address issues with which the public were concerned.

What is strongly evident from this research is that the public base their views not on ignorance or prejudice but on an experience of how past decisions have been taken and on observed outcomes. They are not prepared to reduce the debate to matters of 'neutral' science. They do not believe it is premature to explore 'what if' scenarios and to seek reassurance about what will happen if things go wrong because they know from past experience that institutions are fallible and that safety measures and rules are likely to be breached. The authorities may focus more on probabilities, but the public focus on consequences.

People have also learnt that authorities are loath to admit uncertainties, and often seek to suggest that there is no alternative or there is no evidence of harm. This excludes consideration of matters which the public feel are important – including the involvement of the public in the decision-making process itself. Such decisions they may believe to be dependent as much on value judgements or moral considerations as on scientific evidence.

Assurances that there is either no evidence of harm to human health or that the risks are so low that it would be a wasteful use of resources to mitigate them are often met with scepticism and disbelief. There is a lived experience, which is that the authorities tend to wait until damage has occurred

Keep out! Burden of risk may fall disproportionately on poor areas.
FoE Scotland

before they take action. It has been said of chemical risks that 'control usually follows rather than proceeds any unforeseen and unknowable disaster and society seems willing to pay that price for the advantage that new substances offer. To ban them until they are proved harmless would burden enterprise with extra costs and slow the rate of technical change. The preference seems to be for taking some risks with public health.'[36]

The crucial issue here is that while society may be said to be willing to take the risk, the reality is that the burden may fall disproportionately on a minority. Is society prepared to pay the cost of providing the reassurance and the compensation that those at risk may require?

Personally I have no interest in squandering Scotland's scarce resources on tackling problems that are either insignificant or indeed scientifically demonstrated to be non-existent. But if we are to are to answer the question, 'How safe is safe is enough for this particular culture?', which 'cannot simply be brushed aside,'[37] then we need to accept two things. First, there must be a better engagement of those who are affected and not just leaving safety issues to experts. Second, we have also got to consider the consequences of living with uncertain risks.

It is disingenuous to imply that the process of decision-making on issues of risk is made by politicians on a wholly rational basis, informed by a scientific consensus drawn from timeous and complete research conducted by independent scientists. Nor do I accept that decision-makers marshal all of the available claims upon their resources and then apply a test of prioritisation dependent upon need, urgency, greatest societal benefit and avoidance of risk and so on. A community waging a campaign to force a company to adopt a more rigorous pollution control regime should not be told that the cost of this is somehow subtracted from the sums which may have been made available for more useful improvements to community health, such as tackling smoking or diet. It is simply not the case, as the money is more likely to be returned to the shareholders or spent on improving the firm's competitiveness.

Communities are told that they should not be wasting their time on insignificant, if involuntary risks, compared to the culpability that they may, as individuals, have for the voluntary and significant risks associated with their lifestyle and personal decision-making. This is resented when people are aware that the government has been prepared to take drastic action to remove infinitesimal risks such as banning beef on the bone, even though the risk of that being a route by which an individual would die of new-variant CJD has been described as one chance in one billion in a year.[38]

Some scientists, however, believe that what they regard as a combination of scientific illiteracy and public hysteria means that taking decisions about societal risks should be left to expert bodies. In the UK this has been the approach taken, with the government establishing expert advisory groups and then often seeking to present the subsequent political decision as being inescapable in the light of the scientific evidence and advice that it has received. Paul Slovic has spent a lifetime studying risks and attitudes to them. He is not only sceptical of the political ramifications of transferring power to a technical elite but also believes that it would be misguided, as 'we have no assurance that expert judgments are immune to biases once they are forced to go beyond their precise knowledge and rely on their judgments'.[39] He concludes, 'no approach to acceptable risk is clearly superior to the others ... because hazards are not the only consideration in hazard management decisions. The best we can hope for is some intelligent muddling through.'[40] The current consensus on muddling through seems now to place a greater emphasis on public consultation and engagement with the decision-making process. However, there is scepticism about the degree to which this is being attempted and the scale of response to be expected. According to Julie Hill, Vice Chair of the UK Government's Agriculture and Biotechnology Commission, 'We live in a democracy but that doesn't seem to be enough for those who demand greater public participation in decisions and trust is a commodity in short supply. At the same time life is too short to boil an egg let alone take part in complex discussions about environmental risk and precaution.'[41]

Yet without this engagement, the temptation is to slip back into expert assurances and patronage. In which case, demands of accountability can be resented as a challenge to professionalism. However, as we have seen, communities which are at risk should be included in studies – with a clarity of what is being assessed, what the limitations of the research are and how it may be interpreted. This is still not happening.

Finally, the stress of living in a polluted environment needs to be better considered in Scotland. Communities exposed to toxins or levels of pollution that are associated with potential health impacts find themselves in such a situation involuntarily. The exposure may be unknown, the effects uncertain and their best course of future action unclear.

Where communities are exposed to pollutants which are associated with outcomes which they dread, to which they have been exposed by human action and where they have to depend upon assurances from experts because it is beyond their capacity to establish the consequences for themselves, then there is a significant loss of control over their lives. This is a serious matter – a matter of public health. 'If there is one core postulate in the social psychology of human society, it is the belief that people need to understand, feel in control of and be effective in producing changes in their physical and social environment.'[42]

Public health specialists recognise that a distinction has to be drawn between the physical harm caused by exposure to toxic sites and the effects of stress arising from such proximity. The report of an expert panel workshop on the psychological responses to hazardous substances concluded, 'If higher than normal levels of psychological stress and psychological sequelae are being found in communities affected by possible exposures to hazardous substances, then this presents a public health problem.'[43] This is not unique to toxic sites.

People are forced to make sense of the situation for themselves as 'beliefs are based on the facts available to them, pre-existing opinions, cultural factors, sensory cues, and the beliefs of leaders and others in the community. On the other hand scientists tend to rely on objective data produced by specialised testing that is subject to statistical analysis. The results of surveys and studies are highly technical and may be difficult to explain to a lay audience that may not share the same underlying beliefs and values as the scientists.'[44]

The sense of loss of control is likely to be even greater for poor communities, which will have other issues where the same sense of powerlessness and grievance is felt. These may include poorly constructed, hard to heat homes (where often the blame, nevertheless, for things like condensation and damp is attributed to the residents themselves); neighbourhood issues of crime, drug taking and bad neighbours; problems with public transport and accessing employment, health or social facilities; or as sole carers for children or for the elderly expecting greater assistance from the authorities.

This is where social justice and environmental justice meshes – the stress of living lives which are dependent on decisions by others and where at the bottom line the 'sense of fairness and justice is violated'.[45]

Notes

1. *Sunday Herald*, 18 August 2002.
2. Scottish New Homes Lead Survey, Scottish Centre for Infection and Environmental Health, October 2000.
3. http://www.aeat.co.uk/netcen/airqual/reports/strategicpolicy/2001 socialdeprivation.
4. Cave, *Applying Psychology to the Environment*, p. 146.
5. Johnston and McIvor, *Lethal Work: A History of the Asbestos Tragedy in Scotland*, pp. 1–2.
6. Ibid. p. 213.
7. Ibid. pp. 212–13.
8. Ibid. p. 214.
9. *The Scotsman*, 17 May 2002.
10. Baarsachers, *Eco Facts and Eco-fiction*, p. 6.
11. Falkirk Council, *Inspection Strategy for the Identification of Contaminated Land under Environmental Protection Act 1990, Part IIA*. September 2001, p. 3.
12. 'Assessment of the Risk to Human Health from Land Contaminated by Chromium Waste.' Report by the Department of Public Health, Greater Glasgow Health Board, December 1991.
13. CAS no. 7440-47-3 Chromium, US Agency for Toxic Substances and Disease Registry, February 2001.
14. Canadian Soil Quality Guidelines for Contaminated Sites – Human Health Effects: Chromium Final Report, March 1996. The National Sites Remediation Programme.
15. Domingo Euzigarre-Garcia, Carlos Rodriguez-Andres and C. Graham Watt, 'Congenital Anomalies in Glasgow between 1982 and 1989 and Chromium Waste', *Journal of Public Health Medicine*, vol. 22, no. 1, pp. 54–8; Domingo Euzigarre-Garcia, Carlos Rodriguez-Andres, C. Graham

Watt and David Hole, 'A study of leukaemia in Glasgow in connection with chromium-contaminated land', *Journal of Public Health Medicine*, vol. 21, no. 1, pp. 435–8.

16. Domingo Euzigarre-Garcia, C. Graham Watt and David Hole, 'Lung Cancer in Glasgow and Soil Polluted with Chromium'. (Unpublished, no date.)

17. Peter McCarron, Ian Harvey, Robert Brogan and J. Tim Peters, 'Self reported health of people in an area contaminated by chromium waste: interview study', *British Medical Journal*, vol. 320, 1 January 2000, p. 14.

18. *Glasgow Evening Times*, 14 March 2002.

19. Edelstein, 'Contamination: The Invisible Built Environment', p. 552.

20. 'A Hit Movie is Rated "F" in Science', *New York Times*, 11 April 2000.

21. 'Assessment of the Risk to Human Health from Land Contaminated by Chromium Waste.' Report by Department of Public Health, Greater Glasgow Health Board, December 1991.

22. Setterberg and Shavelson, *Toxic Nation*, p. 162.

23. Dr Raymond Natura quoted in Setterburg and Shavelson, *Toxic Nation*, p. 155.

24. Huxham, 'Science and the search for truth', in Huxham and Sumner, *Science and Environmental Decision Making*, p. 25.

25. Jean-François Viel, Patrick Arveux, Josette Baverel and Jean-Yves Cahn, 'Soft-Tissue Sarcoma and Non-Hodgkin's Lymphoma Clusters around a Municipal Solid Waste Incinerator with High Dioxin Emission Levels', *American Journal of Epidemiology*, vol. 152, no. 1, 2000.

26. Investigation of the incidence of cancer in the City of Dundee and environs – a report of stage 3, prepared by Dr F. L. R. Williams, Dr M. Roworth and Dr A. B. Lawson, 11 June 2002, p. 3.

27. *The Herald*, 4 February 2002. Letter from Dr Helene Irvine, Consultant in Public Health Medicine, Department of Public Health, Greater Glasgow NHS Board.

28. Mazur, *A Hazardous Inquiry*, p. 77.

29. Deegan, *Managing Activism*, p. 94.

30. Bell and Morse, *Sustainability Indicators*, p. 82.

31. Porritt, *Playing Safe: Science and the Environment*, p. 21.

32. Slovic, *The Perception of Risk*, p. 311.

33. Porritt, *Playing Safe: Science and the Environment*, p. 18.

34. 'Public ignorance "limits debate" on science policy', *The Financial Times*, 15 July 2002.

35. Marris et al., *Public Perceptions of Agricultural Biotechnologies in Europe*.

36. Clapp, *An Environmental History of Britain*, p. 64.

37. Scott, 'Risk Society or Angst Society?', in Adam et al., *The Risk Society and Beyond*, p. 43.

38. Porritt, *Playing Safe: Science and the Environment*, p. 45.

39. Slovic, *The Perception of Risk*, p. 119.

40. Ibid. p. 134.
41. 'Scanning the horizon', *Inside Track*, Issue 2, Summer 2002. The Green Alliance, London.
42. Edelstein, 'Contamination: The Invisible Built Environment', p. 567.
43. Tucker, *Report of the Expert Panel on the Psychological Responses to Hazardous Substances*, p. 11.
44. Ibid. p. 2.
45. Edelstein, 'Contamination: The Invisible Built Environment', p. 567.

6

The Right to Know – What is Happening in our Environment?

JUST NOT KNOWING about what is going on can lead to stress, fears and a sense of a lack of control. If you were living next to a factory which emitted strange smells, from which you could see emissions being vented to the air or from time to time into the local water course it would be natural for you to want to know what was going on. Or if living in a community surrounded by industrial activities you might wonder whether the accumulated impact of dust from the opencast sites, and sooty exhausts from the lorry movements could have any impact upon your health and that of your children. People's curiosity to find out what is going on in their area and how it might affect them is wholly reasonable and at the heart of environmental justice.

Getting information in Britain has been notoriously fraught given that attitudes to access have often been shaped by the Official Secrets Act and notions of commercial confidentiality, whether or not these strictly apply. When the deep-water port of Hunterston resumed the import of foreign coal, people in Fairlie wanted to find out whether planning permission for the site permitted the tonnages being accepted. The facility was owned by Clydeport, at that time the recently privatised emanation of the former Clyde Port Authority. The community was told that, as it was a private company, the information was commercially confidential. When it was pointed out, however, that the company was depending upon permissions which had been provided to the previously publicly owned state body, it was then decreed that the information would be withheld under the thirty-year rule governing official secrets. Only after dogged persistence was access to the archived documents provided. However, terms were stipulated: officials could remove anything which they thought was prejudicial, no notes were to be taken by the scrutinisers on behalf of the community and finally the community representatives could not reveal to anybody else what they had seen. In all probability these constraints were challengeable but are typical of the attitudes of officialdom towards those who wish to pry.

Environmental activists should actually be much better off than any other sector when seeking information. In recognition of the public interest into emissions, which by their nature affect air, land and water and can have an impact over a wide geographic area, a European Union directive has provided citizens with access to environmental information. In 1992 the UK put in place the Environmental Information Regulations (EIRs), which for most practical purposes provide reasonably extensive rights to inquire and receive information about the environment.

Long experience, however, has told us that it is one thing to have rights on paper it is quite another to have them properly implemented by the various bodies to which they apply. When local authorities, for instance, were required to set up registers covering air-polluting activities in their area, confusion was evident. A public register gives the impression that somehow this is a large calf-bound ledger into which details have been laboriously transcribed for public viewing or a computer terminal with a searchable database sitting in council reception areas or libraries. Usually neither is the case. The public register is often the filing cabinet with the original working documents and applications sitting in manila folders in hopefully rough date order. Trying to get straightforward information was often thwarted. Sometimes the information was missing because the working file was lying on an official's desk someplace or the register was not available for access because the person responsible was on lunch break. In some instances Councils would refuse to provide the information until the air pollution licensing process had been completed. This was in direct contradiction of the purpose of the process of public registration, which was to allow people to inspect the applications so that their views could be taken into account in the licensing system. There was evidence that training of frontline staff had not taken place, as they would ask inquirers their name and the reason for their enquiry (which sounds reasonable except that the law expressly provides that members of the public should not have to supply such details). However, since then it is probably fair to say that many public bodies have improved their operational systems for dealing with inquiries from the public – at least so far as those requests which appear to be innocuous are concerned. However, the feeling has persisted that whilst they may have got better in observing the letter of the law that is, not resisting requests for information and providing it timeously, the public may still remain dissatisfied so far as the quality of the response to their enquiry is concerned.

The Environmental Information Regulations of 1992 (and updated in 1998) guarantee a right of access to information held by a public authority and relating to the environment to be provided within two months (unless the information falls within certain categories of exemption). Furthermore, this provision is supplemented in Scotland by a Scottish Executive code of practice on access to information, which applies to all public bodies within the Executive's jurisdiction. This states that the target for responding to requests for information should be twenty working days. (This is reflected in a further revision of the EIRs for 2003 by which the legal time limit is reduced from two months to twenty working days for standard requests in conformity with the new Freedom of Information Act.) Better still, certain of these public organisations have developed their own in-house guidelines. SEPA aims to respond within ten days and Scottish Enterprise within seven working days or fourteen if a fuller response is required.

So, on the face of it, the public can expect a pretty good service from public authorities. However, it is not clear that any of these organisations have put in place systems to test whether or not these deadlines are being met.

Sometimes requests are just plain ignored. A perfectly straightforward request was sent to all of Scotland's local authority Chief Executives, asking simply who was responsible for bathing-water issues in their area. Only 17 authorities replied within 2 months, the deadline specified by the EC directive. A reminder eventually prompted another 13 replies, some up to 3 months after the initial request. Two authorities never bothered to reply.

We may not have been given information because of poor systems and procedures within the relevant authority. But sometimes the suspicion has been that the authority has second guessed how this information may be used and finds a reason either not to provide it or to delay its release. Glasgow City Council, for example, refused to release the results of air-pollution monitoring at two assessed sites in the city. One of these was at the then new Buchanan Galleries, where Friends of the Earth had objected to the form of construction that effectively turned part of a major road into a tunnel through which pedestrians were expected to walk. Initially the Council simply ignored the request for three months then it refused the information stating, 'the data were not to be released until a reasonable period of time had elapsed and sufficient data has been gathered'. We formally requested the monitoring results, quoting the EU directive on freedom of access to environmental information and the UK Environmental Information Regulations. Again this was initially ignored by the Council but finally six months after the initial request the Council supplied the information.

Authorities have to balance the right to know with commercial rights to confidentiality. Communities are regularly concerned about what is being dumped and whether it conforms to the site licence. This is always heightened when there are pollution incidents, foul smells and in particular when the local community observes lorry movements happening out of hours. One way of establishing what is moving on to a site would be through having access to the waste transfer notes, which by law are required to be handed from the waste carrier to the landfill operator specifying what type of waste is being dumped, who is responsible for it and where it comes from. Copies are supplied to SEPA. However, requests for access to these notes have been denied, the argument being that if it was supplied to communities it would also have to be provided to rival haulage companies, who might use the information to poach contracts.

Away from the industrial heartland of Scotland, Friends of the Earth Scotland has pursued a high-profile campaign on the environmental impacts of fish farming. Fish farming is now big business – it is no longer, if it ever was, a kind of marine crofting. Indeed, 70 million fish are produced in Scotland annually, with production growing from 30,000 tonnes in 1990 to 130,000 tonnes at the turn of the century. The industry estimates that 6,500 jobs are secured from fish farming and that it is worth £240 million to the Scottish economy. (Although it is worth noting the number of those employed directly in production actually fell from 1,491 to 1,304 between 1989 and 1999 even though tonnage output had quadrupled.) It is a big multinational business with foreign firms dominating production, such as the Dutch giant Nutreco, which operates in sixty countries and owns the Marine Harvest farms in Scotland. (The nineteen aquaculture multinationals represent about 18 per cent of all foreign companies operating in Scotland.)[1]

It takes over 3kg of wild fish to produce 1kg of farmed fish. As a side effect of this, farmed fish may have a higher level of dioxins and PCBs in their flesh, derived and concentrated from this oil-rich diet. This is worrying news for an industry that promotes itself as contributing to a healthy diet. When the BBC broadcast a documentary highlighting these concerns it led to questions in the Scottish Parliament, and the following assurances from the then First Minister Henry McLeish:

On questions of food safety, the Scottish Executive is advised by the Food Standards Agency. The agency has advised that there is currently no evidence to indicate that farmed salmon poses a health risk for consumers. All new research is assessed as part of the agency's continuing review of contamination levels across the food chain from agents such as dioxins and polychlorinated biphenyls. It is important that consumers are fully informed on food safety issues, and the Food Standards Agency will ensure that scientific evidence is made public. The Executive believes in open government and we will do all that we can to give the public the information that they need.

This could not be clearer – the scientific advice was not going to be withheld as having been provided for internal discussion only. But what was the scientific advice? I wrote to the First Minister on 22 January 2001, less than a fortnight after his statement to Parliament, asking how many samples of wild and farmed salmon had been tested for PCBs and dioxins since 1982. Given his assurances that there was no evidence of health risks I asked what levels of dioxin and PCB contamination are considered safe by the government. Was it is safe to eat more than one 100g portion of farmed Scottish salmon per week, and was the advice different for small children and pregnant women. This request was passed to the Food Standards Agency (FSA) in Aberdeen.

We cannot know what the reaction was when it was received. Did they wonder if the information might be used to undermine an important industry? What if the information was 'misused' to give rise to a food scare? In March 2001 the FSA reply provided only partial information of testing and a statement that 'consumption of more than two large portions of salmon per week is unlikely to be harmful'. This did not entirely correlate with its previous statement that eating two portions of fish per week and only one portion of oily fish (including salmon) is safe.

I therefore wrote again in June 2001 to request the testing information and to ask for a straightforward response to the question of whether it is one or two portions of farmed salmon a week which is safe to eat. Under the Environmental Information

Regulations this information should have been supplied within two months. I next heard from the FSA in June 2002 – a full year later and only then to be told that the reason for the delay was due to 'the detail and depth of information you require'. This was not acceptable as an excuse but was even less credible as an explanation in light of the fact that no further information was actually supplied. Instead the suggestion was to contact the FSA in London, which was 'in the process of developing research' on the areas outlined in my letter. Such a response hardly fulfilled the First Minister's assurance that everything will be done to make the scientific evidence available.

The experience of a high-profile campaigning organisation may not be representative of what happens with the general public. So in 2000 over 350 volunteers were recruited and asked to write to a variety of public authorities including the Scottish Environment Protection Agency, Scottish Natural Heritage, local

Farmed fish – public assurances on contamination, so what were the results of tests?
Colin McPherson

enterprise companies, health boards and local authorities. They asked for information on a variety of environmental matters. Overall about 8 per cent of the letters received no reply whatsoever. Furthermore 9 per cent of the letters received responses that took longer than twenty days. The volunteers were asked to assess the quality of the information that they did receive and only 9 per cent thought that the tone of the response was unhelpful, although 18 per cent thought the information was inadequate. The performance of the authorities, however, varied, with local enterprise companies (LECs) performing markedly less well than others who are perhaps used to implementing the environmental information regulations. In the case of the LECs nearly 14 per cent of letters were simply ignored, receiving no reply; 14 per cent of the inquirers thought the responses were unhelpful and 23 per cent felt the accuracy of the responses were poor.

Responding to specific inquiries in this fashion is a passive form of freedom of information, providing access but volunteering little. It depends upon the individual requesting the information precisely enough to be able to receive an adequate reply. It may be that the individual requires a mass of information available from a variety of sources to be fully informed as to what has prompted the inquiry in the first place. Authorities are not anticipating reasonable lines of inquiry. People may want to know what the neighbouring company emits but also for purposes of comparison to know what is coming out of similar plants elsewhere in the country. They may want to be informed of the total emissions coming from a plant or the total emissions of a particular chemical from all sources in the area. The obvious solution is for the regulatory bodies to require polluters to provide them with information and for it in turn to be provided to the public through an electronic database which can be remotely accessed through an individual's computer rather than by having to go to the local office or headquarters of the regulatory body or local authority. In Scotland, we are about to get a database system. This does not necessarily mark a culture change because it is a requirement of

the Pollution Prevention and Control (Scotland) Regulations
2000. These in turn implement a 1996 European Union directive
concerning integrated pollution prevention and control. The
information available to comply with this directive is strictly
limited. There will only be a requirement to report on fifty
chemicals and on this basis an inventory of the principal
emissions and sources will be published only every three
years, at least initially. The information may not be available
on a searchable website but perhaps only by calling at SEPA
headquarters in Stirling.

This compares poorly with existing provision available
elsewhere. The United States Environment Protection Agency
draws up what it calls a Toxic Release Inventory (TRI). The
TRI database was established under the Emergency Planning
and Community Right to Know Act 1986 and as such seems
to provide information which would be of interest and use to
communities concerned about the impact of chemical hazards
in their areas. For instance:

- What chemicals were released into the local environment
  during the preceding year.
- How much of each chemical went into the air, water and
  land in a particular year.
- How much of the chemicals were transported away from
  the facility for disposal, treatment, recycling or energy
  recovery.
- How chemical wastes were treated at the reporting facility.
- The efficiency of waste treatment.
- Pollution prevention and chemical recycling activities.

Even in England and Wales the Environment Agency has
established a database using information gathered under the
Integrated Pollution and Control Regulations dealing with large
industries and their annual release of chemicals to air, water
and land.

So why is it that, yet again, Scotland seems so reluctant to
proactively assist communities who may feel that they are

experiencing environmental injustice or just have a desire to know more about what is happening regarding their local environment?

There is an official reluctance to put extra demands on industry to collect information beyond what is actually required of them. Soon there will be such a requirement when the provisions of the Aarhus Convention are carried into effect. It makes provision for an inventory to cover 131 chemicals with the option of including another 113. It also provides for annual reporting on a publicly accessible website.

A reluctance to divulge more than the minimum of information may arise from concerns over the use to which it may be put by troublemakers. In the United States, campaigners at Environment Defense take the EPA information and turn it into a scorecard of polluters, allowing comparisons of different facilities and states. They also add health-based information to alert citizens about the potential effects of the pollutants being released. Friends of the Earth in England has copied this approach, taking the Environment Agency's database and producing league tables of the worst polluters. It also highlights the link between the location of polluting industries and the socio-economic status of the communities surrounding them.

As a result people living around the Shell plant in Cheshire are able to find out that it emitted almost 11,000 kilogrammes of acetone and 47,000 kilos of particulates into the air, that almost 5,000 kilos of toluene was discharged to water sources and that over 12 million tonnes of special waste was generated by the complex. No information, however, is held on the Shell facilities north of the border.

A more general right to information will come into force in Scotland by December 2005. A Freedom of Information Act was one of the flagship commitments provided by the coalition government when it came to power in 1999. At its centre is the general right to know, without justifying why you need to know. When the Act was finally passed in 2002, it was rightly hailed as a progressive piece of legislation. Devolution had meant that the ability to secure information was assisted by Scottish provisions which were more beneficial than in the UK Act. Authorities will have to provide the information unless they can demonstrate substantial prejudice. This is a much higher test than currently operated by the code of practice, which only requires a possibility of harm to be identified. It is also seen as more stringent than the Westminster provisions, under which public bodies can withhold information if they can demonstrate that their interests are simply prejudiced.

There is no doubt that the legislation will improve upon current Scottish practice by extending the right to information beyond environmental matters and applying it widely across all public bodies and public-service providers in Scotland, including the National Health Service, schools and the police. (Certain categories of information are still automatically excluded such as defence and security issues, matters affecting the royal family and the Honours system.) Underpinning these rights is an independent Scottish Information Commissioner who will be able to order the disclosure of information in the public interest, and resolve disputes between those requesting the information and those refusing to provide it all or in part.

Even so there has never been any question of the archives or filing cabinets of government being thrown open. In drawing up the legislation it was clear that the Executive sought to balance a right to access against what might happen in the worst-case scenario or if a group of people should, from their perspective, abuse the intent of the legislation. Dr Richard Simpson, at that time junior minister for Justice, reinforced this by reminding us that just because the government was introducing the legislation did not mean that it intended to be a soft touch for campaigning organisations.[2]

It was initially proposed that public bodies would have the discretion to charge the full costs of providing information costing over £100. This would have meant that people in Scotland could have been charged significantly more than people south of the border, where it was proposed that no more than 10 per cent of the costs could be levied. So, for example, if it cost £200 to comply with a request in England the charge would be £20. In Scotland it would have been £100.

After consultation, the Executive responded to concerns and in fact the proposed charging regime for Scotland is now generous and better than under the UK Act, providing the information free up to £100 and only charging 10 per cent thereafter.

There are a number of provisions in the legislation where there is the possibility, and indeed likelihood, of public bodies and information requesters not seeing eye to eye. For instance, the Act anticipates that requests may be received from 'different persons who appear to it to be acting in concert or whose requests appear to have been instigated wholly or mainly for a purpose other than the obtaining of the information itself'. In which circumstance the public body can withhold the information if the cost of providing it would be excessive.

Authorities could also withhold information which, if disclosed, would be likely to prejudice substantially the commercial interests of any person. Information, which is being gathered as part of a research programme, may be withheld. (Universities argued that the capacity to tender for, and secure, lucrative commercial contracts with companies commissioning research may be compromised and Scotland would lose out to English Universities, who are not subject to the same potential requirements to disclose.) The Executive's view is that it would be unreasonable for research to be either prematurely disclosed or the intellectual investment to be given away for nothing.

It will be important to ensure that those required to implement the system reasonably interpret the provisions for exemption. The backstop against abuse or misinterpretation is the provision for a Scottish Information Commissioner. There is no doubt that this is a fundamentally important post. The Commissioner has to ensure that the requirements of the Freedom of Information Scotland Act 2002 are met, and is responsible for providing the principal interpretation of the Act. The Commissioner will also encourage the proactive disclosure of information by authorities and will deal with applications from people seeking disclosure of information which has been refused.

The Scottish Information Commissioner is going to have to rule on what is substantial prejudice, what is commercially confidential, what constitutes policy advice, what can be considered as research and what happens when there is an unjustifiable delay.

The experience of the Irish Commissioner, on which much of the Scottish system appears to be modelled, may tell us something about what we can expect to happen here.

In 2001 Irish public authorities received just over 15,000 requests under the freedom of information legislation. Decisions by the authorities, mostly for refusal to provide information, were appealed to the Commissioner in 387 cases. About 30 per cent of these were withdrawn or discontinued after discussion with the Commission staff and in 16 per cent of all the reviews completed settlement was achieved between the public body and the appellant without need for a formal decision.

In Ireland the public authorities refused to supply any information in about 20 per cent of the requests they receive and grant the information in full in less than 60 per cent. When the figures are broken down central government is seen to be the most reluctant in parting with information, with the civil service granting full release in only 38 per cent of cases. This contrasts with the situation in Australia, where the federal government refuses requests only in 8 per cent of all cases.

Clearly the Scottish Commissioner is going to have to look at the experience of counterparts elsewhere and anticipate the difficulties which may arise and provide guidance as clearly as possible for public authorities in Scotland. We should take heed of the Irish Commissioner when he says that 'Experience abroad indicates that the principal barriers to the successful implementation of FOI are inadequate resources, lack of proper training, poor procedures and practices including poor information management and the slowness of the political and administrative system to change the culture of secrecy.'[3] The test of the regime should not be the number of aggrieved citizens who feel compelled to complain to the Commissioner but rather the willingness and ability of the authority to satisfy the request in full or at least in part. Certainly Kevin Murphy, the Irish Commissioner, is in no doubt that the freedom of information legislation has led to better governance:

> I believe citizens are now better informed than ever before about how government works and how decisions are made. I also believe that as a result of FOI and other legislation affecting the public service, the culture of public bodies is changing more rapidly, in some cases than others, to one where they are more comfortable in dealing openly with their clients and citizens in terms of explaining their actions and activities.[4]

People are not just asking for the information out of curiosity. Often they require the information because they are challenging a proposal to grant a licence to a polluting industry or they are objecting to a grant of a planning application. These submissions are usually time restricted – for example there is a limit of twenty-eight days to object to a planning application. If the information comes within twenty days it may be of some use, if it comes belatedly after disputing the failure of the authority to correctly implement the provisions of the freedom of information legislation then it may be of little use.

This is not just the view of disgruntled activists. Looking back over the first year of the Irish regime, the Commissioner there said, 'Very few requesters seek access to records for their own sake. They are looking for information, and worthwhile information at that. If information is released only after a decision has been reached, at a time when it is perceived that the requester can no longer make any effective use of it then one must wonder whether the information is worthwhile and whether the purpose of the Act is being served.'[5]

Getting a decision can be a protracted business. In Ireland the Commissioner was expected to complete a review of each appeal within four months (now reduced to three months). Yet he admits that almost no cases were completed within the deadline and that significant delays of more than twelve months before coming to a decision have become the norm. A finger has been pointed at public authorities, which were held at least partly responsible by failing to provide the necessary information to the Commission's investigators. The Executive can take some comfort that if anybody is aggrieved by an authority's unwitting or deliberate failure to implement the intent of the Act, this can be remedied by an application to the Commissioner. However, it still needs to be acknowledged that the information's purpose may have been negated or degraded by the authority's action. And we should not imagine that the authorities do not consider how the information may be used and whether or not it prejudices their own agenda.

The freedom of information legislation is a major step forward for Scotland but it exhibits some of the characteristics of matters being viewed primarily through the eyes of authorities. The drafters have made what they regard as reasonable provisions for withholding information primarily to avoid it being misused or to avoid the system being abused by obsessive, troublesome or wilful campaigners. However, what concerns campaigners is that the provisions for exemptions will be explored by authorities to deny, delay or make opaque the information which they hold.

Notes

1. See Friends of the Earth Scotland, *The One that Got Away*.
2. *Good Morning Scotland*, BBC Radio Scotland, 24 April 2002.
3. Irish Information Commissioner Annual Report for 2001.
4. Ibid.
5. Information Commissioner's speech given at 'Freedom of Information Act – One year on' conference, Dublin Castle, 23 April 1999.

7

Sustainable Development in Scotland –
Getting beyond the Rhetoric

WHEN SAM GALBRAITH was a minister in the Scottish Executive, I met with him to discuss how we could be sure that the Scottish Executive was living up to its promise to put sustainable development at the heart of its programme for government. In particular we discussed the merits of indicators of sustainable development. The UK government had adopted about 150 indicators. Scotland at that time had none. Galbraith was notoriously dismissive of government by measurement and insisted that 'There is only one indicator which matters in terms of judging whether or not the quality of life in this country is improving and that is life expectancy at birth.' We will return to whether or not Scotland is sustainable and how that may be measured later but let's take it at face value. Recent government figures show that the life expectancy of Glasgow men on average is 68.7 years and for women 75.7 years. Glasgow City is the local authority with the lowest life expectancy at birth in the UK. For both women and men five out of six of the bottom local authorities in the UK for life expectancy are in Scotland. Not unexpectedly no Scottish local authority features in the UK top five for the highest life expectancy at birth, in which men in East Dorset can expect to live to 79, and women in Westminster have 83.5 years of life to look forward to.[1]

Addressing the north–south divide, so graphically illustrated by these figures, has driven and shaped Scottish economic and social policy for decades. It has given rise to a conviction that to serve the people of Scotland is to deliver economic development.

This, it is presumed, will produce, through growth and employment, the household income to lift people out of poverty and the national wealth to provide the infrastructures that will attract and sustain further growth.

It also means the stark causes of early mortality from chronically poor diet, dependency on tobacco and other drugs, alcoholism, lack of exercise, poor workplace conditions, and inadequately heated homes provide a social justice and public health challenge of such a magnitude that other issues are dwarfed by them. It is against this background that concerns about environmental degradation caused by economic activity are dismissed as a middle-class preoccupation or an unfortunate price to be paid for other more important outcomes.

The existence of an actual north–south divide between Scotland and a wealthy south has long been a matter of contention and grievance. The mortality statistics are but one manifestation. Others commonly pointed to over the years are regional unemployment rates, GDP per head by region, relative house prices by region and so on. However, economic figures are illustrative rather than conclusive in this argument. Even if people in the south of England have higher incomes, own more expensive houses and have higher levels of car ownership, they will protest that their quality of life is not significantly better than somebody in the north of Scotland. The strain of congestion, high levels of mortgage debt (and at times in the past negative equity) and the requirements to commute further and further to get to work somewhat offsets, they say, the supposed straightforward economic benefits of living in the south. It is not a protestation that will cut much ice in Ballieston.

It is also important to note that the north–south divide is not just between Scotland and the rest of the UK but is marked, as one author has put it, by a 'fuzzy line drawn between the Severn and the Wash which shows on a wide range of economic measures marked and widening differences between those regions above and below the line'.[2]

The conviction that what matters most is the life chances at birth is particularly potent because, assuming that we find the situation to be intolerable that on average some people in our society die ten years earlier than others, then the question is what do we think should be done about it? On the one hand there are those who suggest, even if not blaming the poor, that it is up to individuals to take responsibility for their own health and diet and that there is no reason why people in poverty are automatically condemned to an early death. The alternative view is that low life expectancy, alcoholism, drug dependency and low levels of educational attainment are simply manifestations of a political and societal failure to spread equitably the benefits of economic performance. This does not just apply to the location of jobs but also social infrastructures such as public-sector housing, health care and access to higher education.

In terms of public policy both of these positions can be maintained at the same time with a greater or lesser emphasis depending upon the political perspective of those in power and arguments as to the efficacy of the means of delivering improvements. Current New Labour thinking has drawn from the tone set by Bill Clinton before he became President in his Democrat Convention speech in 1991 where he talked for the first time of giving 'people a new choice rooted in old values . . . that offers opportunity, demands responsibility'.[3] Traditionally, however, the Left has sought to avoid personal blame and to focus instead on market deficiencies and state responsibilities. Twenty years ago, long before he became Chancellor, Gordon Brown concluded, 'Scotland's poor are not poor because they are Scottish: they are poor because, if they are not unemployed, they are in the wrong job, generation, sex or class – and because a welfare state fails to compensate them for it. In other words Scotland's high levels of poverty are not the result of feckless-ness, incompetence, poor household budgeting, excessive drinking or smoking or personal deficiencies amongst the poor: they are rooted in the industrial and occupational struc-ture of the Scottish economy and in particular they arise from the highly uneven and uncontrolled character of Scotland's economic development.'[4]

Despite the early onset of the industrial revolution in Scotland

and the existence of some major manufacturers, some commentators have seen Scotland's economy as always characterised by uneven development. The nation owed aspects of its former prominence to natural resources and the captive market afforded by the Empire. However, it was also characterised by a relatively few entrepreneurs, a dependence upon imported capital from England and to a certain extent the competitive advantages of a skilled but relatively low-paid labour force. As industry moved away from a dependence upon local reserves of coal towards centrally generated electricity, Scotland found itself geographically peripheral and with relatively poor transport links to new markets. The traditional manufacturing areas of Scotland were also made unattractive because of the poor physical environment bequeathed by the spoils and physical dereliction of old industries.

Postwar, the prevailing attitude in the UK was that proactive state intervention would be necessary to avoid the return to the depression of the 1930s and to mitigate the vagaries of market forces. The feeling appeared to be that 'if state intervention could help defeat the might of Hitler's armies, then surely it was also capable of tackling the evils of poverty, unemployment and social deprivation'.[5] This view had been given a coherence with the publication during the war of the Beveridge report, which had provided a blueprint for the postwar society in which the state would make cradle to grave provision and establish, at least in the popular imagination, a national minimum below which no one should be allowed to fall. State intervention was therefore particularly welcomed in Scotland, where historically unemployment had been higher, wages had been lower and health had been poorer than the rest of the UK. Scotland had also experienced during the the Second World War perhaps the most interventionist Secretary of State for Scotland in the form of Tom Johnston, who had strenuously sought to ensure the dispersal of industrial production away from the Midlands and the south of England. He had brought electricity to the Highlands through the establishment of the North of Scotland Hydro Electric Board, which forged ahead with an agenda by which 'Industry would be attracted into the Highlands by a supply of cheap power and an area wide policy of affordable connections to the Grid for private consumers. These connections were to be made irrespective of real cost, and regardless of remoteness.'[6] It is a policy unlikely to commend itself to Johnston's successors.

The direct state ownership of assets and industries such as railways, steel works, power companies and coal was accompanied by a state-plan-led approach to shaping the built infrastructure of urban Scotland. Slum-clearance programmes saw the proliferation of peripheral housing schemes at Pollock, Castlemilk, Drumchapel and Easterhouse as well as whole new towns being built as far afield as Ayrshire and Fife to act as overspill capacity, bringing Glasgow's population down. The nature of some of these developments were declamatory, making statements and assumptions about the shape of things to come. Cumbernauld was typical of the new towns with a complex layout fused with an 'unprecedented level of provision for car ownership. It was often hailed at the time as a "motor town" an "ongoing laboratory of city making" whose . . . inhabitants could aspire to American levels of mobility.'[7] This built-in car provision was actually cemented in car dependency – a particularly heroic belief in progress given that fifty years later 35 per cent of the Scottish households still have no car. The designers, we are told, could not be expected to anticipate the oil shocks of the 1970s and the consequences of global warming from fossil-fuel emissions.

Nowadays we can see other deficiencies of this investment. Many of the people with whom Friends of the Earth and other voluntary organisations work are having to cope with the fuel poverty caused by impossible to heat homes built in that period. They also face isolation through being cut off from access to increasingly centralised health, educational and retail services and from employment opportunities, stranded in peripheral schemes poorly served by public transport. Yet such developments are still defended strenuously against criticism as if this is simply an affectation of hindsight or the imposition of current-day standards upon decision-takers dealing with more insistent issues. Professor Tom Devine makes clear where his sympathies lie when he says that 'it has become fashionable to criticise the massive post war expansion in Scottish public housing for monotonous buildings, poor construction, the absence of amenity, pubs and entertainment in the large schemes around the cities, inadequate transport and the break up of old communities'.[8] But he gives such views short shrift, on the basis that such criticism fails to appreciate the pressing nature of the challenge confronting the political authorities in dealing with the slum conditions and overcrowding of Glasgow and the west of Scotland. Such outcomes were the lesser of two evils, given that it is all too easy to overlook that 'for the first time large numbers of Scots had a decent home equipped to modern standards. Rising expectations and a continuing increase in standards since the 1950s cannot alter that judgment.'[9] I appreciate his viewpoint, as someone who benefited from being able to move into a council house with modern facilities (such as an indoor toilet) and then later going to live in a new town, where rented homes had central heating. However, for all the gratitude we had for these improvements we were still able to moan at being frozen cold in an uninsulated house, or be in disbelief that we could get nowhere by public transport and had to walk prodigious distances to access the scattered and geographically separate locations of work, recreation and shops. It could have been done better then, and this is not a judgement of hindsight.

For almost thirty-five years governments, Labour or Conservative, were strongly interventionist. State-owned industries were augmented by others, for which large capital loans were provided to modernise or expand (such as Colvilles Steel Works, or the British Motor Corporation at Bathgate). Investment was directed as part of a regional development policy which suffered the setbacks of failed pulp mills, aluminium smelters and oil-rig fabrication yards. In those days, as now, opposition to such potentially job-creating activities, however unlikely to prosper, was caricatured as backward and selfish – as the following assessment of the the battle lines regarding a proposed oil refinery for the Cromarty Firth in the north of Scotland shows. 'In favour of the project were most of the small traders, the shopkeepers, the pub owners, the service industries, the local trade unions, the Labour Party, the entire work force of Highland Fabricators platform yard at Nigg, the Liberal party, most members of the Scottish National Party... lined up against the refinery was a smaller but well financed and well organised army of most of the big farmers, the land owning gentry, the businesses who made their living from tourism, the fishermen, retired people from the south, the handful of youngish middle class dropouts who had moved into the area.' However, the author has the grace to acknowledge that it also included 'everybody who lived right up against the project and who seemed doomed to live in the glare of Daniel Ludwig's flare stacks'.[10]

This particular project was the subject of a public inquiry, which at that time was one of the most complex, expensive and longest running ever heard in Scotland. The reporter finally decided to recommend against the project on the grounds that there was no need for it given the overcapacity elsewhere, but he was overruled by the then Secretary of State for Scotland. It was said he could not turn down the jobs that the refinery might have brought to the north of Scotland. Yet, needless to say, after all the bitter dispute, charge and counter-charge, the refinery never saw the light of day.

If it had, would it have brought the transformation its backers promised? About that time a similar catalytic development was directed to Wester Ross. The Kishorn oil-fabrication yard operated between 1975 and 1986, generating up to 45,000 jobs. A study of its impacts showed that 'it brought widespread material benefits but also profound social disruption in both the short and long term. A majority now say that they would have preferred small scale locally based development, which would have obviated the need for substantial migration of labourers.'[11] The question which we will address ourselves to later is whether we have managed to get ourself off the treadmill of pursuing unsustainable developments, and being beguiled by the promise of long-term jobs despite years of evidence of the fickleness of economic history in Scotland.

Thatcherism brought a strongly free-market government. Not only was there a preparedness to dismantle what were regarded as old and inefficient state-subsidised heavy industries like steel making and mining, but also an unwillingness to pick winners in using state funds to favour new industry. It was the role of the market to determine what would be profitably sited in Scotland. But footloose capital expected states to influence investment decisions by offering attractive locations and favourable financial incentives in the forms of grants, loans, rent-free periods or tax exemptions. In Scotland the government and its agencies strove to offer this more attractive investment climate and physical infrastructure. Part of this did focus on cleaning up the industrial dereliction of the past. Asbestos was removed at the taxpayers' expense from the site of the former Turner and Newall factory in Clydebank to make way for a new controversial private hospital while the Glasgow garden festival was justified as a site-rehabilitation exercise to attract future funders. However, there is no doubt that this environmental activity was entirely to meet the needs of inward investors and was not located within a strategy which considered other environmental impacts. If a foreign company wanted a green-field site close to a motorway then it would get it. Planning permission and public funding was used to make the Hyundai electronics site available close to the M90 in Fife. Even though it was remote from any public transport node serving the neighbouring towns of Dunfermline or Cowdenbeath, the ethereal promise of 2,000 jobs meant the company could literally pick its spot. Road building itself became seen as the panacea for improved access to the market and to attract inward investment. Public spending on rail, buses and provision for cycling and walking was dwarfed by that for new roads, upgrades and extensions. Research has shown that roads contribute little in the locational decisions of inward investors and that in any case they are just as likely to suck jobs out of an area as to attract them, given that regional distribution centres can be set up, closing local suppliers. Yet they remain totemic so far as economic development strategies are concerned.

On this agenda Labour members of parliament and local authorities were just as likely to be as bullishly pro market as Conservative Scottish Office ministers. The battle was on for growth, for jobs – and it was seen as a battle against in particular the Welsh and Irish, who were fighting to attract the same type of investment and had on offer similar if not better packages of state support, local infrastructure and available workforces.

The former Scottish Office minister, Lord Gus Macdonald may have once said that Ireland is a great place to go to for a stag party but not for economic policy but there is no doubt that the success of the Irish in growing its economy was seen as both an example and a challenge. Despite the relative success in attracting foreign investment (through the 1990s Scotland's annual share of foreign direct inward investment coming into the UK typically averaged between 15 and 20 per cent), Scottish GDP growth through the 1990s amounted to 22 per cent. This was contrasted unfavourably with the 100 per cent growth in the Irish economy. That is not to say of course that the Irish government's track record was not causing problems for communities and environmentalists there. Heated protests were voiced over the wooing of companies such as pharmaceutical giants Merrill Dow, and Schering Plough, or the asbestos waste produced by the US company Raybestos Manhattan, as local people often believed that some of this investment had been achieved through less stringent pollution legislation.

In the aftermath of the Earth Summit in Rio in 1992, much was made of the fact that at the very least economic, social and environmental issues would be weighed in the balance. In 1999 when, following devolution, the programme for government was unveiled, it was unequivocally declared that the Scottish Executive was committed to socially and environmentally sustainable development.

How this was to be translated into action was not at all clear. In particular, fears have been expressed that although the language has changed and become more accommodating, the trajectory of policy is little altered. The Scottish Executive published its framework for economic development in Scotland, which was then amplified by a paper, *Smart Successful Scotland*, which set out the Executive's ambitions for the enterprise networks. It promoted a notion of Scotland which was no longer about combating market failure or countering mass unemployment but instead was about 'entrepreneurial dynamism and global connections', fitting Scotland to attract and retain, what it calls mobile direct investment. It argued 'our approach to globalisation must not be to resist change but to embrace it. We need to be globally connected integrating the Scottish economy into the world economy.'[12] Is that so? As Damien Killeen of the Poverty Alliance often asks, 'Where is the debate about development in Scotland?' He has a point. Walk into any major bookstore and you will find texts on world development – should it be bottom up, what is the efficacy of aid, what is sustainable development? But I defy you to find similar range of titles about our own country. Scottish Enterprise portrays globalisation as a given and if there is any negative consequences for Scotland presumably it will be our fault for not having engaged adequately. It has set up a sixteen-strong committee to advise it on globalisation, made up of what have been called heavy hitters – Scots who have made it big on the world stage. These include Crawford Beveridge, the former Scottish Enterprise head who is chief Human Resources Officer of Sun Microsystems, Hugh Grant, Executive Vice-president of Monsanto, Sir Tom McKillop, Chief Executive of AstraZeneca and Euan Baird, Chief Executive and Chairman of oil services giant Schlumberger. It is unlikely that within this group any will argue against a trade-dominated global agenda or question the merits of globalisation. They will expect to exercise influence over Scottish economic policy, with one Scottish Enterprise insider reported as saying, 'You don't pick a panel like that and then ignore what they are saying.' Can we presume from this there is a societal consensus or have we simply not appreciated what is going on?

Globalisation as a concept dominated the World Summit on Sustainable Development in Johannesburg in 2002. It has almost become an article of faith, described as a process by which the 'diffusion of western culture and capitalism is inevitable, carried forward by a deterministic logic beyond any intervening powers'.[13] Some are puzzled that we should find anything objectionable in this, saying, 'surely we see cultures moving toward almost a global uniformity in which individuals, rather than localities, find a distinctness?'[14] This end-of-history fatalism is disputed. But even if it is the case, then we should anticipate that, whatever benefits are thought to accrue from this global economic juggernaut careering across the globe, there will be a price to be paid in terms of road kill of cultures, local economies and natural resources. Yet there is a doctrinal impatience with such concerns because, quite simply, they are not going to deflect the current political and industrial elites from pursuing a globalised free-trade agenda. 'Globalisation is the natural condition of a minor planet, from which politics dislodged it, and to which culture and economy now have the potential to return it.'[15] It seems that 'No amount of human suffering or natural destruction exacted by the doctrine's implementation can alter its prescriptions or prove it false.'[16]

For some reason global enterprise is portrayed as capable of transforming the deficiencies of our current method of doing things, in a way which national enterprise has so far failed to do. It will make up for the sad failings of trickle-down theories of wealth, even though is clear that the polarisation of rich and poor continues apace. (Ironically the World Summit was held in a country which had just overtaken Brazil as the nation with the biggest gaps between the haves and the have-nots.) It will plug the gap in international development assistance, using private foreign direct investment flows, to counter the embarrassing reminder to nations that they were pledged to provide 0.7 per cent of GNP in aid.

Globalisation offers a vision, it seems, of liberalised international trade and of governments working in partnership with global corporations to provide what were once public services such as water and sanitation, energy and health, which are now to be resourced or owned by private capital. But it also raises fears about human rights, food, water and land security and democratic autonomy, and the inadequacies of global regulatory frameworks.

The alternative take on globalisation is of a homogenised world dominated by footloose capital and corporations above and beyond the capacity of international regulation to control and which will take advantage of low labour and commodity costs, and poor environmental standards. Such businesses lose what has been called the ethic of place and become 'global oriented industries that have no place based identity other than to maximise their selection of labour markets, materials transportation, and marketing end point'.[17]

Wolfgang Sachs observes that globalisation undercuts social solidarity since 'through transnationalisation, capital is in the position to escape links of loyalty to a particular society. It prefers not to be bothered by things like paying taxes, creating jobs, reinvesting surplus, keeping to collective rules or educating the young, because it considers them mere obstacles to global competition.'[18]

Prominent neo-liberal economists like Kenichi Ohmae do not see why business should be encumbered with non-commercial demands. He rails against the steadily growing share of the civil minimum expected of government in the form of broad-based social programmes – welfare, unemployment, compensation, public education, old age pensions, health insurance and the like.

His preferred future is a consumerist vision that dispenses with anachronisms like the nation state and national identities and indeed therefore the burden of maintaining those parts of the national population in inconveniently and uncompetitively sited locations. His preference is for region states:

Region states welcome foreign investment. They welcome foreign ownership. They welcome foreign products. In fact they welcome whatever will help employ their people productively, improve their quality of life and give them access to the best and cheapest products from anywhere in the world. Region states also welcome the chance to use whatever surplus these activities generate to ratchet up their people's quality of life still further not to fund the civil minimum or subsidise outmoded industries. In a word they consistently put global logic first.[19]

Scotland has already experienced some of the manifestations of this, particularly in the electronics sector. At the end of the twentieth century electronics was Scotland's big success story. Not in indigenous companies or product development but in attracting foreign investors to set up manufacturing bases here. In 1997 200 electronics companies employed 46,000 people (1 in 7 of Scottish manufacturing employment). We produced 80 per cent of Europe's workstations and 65 per cent of Europe's automatic teller machines (ATMs). We were Silicon Glen. Why were we so attractive? Well, according to Ohmae, it was the same old story: 'Glasgow may have high unemployment and an out-of-the-way location, but it also offers an eager, low-cost source of labour and a convenient entry point to Europe for US investment.'20

It ever was thus. The great demand for Clyde-built ships was attributed not to their technical superiority but to their low cost. This was due, in part, to the cheapness of materials but chiefly, according to an early twentieth-century US Congress study of the international level of wages, to the 'abundance of skilled workmen and the low rate of wages paid to them'.[21]

Criticism that the electronics sector was largely an assembly line where the off-switch could be thrown when economic chill spread through the United States, Korea or Taiwan was dismissed. Major players like Motorola and NEC were here for the long term. Yet between 1999 and 2002 over 10,000 jobs were lost in the electronics sector in Scotland as companies closed or moved operations elsewhere. Questions are being asked about the overall benefit of the public funds used to attract some of these firms in the first place. Motorola was enticed to West Lothian with a grant of over £50 million. When it closed its doors ten years later it paid back less than £17 million.[22]

The view now appears to be that breeding home-grown industries, and improving the rate of commercialisation of innovation and research, should secure greater attention. Foreign funds utilised in this process, however, are more than welcome, such as those from the South African company Sasol, which invested a relatively modest sum to establish a research laboratory in St Andrews University. The stated aim is to develop chemical feedstock for plastics, detergent and other products using less oil. So far as the business press and the Scottish Executive were concerned, this fitted well with their Smart Successful Scotland objective of more effective links between universities and business. Few in Scotland would know much about Sasol, even though it is South Africa's largest oil company with a turnover of £2,240 million and 30,800 employees worldwide. Delegates to the World Summit were welcomed with billboards advertising Sasol's art collection on display in downtown Johannesburg.

If they had travelled 65 miles south of the city to the company town of Sasolburg they would get a different impression. Sasol was established to counter international sanctions against apartheid. It is a major polluter discharging 26,000 tonnes of sulphur dioxide from its Sasolburg operations alone. In south Durban its impact on the local community has been direct – in 2000 three serious chlorine-gas leaks occurred with hundreds of children taken to hospital as a result. The company has sought to improve its image working with the local council in Sasolburg to improve local parks and paying for tractors and mowers. But South African environmental activists say this obscures the company's resistance to new pollution laws. Sasol is a primary target of the environmental justice movement, which sees a major multinational taking advantage of poor regulatory laws and cheap labour. (The company, incidentally, was also the subject of an official Commission of Inquiry as to whether its share dealings with Deutsche Bank contributed to the sudden depreciation of the rand, with one of the investigators recommending legal action should be taken over exchange-control violations.)[23] Pointing out that Sasol has been wealthy enough to acquire assets in Germany and Italy, South African environmental organisations want to see it meeting the same high standards at home. Foreign chemical companies, too, enjoy the same comparative advantage in South Africa – other refineries are owned by familiar names such as Shell, BP, Total and Petronas.

If we are to be serious about environmental justice here in Scotland we have to be aware of the track record, at home and abroad, of companies operating in our midst and establish a position of mutual solidarity with those affected elsewhere.

Globalisation differs from past mercantile or colonial trade in that it aspires to free trade within an international framework that discourages protectionism and subsidies (which is far from saying that they have been swept away). Anything that hinders the free-trade agenda is suspect, such as measures designed to protect the environment, secure decent working conditions or human rights. The weak structures put in place to promote sustainable development are powerless compared to free trade institutions. The Earth Summit in Rio in 1992 produced Agenda 21, a 273-page action programme and established the United Nations Commission on Sustainable Development, which was equipped only to encourage and monitor implementation. This was dwarfed by the Uruguay Agreement two years later, running to 26,000 pages, and setting up the World Trade Organisation (WTO) to rule on and enforce the agreement. As a result of this dominance, some multilateral environmental agreements may be in contradiction with WTO rules. It is certainly clear that the WTO will not countenance any national decisions to deny a market to products simply because of concerns over their production processes – whether it be the use of hormone growth treatments or impact on non-target species such as dolphins or turtles. One of the major planks of Rio, the application of the precautionary principle to permit action to prevent environmental or health harm even in the absence of scientific proof, is under pressure as the WTO only permits trade measures based upon scientific evidence of risk. We may want to reject genetically modified crops or insist upon sustainably sourced tropical timber but the WTO does not permit such national expression.

There is an international environmental justice connection here. Just as it is not acceptable for rich communities in the north to push polluting activities to neighbouring poor areas, the answer is not to displace the impacts to poor, even more vulnerable communities overseas. Yet the fear for southern countries is that free trade rather than fair trade will leave them dependent on rich northern markets. 'And the greater that dependency the greater is the pressure to further lower labour and environmental standards and to police resistance so as to remain globally competitive.'[24]

Criticism of globalisation, as it is currently being pursued, is not just coming from the demonstrators on the streets of Seattle or Genoa. The Nobel Prize winner, and former World Bank chief economist, Joseph Stiglitz notes that the decline in transportation and communication costs and the reduction of barriers to the flow of goods, services and capital is analogous to the processes by which national economies were formed. But what is different is that 'Unfortunately we have no world government accountable to the people of every country to oversee the globalisation process . . . indeed we have a system that might be called global governance without global government, one in which a few institutions, the World Bank, the IMF, the WTO and a few players – the finance, commerce and trade ministries, closely linked to certain financial and commercial interests – dominate the scene, but in which many of those affected by their decisions are left almost voiceless.'[25]

Not only are they voiceless, they will often not even know what is going on as in 'the IMF style of operation, citizens (an annoyance because they all too often might be reluctant to go along with the agreements, let alone share in the perceptions of what is good economic policy) were not only barred from discussions of agreements, they were not even told what the agreements were'.[26]

The World Summit was not just a missed opportunity to address the issue of global governance, which Stiglitz has raised, such debate was actively resisted by nations content with the current trade domination of the agenda. Ideas such as forming a Global Environmental Organisation, as a counter-weight to the WTO, never made it to the official discussions. Nor did suggestions that a permanent court of arbitration be established to remove from the WTO the right to adjudicate in disputes between trade and environment imperatives.

Globalisation has prompted differential responses, which may be categorised as follows:

1. Ideologically committed – a neo-liberal position that sees globalisation as inevitable and desirable. It resists protectionist counter- beliefs based around environment, culture, human and labour rights. It normally dismisses inconvenient concerns such as climate change, or environmental space limits.

2. Pragmatically proactive – presumes that globalisation is likely, and is not ideologically opposed. Believes that, if implemented well, globalisation has the capacity to tackle poverty and improve life expectancy. Recognises some of the potential for harm. Supports a range of measures to work with the grain of progressive market forces such as eco-efficiency, corporate responsibility and eco-taxation.

3. Pragmatically reactive/defensive – concerned that globalisation is being pursued with insufficient regard for negative impacts. Highlights the adverse consequences while at same time working to secure improvements, mitigation or redress for those who are affected. Seeks to put in place mandatory obligations and bolster international and national regulatory structures. Supports and explores alternative forms of economic organisation.

4. Ideologically opposed – does not accept globalisation is

inevitable and regards multinational corporations and structures as incompatible with sustainable development. Unwilling to engage with measures to create better international framework or corporate accountability as these may bolster the very existence of such corporations or globalisation. Reluctant to be engaged in measures to mitigate national or local impacts, preferring to expose and resist.

Bona fide environmental groups will not be ideologically committed to globalisation. However, they will be found spread across the other categories and indeed pursuing policies and tactics which are contained in more than one.

They may comment on sectoral/company initiatives and technologies, propose improvements to international governance through corporate accountability and the implementation of stronger national regulations, promote citizen rights to information, resist loss of public control of services, and advance alternative national and local development strategies.

If there is to be a debate about globalisation and its consequences for Scotland, then we need to assert what kind of Scotland we would like to live in. What do we want to keep and protect, and what do we want to see introduced and expanded?

We have also to question the development model which is being assumed is our place in the world. Do we want to be a consumer nation, one which overconsumes more than its fair share of the world's resources? For that is the current path of economic growth along which we are being propelled. This is inconsistent with protestations of sustainable development and international environmental justice.

Scottish Enterprise declares that it aims, with its £493 million budget and 2,000 staff, to transform the Scottish economy into one of the fastest growing in the developed world.[27] This may all be corporate puff, given our past record and recent dip into technical recession. But if that is the aspiration the question is how this will be done as sustainable development. Is this growth to be achieved within a lesser impact upon the world's natural resources and with a diminution of emissions of climate-change gasses and pollutants? That is what should happen, but does not.

When considering how to measure whether Scotland is becoming smart or successful, the team charged with implementing the agenda came up with three overall parameters which, taken together, could gauge the delivery of what it called balanced economic development. The selected measures were standard of living, output per head (productivity) and the employment rate. As a standard of living index was not available to measure what sustainable economic development is ultimately trying to achieve, it was proposed that income per head be used as a proxy.

It would appear from this model that the most desirable state of affairs would be for per capita GDP to grow, closing the gap with not just the rest of the UK but with the foremost OECD nations, so that close to full employment is achieved, and that output per worker is increased to the levels seen in the USA. Surely this represents a long-held aspiration little affected by recent notions of sustainable development? It does not accommodate any consideration of the appropriation of raw and manufactured materials and the ecological impact of their extraction, emissions from manufacture, or scale of consumption. Within the limitations of this model it would be possible for Scotland to profligately appropriate more than its fair share of natural resources, and despoil its environment, yet still be regarded as smart and successful. What's missing from this model? It's the environment, stupid.

It is not inevitable that growth is unsustainable. As the economist Michael Jacobs has pointed out, just 'because current patterns of economic growth are environmentally damaging, it does not follow that the solution to environmental problems is no growth'.[28]

But historically and currently the economic growth of developed nations has been environmentally harmful. If globalisation intends to use conventional growth as a model for development elsewhere then the consequences are unsustainable, in terms of the capacity of the planet to replenish stocks, the rate of extraction and consumption of finite resources, and the ability to absorb pollutants and emissions.

This is not because of illegal activity or gross pollution – although these still exist – but simply because of the scale of resource consumption, appropriated by our everyday western lives. The figures are well known by now but we should remind ourselves. The OECD countries are home to only 19 per cent of the world's population, but account for 82 per cent of world GNP. We consume 50 per cent of global grain production, and use 75 per cent of the world's energy, 80 per cent of iron and steel, 85 per cent of chemical production and own 92 per cent of private cars.[29] Self-styled sceptical environmentalists like Lomberg suggest there is no need to worry as at present levels of consumption, there are many years left of the raw materials feeding the maw of consumerism. Despite his impressive 3,000 footnotes he misses the point. Present levels of consumption can only continue if many nations live in poverty. If development aspirations are met, then they too will wish to consume at western levels. This would rapidly deplete relatively scarce minerals and fossil fuels. For abundant materials, such as rock which can be turned into cement, the consequences are not scarcity of the raw materials but of the ancillary effects on water demand and climate-change emissions. If the globe could provide the arable land to grow nearly three times as much food as it does currently, the seas and aquatic ecosystems could absorb the fertiliser runs-off and withstand the depletion of stocks for consumption and aquaculture; if the atmosphere could accept the CO_2 emissions of 4 billion cars (presuming the rest of the world aspires to US levels of car ownership) without global warming, then an argument might be made that the Western development path is sustainable. But we know that this is not possible.

However we wish to measure it, the answer is the same. Our ecological footprint is too big. We are occupying too much of the available environmental space. (Assuming by 2050 each person on earth would have the same entitlement to the world's resources and that these were utilised within the carrying capacity of the planet, then in the case of Scotland it is estimated that we would have to reduce our raw-material consumption by 80 per cent or more to live within our environmental space.) Rich nations are overconsuming their fair share of the world's resources, which have to be distributed more equitably to allow poor nations to develop and which have to be stewarded against profligate overuse to leave a legacy to future generations. We owe a huge ecological debt to the south.

We, in the north, are the 'fortunate fraction of humanity'[30] which capitalism has allowed to achieve 'undreamed of material standards of living'.[31] But as former World Bank economist Herman Daly and his colleagues have signalled, this has been achieved by adopting 'an overarching ideology of growth, expansion and fetishistic moneymaking for its own sake and at whatever social and environmental cost'.[32] Capitalism does not distinguish between necessary and trivial consumption, and they ask exasperatedly, 'Do we really need automobile air fresheners to lead civilised lives?'[33] Clive Ponting takes up the same theme of artificially created needs or wants saying that 'Companies . . . develop new products to create new markets where none existed before or where perfectly adequate cheap alternatives were already available' before going on to illustrate it with his particular *bête noire*, the development of the electric toothbrush.[34] Richard North, arch critic of the environmental movement, acknowledges that 'The most environmentally-conscious move many firms could make would be to cease to produce products of small usefulness and some or great ecological cost.' But candidly he says, 'It is not reasonable to ask capitalists to make that sort of choice . . . One should not expect industry to be Green only to be good citizens.'[35]

Without product innovation, it is said, we would up to our waists in horse dung and that by questioning growth we are condemning those who have so far missed out on wealth to perpetual poverty.

It is quite the opposite. Conventional development has proven to be incapable of eradicating poverty. It is highly inequitable – the poorest 40 per cent of people in northern industrialised nations receive only some 16 per cent of the total national income. If the model worked, then in Scotland of all nations poverty would be unknown. We have had bountiful natural resources, early industrialisation, enjoyed access to the unearned benefits of Empire and a protected market, as well as redistribution of resources through regional development assistance. Yet as we have seen poverty is widespread, and in the pursuit of economic growth negative environmental impacts are experienced by our poorer communities.

The proposition that we should consider more deeply, than is currently evident in Scotland, what constitutes sustainable development, and consequently alter the trajectory of economic activity, does not indicate a preparedness to ignore the needs of the poor in our country. It is precisely about how we can provide for the legitimate needs of everyone, here and abroad, within the carrying capacity of the planet.

To do so, we have to tackle the self-evident inefficiency and profligacy of northern nations. As our GNP increases, so do waste levels, which indicates our failure to decouple the link between economic growth and material consumption and pollution emissions. No one now disputes that such decoupling has to take place. It is explicitly part of the OECD agenda and even at the World Summit the need to transform current patterns of unsustainable consumption and production was accepted. As Michael Jacobs has argued, we need to be able to identify the environmental impact coefficient (EIC) of GNP. If the content of economic activity is changing, so that an extra unit of GNP tends to consume fewer resources than last year, EIC can be said to be falling.[36] But this is not happening in many sectors and where it is evident, it is not progressing fast enough.

There is substantial evidence of market inefficiency – that is, companies are not altering their environmental impact even where it is cost effective to do so. In some instances, efficiency gains are being encountered – the shift in the UK away from coal-fired power stations to more efficient gas fired has meant that each unit of GNP was produced with fewer tonnes of CO_2. There are several examples of eco-efficiency, which regularly appear in the literature, to encourage the belief that the market is responsive. These include the packaging industry lightweighting its products so that we get the same strength, durability and safety for a reduced use of materials. Bottles today are 25 per cent lighter than they were in 1984. Plastic grocery bags had a thickness of 30 microns in 1976, today most are 18 microns.[37]

Enthusiasm for eco-efficiency and the benefits of constant innovation are at the heart of technocentric optimism. There is a problem, however, as this efficiency is not being pursued for environmental purposes alone and so is often not accompanied by any change in business or consumer attitudes. The supposed or potential environmental benefits are negated by increased volume of sales, or higher specification of the same product. This has a discounting effect which means that the promise of eco-efficiency is unlikely to be realised by a technocentric approach alone. As iconoclastic right-wing critics of the soft green agenda have pointed out:

> More efficient means much the same as less expensive. Most of the cost of owning a refrigerator lies in running it and refrigerators do indeed run much more efficiently than they used to. So people can now buy bigger ones and that is exactly what they do. It is the same with planes, cars and just about everything else. More efficient engines mean cheaper travel so you travel more. Today's soda cans contain one fifth of the aluminium they did three decades ago but the number of cans purchased has grown by an even larger multiple.[38]

This so-called rebound effect is not a novel finding, but is often not taken into account. Scottish academics have built models that, on a range of scenarios, show that since increased resource efficiency leads to greater output per unit capital stock, then output will rise. Is it inevitable that increasing efficiencies should lead to yet more resource consumption?

The answer depends upon how we choose to spend the spare human made capital (HMC) released by efficiency measures. We could spend it on making more consumer goods, which would in turn expand the industrial sector and so expand economic activity further with all the downstream effects like more pollution and more consumption. We could also choose to spend it on non expansionary activities such as more hospitals, more old folk's homes, public transport, educational facilities or environmental protection ... moreover if we are to develop sustainable energy systems as oil and gas run out, we shall need all the spare HMC we can lay our hands on to create those renewable systems.[39]

The consequence, it is argued, is that we need to move beyond the illusion that efficiency measures alone will produce a decoupling and the necessary reduction in environmental pressures and face up to what has candidly been called the management of greed. Others characterise it as a move beyond efficiency towards a notion of sufficiency.

It should be clear that if governments, including the Scottish Executive, are making claims to pursue sustainable development, then we need to have some commonly agreed idea of what this means. How are we to gauge progress and how do we ensure in the process that those currently disadvantaged in our society have their needs addressed, including the need for environmental justice?

We are not homo economicus – life is more than what we earn, acquire or consume. Even in the United States it was life, liberty and the pursuit of happiness that was the cornerstone of the Declaration of Independence. (Jefferson, it is said, was influenced in this choice of phrase by the Glasgow philosopher Frances Hutcheson, although others suggest it could have come from the Rev. James Witherspoon, the Paisley minister who established Princeton and who was one of two Scots to sign the Declaration.)[40] We have known for years that happiness cannot be crudely equated with increasing national wealth. We need a more refined measure.

Over thirty years ago the OECD accepted that 'increasingly sophisticated social indicators should be evolved to monitor trends and impact and to provide a system of early warning of growing imbalances, social disbenefits, dissatisfactions and emerging social needs.' Researchers in the USA at around the same time proposed general criteria of social well-being with the classifications of:

- Income, wealth and unemployment.
- The living environment (housing, neighbourhood and physical environment).
- Health (physical and mental).
- Education.
- Social order (such as crime, delinquency, family breakdown).
- Social belonging (for example, democratic participation, segregation).
- Recreation and leisure (culture and the arts, recreation facilities).[41]

This is a list that would be still acceptable today and indeed bears comparison with some that have been produced in Scotland. It has also been long understood that simply measuring external objective data on pollution or traffic congestion or the extent of ownership of consumer durables and so on is not sufficient for ascertaining quality of life. It would be quite possible for the external conditions of life to be said to improve while people's sense of well-being declined. It has always been the case, however irritating and uncomfortable to scientists and economists, that perceptions are as important as objective measurements.

The challenge is to come up with some way of assessing whether or not we are a happy, healthy society. By what measure can we gauge whether we have a society in which there is the provision of the necessities of life for all, a reasonably equitable sharing of wealth, while living within the constraints of a fair share of the earth's resources? This is beyond the capacity of a single crude indicator such as per capita GNP.

In Scotland we have made heavy weather of coming up with tests of the general criteria of social well-being proposed thirty years earlier, or of sustainable development as set out at Rio ten years ago. There has been agonising and frustrated discussion over what sustainability means for us, should we have a definition and even whether or not the term sustainability rather than sustainable development is appropriate (an argument we will not go into here). A senior civil servant once provocatively told a room full of Cabinet ministers, who were taking to task government departments on their lack of progress on implementing the Scottish Executive's commitment to sustainable development, that a view existed among his colleagues of 'define it and I'll do it'. He would find some support from commentators who have agreed that 'while one can sympathise with the view that a simple concise definition may not be possible, surely some idea of where one is trying to go is an absolute necessity'.[42] A bloody-minded insistence upon carrying out business as usual until a definition is agreed should not be acceptable. We know enough of what we are doing wrong and are agreed enough on what would be an improvement without requiring a universally accepted definition to sanction the change of policy, investment or culture. Nevertheless it would have been useful in Scotland at a much earlier stage to have a sophisticated official analysis of, and policy on, sustainable development, accompanied by a set of sustainable development indicators.

The challenge, however, has been to come up with indicators that, incorporating social, economic and environment elements, provide a coherent measurement of where we are, and what progress we are making towards where we would like to be. There is no end of such indicators scattered across the globe and advice, templates and international comparators from which to derive a Scottish set. It was not desirable to simply take one of these off the shelf and begun to slot Scottish statistics into it. Sustainability is not out there waiting to be discovered by punching in some selected numbers.

But the frustration at the late development of a bespoke Scottish set and lack of agreement over what would be included meant there were strong arguments made for short circuiting the process by adopting and where necessary adapting the 150 indicators that had been drawn up by the Department of the Environment Transport and the Regions. These mirrored and even went beyond the working list of 131 indicators of sustainable development that had been drawn up by the UN Commission on Sustainable Development following the Earth Summit in Rio in 1992. However, there is a view that lists of such detail do not allow us to grasp overall whether sufficient progress had been made towards sustainable development. Nor are the indicators weighted one against the other to know whether or not some fundamental failing undermines the progress in others. The alternative therefore is to adopt a smaller, representative, set such as the thirty-five indicators drawn up by the OECD.

It is noticeable that environmental indicators are prominent in all these sets. This is resented by those who believe that environmental issues dominate sustainable development and that some redressing of the balance is necessary. They are wrong. The reason why there is a consistency of indicator profiles is straightforward. The concept of sustainable development has grown out of the environmental movement, which has alerted humankind to notions of depletion of natural capital, exceeding carrying capacity and living outwith our environmental space. Environmental indicators predominate not because the environment is more important than concerns over poverty but because they measure whether we are pursuing social and economic ends in a way which can be continued indefinitely. This balances the right of current generations elsewhere in the globe (especially in poor nations) to expand their share of world resource use with the right of future generations to inherit a viable ecosystem. So for example the 'Quality of Life Counts' DETR set has 94 environmental indicators, the UNCSD set has 72 and even the OECD set has 24 environmental indicators.[43]

In Scotland, having decided not to adopt the UK set, a tortuous and fraught process was pursued. External consultants recommended the adoption of 42 indicators. However, this ran counter to a ministerial inclination to have an even shorter list, so only 12 of the indicators were actually adopted in a public consultation document *Checking for Change* issued by the Scottish Executive. Indeed the prospect was floated as to whether or not a single indicator such as CO_2 emissions per capita might be adopted, to provide a headline indicator of Scottish performance (to match Sam Galbraith's preference for a single quality of life indicator).

Following adverse criticism from government agencies, NGOs and local authorities and another reshuffle at a ministerial level, this set was withdrawn and was eventually replaced with an expanded set, which drafted in some of the existing social justice indicators. Arguments flared again, this time as to whether each of the indicators would require to be accompanied by targets. Insisting, however, that indicators without currently agreed targets should be stripped out of the set would mean that many critical issues that had constantly appeared in all of the various draft lists would now disappear, such as percentage of waste recycled, for which no target had yet been set. On climate change Scotland has a target of sorts but which is untestable as the Executive simply promises to contribute an 'equitable share' to meeting the UK's Kyoto commitments. A process of political hokey cokey ensued with indicators being in, out and then in again before finally in April 2002 the Scottish set of 24 was unveiled nearly three years after it had been commissioned. Whatever the deficiencies, it is still useful that the indicators are now in place.

The question has to be whether the indicators selected for Scotland and the manner in which they have been presented will make an impact upon public policy. The OECD suggests that for indicators to have policy relevance and utility for users they should:

- Provide a representative picture of environmental conditions, pressures on the environment or society's responses.
- Be simple, easy to interpret and able to show trends over

time, be responsive to changes in the environment and related human activities.

- Provide a basis for international comparisons.
- Be either national in scope or applicable to regional environmental issues of national significance.
- Have a threshold or reference value against which to compare it, so that users can assess the significance of the values associated with it.[44]

Table 7.1 Indicators of sustainable development for Scotland

1. Sustainable prosperity: Index of CO_2 emissions divided by GDP.
2. Work: percentage of unemployed working-age people.
3. Population structure: proportion of population that is working age.
4. Waste: municipal waste arisings.
5. Waste: percentage of total household waste recycled.
6. Waste: biodegradable municipal wastes landfilled.
7. Climate change: million tonnes of greenhouse gases carbon equivalent.
8. Air quality: number of air-quality management areas.
9. Water quality: kilometres identified as poor or seriously polluted.
10. Biodiversity: % of Action Plan species and habitats stable or increasing.
11. Sea fisheries: proportion of fish stocks within safe biological limits.
12. Energy: electricity consumed.
13. Energy: % of electricity generated from renewable sources.
14. Travel: total vehicle kilometres.
15. Travel: freight intensity (tonne kilometres moved and GDP).
16. Travel: % of journeys to work not using car.
17. Travel: % of households within 6-minute walk of a bus service.
18. Home life: % of children living in workless households.
19. Preparing for life: % of 16–19-year-olds not in education, training or employment.
20. Fuel poverty: total living in fuel poverty.
21. Social concern: number of homeless people entitled to permanent accommodation.
22. Crime: total number of crimes.
23. Volunteering: % of people taking part in voluntary activities.
24. Health: life expectancy at birth.

Source: Scottish Executive (2002), *Meeting the Needs*.

Indicators, therefore, have to be chosen carefully to perform a number of functions and, in combination, provide an overall picture of the progress towards or away from sustainable development. But before we got as far as indicators we should have had a view as to what sustainable development means for us in Scotland. It is not seen as good practice to 'develop a host of sustainability indicators then test them to see whether they adequately describe sustainability. Rather, the starting point is a description of sustainability with all of its human subjectivity followed by an identification of sustainability indicators to gauge attainment of that description.'[45]

We need to have a more sophisticated concept of sustainable development. Simple models portray the task as achieving the increasing overlap of economic development, social welfare and environmental protection. This is true but it gives no impression of urgency, the limits to the global resources to be commandeered in meeting this goal nor who is to be included in the decision-making when trade-offs are made. The utilitarianism of this could still affect the poorest.

All models have their deficiencies of course and so long as the intent is there and the model is illustrative of a deeper analysis then we should not get hung up. But we lack that deep analysis from official or business sources.

To be frank we do not yet have something for Scotland that fits the bill. There was a statement attached to the indicators called *Meeting the Needs*,[46] which set out a vision, priorities and action. The language is encouraging. Development, it says, should have regard for others who do not have access to the same level of resources and the wealth generated. We should curb the effect of our actions on future generations by radically reducing our use of resources and by minimising environmental impacts. We should live within the capacity of the planet to sustain our activities and to replenish the resources that we use. However, the document runs to only some nine pages. It is insufficiently inclusive in its scope or strategic in its goals to have significant impact on the vested interests of government departments, which were producing far weightier departmental or sectoral strategies of their own. Unfortunately the focus on waste, energy and travel can also encourage a view that what is being addressed is the housekeeping impact of a department's own activities on the environment as opposed to the policy and agencies with which it is engaged.

This confusion was evident when Executive departments were required to furnish a statement on the contribution which their programmes would make to sustainable development, when making their bids as part of the Spending Review 2002. The results were patchy. The Justice department noted that the Scottish Courts Service has reduced energy use by 35 per cent. It mentioned that the department contributes directly to environmental protection through the pursuit of environmental crime, but there is no recognition here or from the Crown Office of the issues raised earlier of the proportionately lower prosecution of environmental offences.

Some do acknowledge that they are confronting issues that have to be reconciled. Tourism, Culture and Sport noted that VisitScotland's mission to make Scotland a must-visit destination, and so to increase the number of visitors to Scotland, at first appears to conflict with sustainable development. However, it then went on to say that the CO_2 emitted by visitors' coaches and cars is very small compared with the total emitted by all cars on Scotland's roads, without attempting quantification.

Reading the statements, you could be forgiven for believing that Scotland was gamely doing its bit and must surely be up there in the top performing countries in delivering on the Rio commitments. But, wait a minute, is this not the same country which has been unable to get recycling beyond 6 per cent, where CO_2 emissions overall are barely reducing despite Kyoto commitments, where car ownership and miles travelled are on the increase; where we do not even know what our resource use per capita GNP is, and where we are projecting a massive increase in air travel over the coming decades?

If we are serious about sustainable development then we need to confront ourselves with the failings not just the achievements and to contribute to a different trajectory, as it seems unlikely that our current development path will deliver.

There are issues to be addressed. This is a small country – what do we do when there is market failure, in a market where there may only be a few key players? At one time in central Scotland there was a reasonably sophisticated office paper collection scheme run by a charity. This was taken over by Weir, a privately owned Australian paper company, but which, in turn, was then bought by Inveresk Papers. This was a successful Scottish operation that had been formed from a management buy-out and was then floated on the stock market. However, when the price of virgin pulp was cheaper than collecting recycled paper the office scheme came to a juddering halt. People were left with bags of paper uncollected and the prospect of having to pay to have them taken away. Not surprisingly a jaundiced view was taken of future schemes. We need to consider how we can use the purchasing power of the public purse to create a market for recycled and green products.

We have to ensure too that adequate environmental information is available for decision-making. How is it that the energy efficiency performance of white goods such as washing machines and fridges is now prominently displayed, but that a potential house buyer has no idea what it takes to run a house.

Clearly, getting the right mix of regulation, fiscal incentives and penalties can change behaviour. The requirement on electricity generators to produce 10 per cent of their power from renewables has stimulated a far greater level of investment in windpower than previous schemes. The cost of that can be hidden away in bills, which in any case are falling after deregulation. But politicians are nervous when it comes to confronting the public with direct costs such as congestion charging or separated waste collection.

Whatever measures are suggested are cramped by a political and bureaucratic culture which is disinclined towards principled policy choices or sweeping statements of intent. This is not a peculiarly Scottish trait.

Whether it be 'back to basics' or 'ethical foreign policy', these stances can be seen as hostages to fortune. Sustainable development has stayed the course as a claimed core value but perhaps only because it has been interpreted so cavalierly by so many actors and has not been prescriptive in its requirements. This fits with what has been seen as a UK political tradition whereby 'general norms are to be avoided if the decision can be left to the exercise of continuous administrative discretion'.[47] But without a more systematic attempt at change then isolated initiatives will founder.

Scotland faces a dilemma which is not unique but which we should not wait for others to resolve. Despite the lived experience of how difficult it has been to secure redistribution even in a time when politically and commercially the state predominated, we are still committed to attempting that redistribution. At the same time we are having to face up to the profligacy of our resource consumption and extending our aspirations to a global not just national redistribution of wealth and resources. All of this is to be achieved within the limited carrying capacity of the planet.

We have to assume the responsibility for past mistakes, and safeguard the rights of future generations as well as attending to our current generational inequalities. Yet even at this realisation our levers of change are being wrested from our grasp, or simply let go. We have been signed up to a globalisation agenda which returns to a simplistic view of economic development that what is good for the firm is good for society. Wealth it is hoped will inevitably trickle down even if inequalities grow.

It is not inevitable, and may not be the best route as the United Nations Environment Programme has illustrated when considering what kind of world we are going to live in. Its GEO3 report looked forward over the next thirty years, projecting different outcomes that are likely to emerge based upon four differing value systems. It envisages a 'markets first' approach, where most of the world adopts the values and expectations of the industrialised nations, by which globalisation and liberalisation are expected to generate the resources to tackle environmental and social problems. Under a 'policy first'

Economic development – 'we have to assume the responsibility for past mistakes as well as safeguard the rights of future generations.'
FoE Scotland

rubric, governments intervene to factor anti-poverty and pro-environmental outcomes into economic development through the use of regulation, fiscal levers and planning processes. 'Security first' is a dark world where the drawbridge of self-protection is pulled up and inequality and conflict is seen as a fact of life. And finally there is a 'sustainability first' scenario, which imagines a value-shift based around equity and corporate accountability and a 'consensus is reached on what needs to be done to satisfy basic needs and realise personal goals without beggaring others or spoiling the outlook for posterity'.[48] Not surprisingly the market first approach consistently entails the highest environmental impacts – generating 15 billion tonnes of CO_2 per annum by 2030 compared to 7 billion tonnes under the sustainability first scenario. Market forces would reduce the percentage of population living with hunger by about 25 per cent but not nearly by as much as more conscious effort through a policy-led or sustainability-driven approach. The markets first approach would induce environmental problems – in Europe nearly 50 per cent of the population would live in areas with severe water stress, compared to less than a third of that under a policy first or sustainability first scenario.

We can point to aspects of each of the four approaches being current in present-day national and international policy. No single scenario is likely to emerge over the next thirty years. Yet it is clear that 'markets first' is the dominant paradigm. Even where policy initiatives are taken, the best that may be achieved is mitigation of the negative impacts of a market-led approach. Sustainability initiatives may be in conflict with or cancelled out by competing trade liberalisation measures. The privatisation of energy was motivated by the drive to lower energy prices through competition, pulling in the opposite direction for the desire to cut CO_2 emissions and to promote investment in renewables and energy efficiency. What is clear, however, is that these outcomes are not pre-ordained.

We hold to our old desires but hope that the new forms of economy will deliver. In part we can do so because there is no absolute break with the past. We have some companies who exhibit a social engagement alongside others who regard Scotland as a temporary depot. We look to juggle the remaining powers we have to affect the operations of the market whether through legislation, specification, best-value principles or contractual obligations. But sustainable development is not about pointing to pilot projects, sectoral initiatives or preambles to government policy documents. It will be tested on outcomes and will require us to address irreconcilable objectives. Serious debate in Scotland on how we deal with the diverging trajectories of globalisation and a sustainable small nation is absent. Instead we seem capable of claiming to pursue both ends at the same time. In which case we have to ask ourselves whether this is likely to bring about the kind of Scotland we want to live in. We have choices and if we want to bring about sustainable development, and within that environmental justice, we need to plan for such a future, not leave it to happenstance.

Notes

1. Office of National Statistics, *Health Statistics Quarterly*, 13, Spring 2002, p. 85.
2. Smith, *North and South*, p. 32.
3. Klein, *No Logo*, p. 39.
4. Brown and Cook, *Scotland: The Real Divide*, p. 12.
5. Devine, *The Scottish Nation, 1700–2000*, p. 554.
6. Woods, *The Hydro Boys*, p. 58.
7. Glendinning and Page, *Clone City: Crisis and Renewal in Contemporary Scottish Architecture*, p. 44.
8. Devine, *The Scottish Nation, 1700–2000*, p. 561.
9. Ibid.
10. Rosie, 'The Cromarty Firth: The Tale of Multinational Business in Scotland' in Maxwell (ed.), *Scotland, Multinationals and the Third World*, p. 151.
11. Warren, *Managing Scotland's Environment*, p. 309.
12. *A Smart, Successful Scotland*, p. 7.
13. Glover, 'globalization.com vs. ecologicaljustice.org: Contesting the End of History', in J. Byrne et al., *Justice Discourses in International Political Economy*, p. 235.
14. North, *Life on a Modern Planet*, p. 212.
15. Shipman, *The Globalization Myth*, p. 227.
16. McMutry quoted in Glover, 'globalization.com vs. ecologicaljustice.org: Contesting the End of History', p. 235.
17. Gottlieb, *Environmentalism Unbound*, p. 276.
18. Sachs, *Planet Dialectics*, p. 163.
19. Ohmae, *The End of the Nation State*, p. 89.
20. Ibid. p. 63.
21. Smout, *A Century of the Scottish People*, p. 112.
22. *The Scotsman*, 2 June 2002.
23. Ibid. 20 August 2002.
24. Butler and Hallowes, *Corporate Accountability in South Africa*, p. 69.
25. Stiglitz, *Globalization and its Discontents*, pp. 21–2.
26. Ibid. p. 51.
27. *The Scotsman*, 31 May 2002.
28. Jacobs, *The Green Economy*, p. 54.
29. Carley and Spapens, *Sharing the World*, p. 42.
30. Prugh et al., *The Local Politics of Global Sustainability*, p. 70.
31. Ibid. p. 70.
32. Ibid. p. 7.

33. Ibid. p. 160.
34. Ponting, *A Green History of the World*, p. 334.
35. North, *Life on a Modern Planet*, pp. 265–6.
36. See Jacobs, *The Green Economy*, p. 54.
37. Rathje and Murphy, *Rubbish: The Archaeology of Garbage*, p. 102.
38. Huber, *Hard Green: Saving the Environment from Environmentalists*, p. 72.
39. Slesser et al., *The Management of Greed*, p. 165.
40. Ascherson, *Stone Voices: The Search for Scotland*, p. 264.
41. See Andrews and Withey, *Social Indicators of Wellbeing*.
42. Bell and Morse, *Sustainability Indicators*, p. 101.
43. See Dunion et al., 'The Role of Indicators in Reporting on the State of Scotland and its Environment', in Usher et al. (eds), *The State of Scotland's Environment and Natural Heritage*.
44. OECD, *Indicators to Measure Decoupling of Environmental Pressures from Economic Growth*, p. 20.
45. Bell and Morse, *Sustainability Indicators*, p. 32.
46. Scottish Executive, *Meeting the Needs*.
47. Weale, *The New Politics of Pollution*, p. 81.
48. UNEP, *Global Environmental Outlook 3*, p. 344.

8

Best-Laid Plans

W E ARE NOT GOING to have a convincing strategy of sustainable development, which includes notions of civic engagement and environmental justice, unless we consciously change the way we plan for the future and question how we currently permit development. We cannot have a persuasive claim to sustainable development if we rely upon a few isolated examples of good practice or pilot projects set against a backdrop of activity which is largely business as usual. We will have to develop a better awareness and knowledge of the impact of activities on key indicators, so that we can know if we are being moved away from or towards sustainable development. At present we have a system that is not delivering declared commitments to sustainable development nor are we equipped to gauge the impact of specific proposed developments.

The alternative is not about rigid state planning or prohibiting choices. It is about anticipating scenarios and exercising informed choice. It is about having a view as to where we wish to go and encouraging and stimulating positive investment. It also requires humility and a recognition that all negative impacts for a community may not be anticipated. Thus the planning approval system has to be made more sensitive to local people's concerns and they should be assisted to more effectively represent those concerns where developments are the subject of dispute.

It may not be the case in Scotland that we have 'a jobs at all costs' approach or a market free for all. Nevertheless, it seems that where economic, social and environmental considerations are weighed in the balance, the scales are heavily tipped in favour of permitting new developments even with a known deleterious environmental effect. In part this is because we are not sufficiently robust in shifting policy and planning approaches to discourage them. There has still been a prevalence to adopt a predict and provide approach – predict what the industry may want and make planning provision in terms of permissions and infrastructure to let it come about.

It is said that we are moving away from this approach. Projected car ownership and usage used to form the basis for providing the investment in roads infrastructure. In part this was a self-fulfilling prophecy along the lines of Kevin Costner being told in *Field of Dreams*, 'if you build it, they will come.' (It is notable that the film portrayed the success of his wild gamble to build a baseball field as a long traffic jam snaking out far into the distance, as fans drove out to his farm.) The projected figures for the numbers of cars which will be competing for road space has led government to accept that it can no longer build its way out of the problem. There is increasing emphasis on rationing existing road space, tackling congestion and shifting freight and passengers off the roads where possible. However, whilst this may be accepted intellectually, it is far from being accepted by the roads lobby.

And when it comes to air travel the old predict and provide policy stills seems to reign supreme. Forecasts for passenger numbers coming through Scotland's airports are being projected to grow at between 3.5 per cent and 4 per cent per annum in the period to 2030. This would mean that Edinburgh, Glasgow and Aberdeen airports would be expected to handle 48 million passengers annually, compared to just over 14 million passengers in 2000.[1] What are the implications, if such predictions come to pass, for climate-change emissions in Scotland not only from the aircraft movements but also from ferrying people to and from the airports? Is this sustainable, and if not what interventions are being considered to mitigate this increase?

Predict and provide is not going to deliver sustainable development. It may not even deliver economic development if predictions are wrong, so that the projected demand does not materialise and communities are left with an undesirable and unneeded activity.

When the then Leicestershire-based company Redland Aggregates submitted its proposals for the Harris superquarry, it insisted that it should be permitted to satisfy national need for aggregates. Roads and building work would be hampered, they claimed, from a lack of material and balance of payments would suffer as the UK would have to import from abroad to meet demand. At the public inquiry the developers used forecasts prepared for the Department of the Environment in 1991 and 1992. These predicted that aggregate demand would rise steadily, requiring between 370 and 440 million tonnes per annum (mtpa) by 2011, compared to (at that time) annual demand of 215 mtpa. When the Department issued its guidelines for aggregate provision in England in 1994 it used these forecasts to make specific provision for the period up to 2006, anticipating on average annual demand of 280 million tonnes per annum. The Lingerbay quarry at full production would produce up to 15 million tonnes per annum.

In some ways this was an article of faith, as aggregate demand seemed directly connected to the robustness of the economy. To anticipate flat demand was tantamount to suggesting that economic growth was not on the cards. Yet even by the time of the public inquiry, demand had begun to fall and as the years ticked by, waiting for a decision on whether the superquarry would get the go ahead, aggregates supply consistently remained 65 million tonnes below the government's annual forecast. The forecasting system was described as 'discredited and pointless' even by the industry, which called upon the government to abandon fifteen-year forecasting and to stick to five-year projections. The Quarry Products Association, of which Lafarge Redland is a member, called the 1991/2 forecasts 'infamous' and suggested that the government would do well to rein back primary aggregate demand estimates to 215 mtpa for the next five years.[2]

The passage of time and the stubbornly flat demand figures did eventually oblige the government to admit that its estimates were much too high.[3] In 2002 the government let it be known that it was now assuming that demand would average 212.5 mtpa between 2001 and 2016, 24 per cent lower than the projections that had been used in 1994 and that had been deployed by Redland Aggregates at the inquiry (and which the company have given no official notice of altering). More significantly government forecasts now assume that net imports to England from Scotland and elsewhere will be insignificant at 3.5 mtpa – well below the capacity of Scotland's existing exporting superquarry at Glensanda.[4]

There never was any national need for the Harris superquarry: it was entirely an opportunistic commercial enterprise. The driving force for the company was the need to secure a supply source which could replace its assets in England if, as seemed likely, planning authorities there were less inclined to grant permission to applications for new or extended quarries. (As it turned out, this concern was misplaced as Redland's massive quarry at Mountsorrel in Leicestershire was given permission to extend its output.) The prospect of sales outside of England was speculated upon, such as into Germany, except that, there too, demand collapsed and in any case cheaper sources in Poland meant that a remote Scottish quarry was unlikely to be competitive. However, getting permission would still be no bad thing for the company – it would be good insurance to have a sixty-year consent and a landbank of up to 600 million tonnes should things ever pick up in the future. Indeed, that now appears to be the position of the parent company. Its Chairman, Bertrand Collomb, has resisted calls for the superquarry application to be withdrawn, saying, 'it is true that past forecasts of demand in the UK were well above actual outcomes. But that does not alter the fact that we will sooner or later need to find new quarries to replace those that run out.'[5] A dormant permission would be an appreciating asset for the company, which is used to dominating the market. (In fact it is too keen to do so having twice been fined by the European Commission for operating a price-fixing cartel for cement and plasterboard. The £156 million fine for the latter offence in 2002 is the third largest imposed on any company by the Commission.) Bolstering a multinational's balance sheet would do nothing for the community. The meagre number of thirty-three local jobs projected at full production would not materialise. The community benefit fund, tied to each tonne of output, and offered as an inducement for the support of the islanders, would receive nothing.

Redland's view that planning permission would be easier to come by in the Western Isles represents just one example of an attempted displacement, from England to Scotland, by what are seen as developments which may give rise to significant environmental effects. This is a process which is not new, especially where mineral extraction is concerned.

Scotland has for years been a mineral-extracting country and indeed the industrial revolution was based upon ready availability of coal reserves. Most British coal was produced from deep mines. For instance in 1965 Scotland produced 15

Roineabhal on Harris – a mountain, or 600 million tonnes of rock for construction?
Sam Maynard

million tonnes of coal, of which only 5 per cent came from opencast production. This was transformed within twenty years. By 1998 coal output had fallen to 8.2 million tonnes, of which 77 per cent was produced by opencast mines. With the closure, in 2002, of the last deep mine in Scotland, future output will be exclusively opencast.

Throughout the 1980s Scotland had produced roughly 20 per cent of the UK's opencast coal output but the figure crept up in the 1990s and seemed set to continue into the new millennium. Even though the Scottish coal field represents less than one-fifth of the UK coal field, the Scottish opencast coal figure of over 8 million tonnes per annum by 2001/2 represented almost 57 per cent of the UK's opencast coal output.

Table 8.1 UK opencast coal production (thousand tonnes)

	1995/6	1996/7	1997/8	1998/9	1999/ 2000	2000/1	2001/2
England	8,908	8,401	8,136	6,956	6,163	4,768	5,111
Wales	2,071	2,271	1,753	1,507	1,540	1,401	1,178
Scotland	5,111	5,592	6,326	6,434	7,224	7,978	8,186
Total	16,090	16,263	16,217	14,897	14,927	13,247	14,475

Sources: County Planning Officers Society, 'Opencast Coal Statistics' 1995/6–1999/2000; Coal Authority Statistical Returns 2000/1 and 2001/2.

In 1997, on a tonnage basis, Scottish planning authorities approved 87 per cent of applications for opencast coal extraction, compared to just 11 per cent in England. This was not because sources in England were exhausted but, quite simply, due to the refusal of planning authorities there to permit new sites to be opened up. Popular resentment there over the impacts of opencasting saw applications being turned down. As a result, companies turned their attention north of the border. A UK government White Paper, on the review of energy sources for power generation, forecast that opencast coal output from England, which in the early 1990s had reached almost 14 million tonnes per annum, was now unlikely to

exceed 3 million tonnes per annum as a result of planning constraints. However, it concluded that Scotland 'has the capacity
and currently the mineral planning climate to produce in the
order of 9 million tonnes per annum. If this came to pass it
would mean Scotland producing 75 per cent of the UK's output.' The low figure for England has not yet been reached but
Scottish opencast production in 2001/2 exceeded the 8 million
tonnes mark for the first time.

Globally, about 70 per cent of the world's ore is obtained by
opencast extraction. At a UK level, the House of Commons
Select Committee on Energy in 1987 described opencast mining
as one of the most environmentally damaging processes being
carried out in the UK. To access shallow coal reserves requires
the removal of large swathes of land – the ratio of soil to coal
can be 20 to 1 or more. The opencast coal companies of course
justify this as a 'temporary' use of land which will be restored.
However, for the communities living around about them they
have to live with a despoiled landscape, noise, blasting, heavy
lorry movements and concerns about the respiratory impacts
of inhaling mineral particles. Whilst some opencast mining
may be a precursor to improvements to otherwise derelict or
poor-quality land, it also encroaches on more complex and
valued habitats such as heath, meadow, bog, ancient woodland
and moorland.

These 'temporary' uses can be prolonged. When planning
permission is sought, the average proposed duration of an
opencast site in Scotland is four and a half years. However,
some sites can be worked for a generation, with the 1,300-
hectare Glentaggart site in South Lanarkshire scheduled to
operate for twenty-two years. Also sites may regularly seek
extensions to the initial planning permission. Blindwells in East
Lothian was scheduled to operate for a fairly lengthy ten years
from 1977 to 1987 but was given an extension to 1997 and did
not finally cease until 2001, twenty-four years after starting
work.

Site restoration may often mean, at best, not much more
than sterile grassland, but could be much worse. At the

Lambhill site, in Perth and Kinross, the people of Blairingone were promised that the site would be completely restored to woodlands, wetlands and agriculture by 1996. Schoolchildren were encouraged to take part in planting trees, each bearing a child's name. However, the 560-acre site was subsequently sold to a waste disposal company and the young trees disappeared, to be replaced by a cocktail of wastes being applied to the land, including human sewage sludge, tannery, fishery, distillery and food-processing effluent, abattoir waste and septic tank contents. (This was one of the companies which has been successfully prosecuted by SEPA for allowing blood and animal remains to leak from the site into a water course, which in turn feeds into Gartmorn dam, the water supply for the town of Alloa.) The local MSP has campaigned for an end to 'fields of filth' and challenged the Environment Minister to 'walk through frozen fields with a gelatinous red goo lying on top, gulls pecking at it ... through silage destroyed in the so-called process of fertilisation with blood and guts smeared thick on it – foxes running through it and cats trailing it into the house.'[6]

Elsewhere, the holes in the ground left from abandoned opencast sites become attractive for waste disposal companies. The landfill operator Haul Waste for instance acquired three former opencast sites in Ayrshire, East Kilbride and Motherwell. Even where sites are filled in and levelled these can become available for house building, thereby introducing permanent development into what was countryside before mining started.

In the UK at the beginning of the twenty-first century there were 48 opencast sites in production in the UK of which 22 were in Scotland, operated by 11 different companies. The justification for this disproportionately high presence in the Scottish economy and for requiring communities to live next to the disruption and physical degradation caused by opencast mining has usually been given as jobs. Scottish opencast mines employed 1,600 people directly as compared to less than 800 in deep mining when Longannet was still open.

Since the dramatic demise of Longannet after catastrophic

*Opencast coal mining – Scotland now produces over half
of the UK output.*
Sunday Mail

flooding of the deep mine, opencast companies now want the relaxation of planning rules to make up for the lost output. In particular they want to see changes in national planning policy guidance to local authorities, which, unusually, presumes against opencast development, following years of campaigning by affected communities. Brian Rastron the director of the Coal Producers Federation has said, 'The only thing we really want is the removal of the presumption against opencast coal mining.'[7] What he also wants, in fact, is that new permissions be granted so that the industry has a guaranteed landbank of ten years' production. Yet current Scottish opencast production exceeds the requirement of the power companies and demand is set to fall with the expected closure of the Cockenzie power station within the next decade.

Even though the jobs card is played by the industry, increasingly communities feel that the coal producers have over played their hand and that very few local jobs are being created in the areas in which the industry is located. The most skilled portion of the workforce is migratory and often the projected levels of employment are either short term or fails to materialise. (Two opencast sites in Northumberland forecast a total of 620 jobs when applying for planning permission. However, once coaling started only 102 men were actually employed.)[8]

Communities began to question whether they were bearing all of the costs and seeing few of the benefits. Looking around them they have seen a succession of sites where their bit of the planet was being scoured, blasted and excavated. The novelist Jonathon Franzen describes the landscape of New Jersey whose 'deep ruination gave the impression of a kitchen floor with the linoleum scraped off'.[9] It is a topography with which people ranging from Ayrshire through to the Lothians and Fife will be familiar. Although the Scottish coalfields are not equated with areas of exceptionally high landscape value, for many communities they represent the local countryside. They are familiar places, close to the edges of towns and villages, which, if not irreplaceable, in terms of uniqueness and international value, can ill afforded to be lost as far as local amenity is concerned. The concentration on extracting coal at the expense of all other considerations is now being challenged. As Thomas Power recognises, 'mineral deposits do not necessarily represent a concentrated form of economic wealth that outweighs the non consumptive values associated with natural landscapes'.[10] There is a dawning realisation that industries and activities such as opencasting and their associated economic bedfellows such as landfilling do not represent the basis for economic development but are dependent upon a desperation borne of being told there is no alternative, no matter how meagre the jobs and financial returns to the local community. As Power has noted, polluting activities are associated with higher unemployment, greater poverty and lower disposal per capita income. He says, 'these correlations do not establish causality. Rather than environmental quality stimulating economic development it may be that poorer areas are more willing to sacrifice environmental quality in the pursuit of jobs and income'.[11] Yet drawing upon the US experience, he concludes that 'examples of areas that have prospered in the midst of environmental deterioration are difficult to come by'.[12]

Speaking up in opposition to proposed opencast coal sites often means taking on the local authority, developers and those within the community who see the prospect of benefiting from either new jobs or the continuation of jobs on sites elsewhere. However, many communities in Scotland are saying enough is enough. North Lanarkshire Council was inundated with objections to an application from Law Mining. The company wanted to mine over half a million tonnes of coal only 500 metres from the community of Fauldhouse in neighbouring West Lothian. Local community activists have described the village as a 'Community under siege from major land use developments'.[13] It is already surrounded by four landfill sites; and within a two-mile radius there are applications for six opencast coal mines, two wind farms, and a land-reclamation scheme which would import 50,000 tones of sewage sludge every year. Every twelve minutes a lorry would have passed through the village, and other roadside communities between the site and the coal's destination, if the Law Mining application had been permitted. However, despite a recommendation for approval from council officials, the planning committee refused it.

Others have not been so fortunate with the same committee. The benighted community of Greengairs, also in North Lanarkshire, has already had experience of living next to open-casting. The Drumshangie mine was a source of local anger when the operators extracted thousands of tonnes of coal without permission, causing a road to collapse. It remained closed for over two years, forcing parents who were taking their kids to school to use a longer route and to share the roads with large haul lorries. When the area was targeted for yet another opencast mine, the developers warned local people that if they objected and the application went to a public local inquiry, then they would forfeit any community benefit on offer from the company. Despite this, the community was adamant that the application should be rejected but were dismayed that the local authority planning committee heard the application during the traditional Glasgow fair fortnight summer holidays. Instead of 30 councillors present, only 12 turned up and the application was approved by 7 votes to 5. With no right of appeal, the local people were dependent upon the Secretary of State (in that pre-devolution time) to call the application in for consideration.

At first the residents were delighted when it was duly called in. Ann Coleman takes up the story: 'People felt that a planning local inquiry would be a democratic and just process dealing with all the aspects of the proposal in the public domain. That is not how it went. The public were treated as if they were naive, and ill informed.'

Like many ordinary citizens who experience a planning local inquiry (PLI), she felt that the odds were stacked against them, not least in terms of their knowledge of how the planning and inquiry systems operate and the resources that the developers could mobilise compared to the local community. Ann found that 'there is nothing written down anywhere in layman's terms that gives you the remit of the PLI and how to take part. I phoned the Scottish Executive and was passed to the Reporter's Office and then to the Ombudsman. Nobody is aware of any such publication. We need somebody to prepare us better for it and to access expert witnesses who will provide testimony for a minimum cost. We managed to raise over £30,000 to be represented. We would need £150,000 to be on par with the developer.'

The attitude of some of those in authority is that if third parties wish to intrude they can do so, but can expect no assistance. When inquiries are convened, residents opposed to opencast mines are often portrayed as old fashioned, not-in-my-backyard objectors. As one commentator wryly has pointed out, 'Concerns by local residents for the effects of mining on their property, the local environment and their health are frequently denigrated as selfish and self-seeking. The fact that these charges are made by barristers on exorbitantly high fees, living miles away from any opencast site is deeply ironic but rarely a matter of comment.'[14]

Improvements to the planning system have to be made if the aims of environmental justice are to be served. The experience of Ann Coleman and others convinces me that there must be some advisory service which assists third-party witnesses to understand the system and to present their case. Being able to afford a QC should not be the price of having your voice effectively heard. There is no reason why individuals or community organisations should not be able to represent themselves. Many already do but can find it intimidating, and unsatisfactory. Guidance on how the inquiry will be run is not available in written form; there is no glossary to explain what technical terms like 'productions' and 'precognitions' mean. The atmosphere is quasi-legal with QCs on opposite sides of the room addressing each other with the studied formality of 'My learned friend . . . '

There can be a ritualised humiliation of objectors at public local inquiries with one senior inspector in England dealing with an opencast inquiry saying, 'the manner in which many members of the public were questioned by the appellants . . . varied between the aggressive and the offensive'.[15]

Community representatives may be tolerated but patronised for their ignorance of procedures. Joan Higginson from Midlothian represented her local roads campaign group at a public inquiry into a biotechnology park. 'I was told it would be like a courtroom – so I was nervous and scared. The language acts as a barrier, and I did not know the format or what my rights were. I was treated like a wee wifie from the streets.'

A publicly funded service should assist groups to understand the system. There should be access to financial resources, which would allow alternative experts to scrutinise the proposals, acquire technical documents, and legal advice on submitting a case. Such a provision exists elsewhere and there is no reason for it not to be introduced to Scotland if we are really serious about local voices being heard in contentious developments.

The other change that must happen is to give communities the same rights as developers when it comes to the planning system. As mentioned above, the Greengairs residents had no right of appeal against the decision of their local planning authority to permit the development; if the decision had been to turn down the application, the company would have had the right of appeal.

The planning system is weighted heavily in favour of developers, although applications nowadays have to be consistent with the local development plan. Planning policy used to operate on the basis of a presumption in favour of development. This reflected the view that property rights mean that owners should be allowed to utilise their assets without being unreasonably constrained and that such development equals societal benefit through economic growth, creation of jobs and stimulation of market activity. Where a development may give rise to negative impacts upon the environment or neighbours, then it is presumed that the local planning authority will act to protect their rights, mitigate pollution, or disturbance and minimise impacts upon other property values. They can impose certain planning conditions or, if necessary, refuse the application. In certain circumstances where the project is large or particularly controversial then Scottish ministers can step in and 'call in' the application for determination.

The experience of some communities, however, is that the system does not provide them with adequate protection or represent a fair approach to assessing proposed developments. What if for example the development is actually being undertaken by the planning authority or on its behalf? That could be a major road infrastructure project or it could be one like the

Kaimes quarry where the outcome of a planning application has a material bearing upon the finances and the waste-management policy of the local authority. What if the local community thought it was protected by a local plan which either made no provision for the development or the development was indeed contrary to the provisions of the plan?

What is needed is equity so that communities have similar rights to developers. If developers can appeal against the decision of the local planning authority and expect their case to be considered by Scottish ministers, including the establishment of expensive public local inquiries, then so should communities. We need what has come to be known as third-party rights of appeal. Traditionally planning professionals have been implacably opposed to third-party rights of appeal. They believe that the system adequately takes community views into account by allowing objections to be heard by the local planning committee. Far more pertinently, they believe that third-party appeals would clog up the planning system so that planning decisions would take longer to arrive at, delaying or even putting in jeopardy developments. Some people may make frivolous use of a modified appeal system, seeking to delay or increase the costs of developments to which they are opposed.

The bottom line is, as ever, that those in authority are unwilling to provide a troublemaker's charter. Aggrieving people with reasonable concerns appears to be the price to be paid for stifling what those in authority would regard as unreasonable or organised campaigns of resistance. As a consequence we have a planning system that is inherently unfair, giving one side rights denied to another. The Royal Commission on Environmental Pollution (RCEP) agrees. In its report on environmental planning it argued that there is a 'pro-development bias in the system and the time has come for change'.[16]

We can come up with intelligent provision for third-party rights of appeal, which address the worst-case-scenario concerns of the professionals, without at the same time restricting unfairly the rights of communities. No one really wants to see every single application capable of being appealed to Scottish ministers. What we want to identify are those types of planning application where it is reasonable, and indeed essential, that there should be some form of review by a higher authority.

Let us say, first, that the third-party right of appeal should apply to those applications which are contrary to the approved structure plan or adopted local plan. That would seem to be fair; these plans are now subject to approval by the Scottish Executive. If they are to be departed from, then any variation should be considered, and consequently approved by the Scottish Executive.

Second, any planning application in which the local authority has an interest should be capable of being appealed. Again this seems only fair – if the perception exists that the local authority has a stake in the successful outcome of a planning application then it is not an unreasonable requirement that this decision should be subject to review by a separate and higher authority.

Third, major applications, particularly those requiring an environmental impact statement, should also be subject to appeal. If the concern of the planning authorities is that applications for the minor building amendments, or the erection of domestic garages should not be permitted to be appealed, we should not at the same time disallow appeals for developments which have a major significance for the community.

Finally if the local authority permits an application recommended for refusal by its own planning officers, then again it is reasonable to suggest that this is controversial and should be capable of review.

If the basis for appeal was restricted in this form then the test of inhibiting frivolous or voluminous appeals would be satisfied. Other administrative provisions would also ensure that the system was not unduly disrupted such as restricting the right to appeal only to those who had objected to the original planning application. (Those waiting to see the outcome before expressing their opinion or entering into the system would be too late.) It would be justifiable to have a modest fee for lodging an appeal, which would also stop any frivolous abuses of the system. A recent report suggested a flat fee of £30.00

would be sufficient. There should be a time limit, of say twenty-eight days, for lodging an appeal.

Certainly the experiences of countries like Ireland, Denmark, Sweden, New Zealand and Australia are that third-party rights of appeal can be provided, without the planning system becoming choked or development hindered. In any case where planning decisions are delayed it is often due to the actions of the developers who pursue hopeless appeals to Scottish ministers simply because they can – at present only 30 per cent of appeals by developers are successful. Nevertheless this unilateral ability to pursue appeals can have an affect upon the original decision of the planning authority. There can be little doubt that local authorities have been inclined to come to an agreement with developers over schemes which they might otherwise refuse but which they feared that would be permitted without community benefit or mitigating conditions if appealed to the Secretary of State.

The provision of third-party rights of appeal is also consistent with the drift of European and national legislation which seeks to ensure public participation and access to justice, in particular the Aarhus Convention 1998 on access to information, public participation in decision-making and access to justice in environmental matters. Article 9 requires that citizens have the right to a review procedure before an independent and impartial body, established by law, to challenge the substantive and procedural legality of decisions. It could be argued of course, both in human rights terms and in respect of Aarhus, that if people feel sufficiently aggrieved they can take the matter to court. The RCEP, however, does not regard this as adequate, saying, 'we have concerns that existing arrangements for the involvement of objectors in the decision making process may not be consistent with the spirit and objectives of the Convention'.[17]

For as we have seen before, for all practical purposes, to challenge the decision of a local authority can only be done through judicial review, in which case the court would not concern itself with the merits of the planning application but only determine whether the decision was made in accordance with legislation. Establishing the illegality of a decision is a high test and in any case in Scotland the right to petition for judicial review is not available to all objectors to a planning application. For instance Friends of the Earth Scotland, as a non-governmental organisation, is able to lodge objections to planning applications which may affect the environment. We are allowed to present evidence and to speak at a public local inquiry. But, unlike our counterparts in England, we would not be allowed to take a case for judicial review, as at present the courts in Scotland narrowly interpret the rights in this respect. Unless Friends of the Earth as an organisation was materially affected by the decision (for example, if property that we owned was affected) then we have no right to judicial review. The provision of third-party rights would provide a consistency in that any individual or organisation, whether directly affected or not but had been involved in the planning-consultation process up to the point of decision, could submit an appeal.

Yet the Scottish Executive has so far been implacably opposed to third-party rights and despite submissions from voluntary organisations and others has excluded it from consideration. As one member of the public, responding to a public consultation entitled 'Getting involved in the planning process', has complained: 'In the consultation paper, third party right of appeal is mentioned, but not favourably by the Executive . . . Why has a question on the matter, and the opportunity to answer and comment, not been included in a questionnaire? Is the Executive afraid of public opinion?'[18]

The answer has to be yes, with the Executive unwilling to provoke or stimulate an expression of public support for a measure that it believes offers the prospect of well-organised, and resourceful, voluntary organisations in Scotland acting in concert with communities.

By putting too much power into the hands of local people it is presumed that effective resistance to developments, which the authorities may deem to be nationally necessary but will always be locally unpopular, will be bolstered.

Authorities everywhere struggle to secure acceptance of problematic proposals such as toxic-waste dumps, and seek methods which will speed up decision-making and reduce delays from local opposition. One way which has been proposed for achieving this would be to require planning authorities to find suitable sites but to enhance the compensation to the particular local communities who 'volunteer' to accept the dump.

This would be done by the government, or the developer, 'auctioning' the proposal for, say, a hazardous waste site. Planning authorities would be invited to bid to establish a site in return for the financial compensating figure in the auction. If no planning authority came forward then a higher bid price would be offered until there were acceptable bids. If the offer site was deemed to be technically suitable then the proposal would then go to a local referendum in the municipal area that encompasses the community affected. If the community rejects the scheme then it would not go ahead. If the referendum is in favour of accepting the proposal then those who are opposed will be offered the option to sell up at a pre-proposal value of their property plus relocation costs.

The compensation fund may be used to benefit people directly (for example, through a reduction in the rates) or it may be used to improve local services in education or health, or invested in capital investments like new schools or hospitals.

To ensure that there is a public acceptability of the need to have such sites in the first place, proponents argue that the government should carry out a needs assessment to establish what level of toxic waste has to be produced and take necessary measures to minimise or avoid its generation. Having established what is still likely to be produced and the number of sites that will be required to accommodate the wastes, then the government can instruct planning authorities to come up with suitable sites. This 'allocation' approach is intended to avoid a laissez-faire attitude by planning authorities that may mean insufficient sites come on-stream or that they tend to cluster in a geographical part of the country.

There are examples already of communities procuring

considerable 'planning gain' from developments, but the scale and the local autonomy which the volunteer community approach envisages is of a different order. Clearly for some it will be attractive – the remaining members of the Goshute Indians have offered to provide a temporary nuclear waste repository on their reservation in Skull Valley, Utah, which would, it is thought, provide them with £33 million over the next forty years. However, the principle of local autonomy clashes with the efforts of Utah's state governor to employ the proximity principle as he argues that as the state does not produce nuclear waste, it should not have to store it for those who do.[19]

In Finland the European nuclear industry has at last found a community willing to host a nuclear waste repository. The town of Eurajoki has volunteered, encouraged by the offer from Posiva, the nuclear generator, of 6.73 million euros in credit. The company has told the Council that it does not need to pay this sum back but instead could use it to establish a home for the elderly. The Council can also look forward to additional local tax revenues from the nuclear dump of 1.68 million euros. There was no local referendum but the Council was bolstered in its decision by an opinion poll (carried out by Posiva) showing that 59 per cent of the residents could accept a waste repository. The outcome may have been affected by the fact that Eurajoki is already home to two of Finland's nuclear reactors.

Advocates of the volunteer community proposal view it as being both utilitarian – finding a pragmatic solution to the current problem – and egalitarian by not imposing the solution on an unwilling community and by compensating the volunteer community and those who are disaffected by the decision.

Yet we can see how outcomes would be disputed. Arguments would rage over the government's assessment of future need. As previously noted, forecasting on the basis of predict and provide can go badly wrong. The government may fail to legislate to minimise the waste or fiscal measures may be ineffective. There would be controversy over the method of disposal proposed – in the case of domestic and commercial rather than toxic waste, the argument against incinerators is that the huge capital investment requires a throughput of material which is likely to undermine efforts to recycle waste. It is also likely that the planning authorities bidding for the site will look for communities which are used to undesirable neighbours or which already have contaminated or degraded land. This is seen as a positive benefit by those who are less concerned with spreading the burden as opposed to a utilitarian view that 'although we must regret the initial loss of land, the past cannot be undone. We should focus now on minimising the risks at existing sites and avoiding the contamination of new sites.'[20] So they argue that 'to the extent that waste needs to be moved from one place to another it should go to places that are already contaminated and unlikely ever to be thoroughly clean.'[21]

This would tend to cluster more contamination next to poor communities, which perhaps would be thought more tempted by the compensation on offer. As the British Medical Association has argued, more affluent areas can afford to forego the financial incentives to take on an undesirable waste site.[22]

The 'volunteer communities' approach would also raise questions of civil rights. Who acts on behalf of or defends at-risk groups in the decision-making process? (For example, if the proposed development exacerbated air pollution, this would not affect the healthy majority but may put at risk those already vulnerable to poor air quality through bronchial or asthmatic conditions.) Is it acceptable that those who are opposed are given the option of selling up or shutting up, as if financial compensation for the value of the house made up for the upheaval?

The volunteer communities approach is likely only ever to apply to really controversial developments. But those are precisely the schemes – the nuclear power stations, incinerators or airports – where discussion cannot be confined only to site-specific issues.

In Scotland we need a thoroughgoing national debate over what constitutes sustainable development. It may seem odd to still be calling for this more than ten years after the Earth Summit. But the reality is that economic and development strategies are little affected by rhetorical commitments. Providentially, where legislation requires or professional practice makes commonplace, there may be some efficiencies in resource and energy use. But these are often negated by expanding markets, increased propensity to travel and higher than necessary product specification. We need to have a more substantial and coherent strategic direction than currently, leading to clear aspirations embodied in a national planning policy framework. At a local planning level, there has to be explicit consideration of the likely environmental justice consequences of the plan. Cumulative impacts have to be anticipated and accounted for.

Without this, efforts at local mediation or promoting planning gain may prove fruitless if communities believe that unpopular developments are unnecessary or unfairly distributed.

Notes

1. Arup Transport Planning (2000), Edinburgh and Glasgow Airport Study – Appendices Tables 25 and 26, Wetherby: Department for Transport.
2. Duncan Pollock, 'The review of MPG6 and related issues: A QPA view', *Mineral Planning*, 81, December 1999.
3. 'Planning for the Supply of Aggregates in England: A Draft Consultation Paper', DETR, October 2000, p. 7.
4. Consultation Paper on Draft National and Regional Guidelines for Aggregates Provision in England 2001–2016, Office of the Deputy Prime Minister, July 2002.
5. Letter from Bertrand Collomb, 23 September 2002.
6. *The Herald*, 11 October 2002.
7. Ibid. 30 March 2002.
8. Beynon et al., *Digging Up Trouble: The Environment, Protest and Opencast Coal Mining*, p. 85.
9. Franzen, *The Corrections*, pp. 225–6.
10. Power, *Lost Landscapes and Failed Economies*, p. 119.
11. Ibid. p. 22.

12. Ibid.
13. *The Scotsman*, 31 January 2002.
14. Beynon et al., *Digging Up Trouble*, p. 140.
15. Ibid. p. 138.
16. Royal Commission on Environmental Pollution, *Environmental Planning*.
17. Ibid.
18. *The Scotsman*, Letters page, 14 January 2002.
19. *The Guardian*, 30 May 2002.
20. Gerrard, *Whose Backyard, Whose Risk*, p. 175.
21. Ibid. p. 174.
22. British Medical Association, *Hazardous Waste and Human Health*, p. 184.

9

Bridging the Gap

ENVIRONMENTAL JUSTICE challenges authority structures by claiming rights, requiring tougher action on pollution and demanding a greater appreciation of the circumstances of people living in polluted or degraded environments.

It is a challenge that may go down badly with some professionals in Scotland. Scientists will defend the neutrality and validity of their research. Public health officials will insist that epidemiological studies have to be insulated against the biases that concerned citizens exhibit in their own popular epidemiological research. Industry will retort that it is already well regulated – indeed too much so. Regulators will claim that it is only right that they should seek co-operation but that they do not shrink from prosecution where necessary. The judiciary would probably tell us – not that they have a mind to – that cases which have sufficient evidence will go to court. Decision-makers will say that they respond to the best scientific advice when protecting the environment and remind us that they have got to achieve a balance between competing claims on economic development, social justice and environmental protection. They will protest that their side of the story is not being adequately taken into account. But the reality is that it is nearly always their side of the story that is articulated to the point that it is the norm, and alternative interpretations represent a deviation.

The intention of highlighting grievances and deficiencies is not to offend or estrange decision-takers. Unapologetically, however, it is to say that the views of those most often affected by their decisions are not sufficiently taken into account. The consequences of the decisions themselves may not be properly appreciated, especially where there are cumulative impacts. There can be a breakdown of trust that is not just due to bloody mindedness and scientific ignorance on the part of the community, as it is often portrayed. It can be as much due to the lack of sympathy shown to people who are living in circumstances that professionals would ensure they avoided. All too often there is a willingness to side with fellow professionals in dispute with what are perceived as local troublemakers.

Where subsequently the judgement of professionals is found to be wanting, the rationalisation is that on the best available information and as far as a consensus of views existed, decisions taken were not unreasonable. Perhaps so, but there is a societal claim for environmental justice to be considered when seeking a consensus, and to be integral in the delivery of sustainable development.

The very fact that we have not sought to determine the extent to which environmental injustice is geographically manifest in Scotland should ring alarm bells. It seems likely looking at US experience and also the data held by the Environment Agency in England that those living next to the most polluting industries will be in low household-income brackets. But as we noted above, such analysis still has to be done for Scotland. But what does it tell us about our attitudes that we cannot answer the reasonable question as to whether or not some part of our communities are more or less exposed to pollution than others? Our inability to do so is the first indication that we are complacent about environmental justice concerns.

Even if it was the case that low-income populations were more often to be found next to polluting industries, does it mean that the consequences have been negative? Should we focus on the effects not the risk arising from such proximity? The official line is likely to be that, even if there is a demographic correlation between pollution and socio-economic status, any siting decision will have been scrutinised. This will have determined that there is no likelihood of health impact upon local people.

Other less than desirable consequences, such as noise, loss of habitat, traffic generation, are justified in terms of the societal and economic benefits of developments. What I have argued is that this scrutiny is partial, may exclude local concerns, and that undertakings and guarantees are inadequately monitored or enforced after permission for development has been given.

It is said, communities often rely upon an intuition that something is wrong and hold to that view no matter what scientific evidence is presented, or they carry out their own health surveys, which do not stand up to rigorous assessment.

There are of course epidemiological studies which do show a co-relation between exposure to certain sources of pollution and adverse health outcomes in the surrounding community, for instance the studies of landfill sites published in 2001 showing lower birth weights and increased levels of birth defects in babies born to families living within two kilometres of landfill sites. These findings can alarm or vindicate communities living next to such facilities, who have long felt that they have been unfairly exposed to risks and have suffered the consequences. However, Professor Paul Elliott, who led the study, said: 'we know of no causal mechanism that might explain our findings, and there is considerable uncertainty as to the extent of any possible exposure to chemicals found in landfills. We need to know an awful lot more about what goes in and what comes out of landfill sites and what gets into people.'[1]

Yet on a site-by-site basis when professional research is carried out often no local co-relation is discovered. You would expect the communities around the Paterson's landfill to be reassured as much as the mothers of children living next to the chromium dumps in Rutherglen that public health officials can find nothing to suggest that they have been affected by living next to pollution. As discussed above, however, what few studies are conducted in Scotland often come too late, are not fully published and may not have addressed community concerns or engaged with them beforehand. The statistical power of them is such that they may not be able to detect instances of ill-effects.

The US academic Christopher Foreman in his book *The Promise and Peril of Environmental Justice* believes that public authorities are at a disadvantage. In the face of complexity, uncertainty and limited resources, their response is often marked by hesitancy, half-measures and the requirements of further study, all of which may seem evasive and inadequate to desperate, fearful citizens.[2] Nevertheless, he believes that the failure to accept the conclusions of research demonstrates that environmental justice activists, or troublemakers, are hell bent on securing an outcome which is more to do with a political challenge to authority, rather than a rational consideration of all the available facts.

This assumes that all the available facts encompass issues raised by communities and not just the research preferences of the scientists, and that decisions are taken rationally, excluding the values, judgements and biases of the decision-makers. As others have pointed out, when authorities insist that disputes should be resolved through the application of 'opaque analyses that effectively transfer power to the minute technical elite who perform them' then public interest advocates 'may resist formal analysis, feeling that avoiding disenfranchisement is more important than determining acceptable levels of risk'.[3] There can be a lack of trust as to the purpose, scope and capacity of some research.

As Beck states, 'The discourse of risk begins where trust in our security and belief in progress end. It ceases to apply when the potential catastrophe actually occurs.'[4] It is the perception of threatening risks which determines thought and action. In recent times, the breakdown of trust appears to have accelerated and this has been linked to the uncertainty and indeterminacy arising from globalisation, where recognisable structures of regulation are absent.[5]

Citizens should not have to bring out their dead before they can persuade those in authority that there is something to be concerned about. The insistence that we address only the effects not the risks is useless when the pollutants we are dealing with may have subtle, cumulative and long-lasting impacts, rather than gross and immediate responses. As scientist and cancer survivor Sandra Steingraber has said, 'When carcinogens are deliberately or accidentally introduced into the environment, some number of vulnerable persons are consigned to death. The impossibility of tabulating an exact body count does not alter this fact.'[6] Who knows how many cancers are caused by environmental exposure? A former US governmental health adviser put it as high as between 10 and 20 per cent of cancers; eminent British scientists suggest it is no more than 1–5 per cent.[7] Even at 2 per cent, then, it is said, over 10,000 people in the USA would die annually as a result.[8]

We can identify people in our community who have succumbed to cancer but we cannot attribute it to specific local exposures. Even where we establish that in some circumstances populations close to sites of toxicity have elevated levels of cancer, we cannot be sure there is cause and effect. Epidemiological studies are not designed to identify such individual tragedies from a multiple of exposures.

It is for precautionary reasons that we establish pollution levels. Consequently in many instances communities are demanding that existing safeguards and threshold levels be applied and want authorities to uphold their rights. If under EC directive or national laws a limit on exposure has been set, then it is not up to the community to go back to first principles and demonstrate the level of harm. The grievance in Scotland is that all too often the regulator is unable or unwilling to enforce limits and that the courts are uninterested in punishing polluters.

But the notion of justice goes beyond the punishment of polluters and the application of statutory regulation, to encompass concepts of fairness and decency. As we have noted before, it is perfectly possible that pollution is emitted legally and at levels for which there is no proven cause and effect between the discharge and any impact upon the local population. However, we need to consider the combination of degrading impacts upon quality of life. This should include other polluting activities, but also the condition of housing, the availability of employment, the incidence of poor health, such as asthma, bronchial conditions and others, which may be exacerbated by environmental conditions. In circumstances of poor social and health circumstances, there may be a real deleterious effect of living next to an industry, which through episodes of poor management performance or regulation, represents a recurring public nuisance and undermines mental well-being.

On quality of life issues even those who are sceptical of environmental justice may agree that something should be done. However, they will add the caveat that we should be concerning ourselves with those issues that have the greatest consequences. In Scotland it seems everything is eclipsed by the need to tackle ill-health arising from smoking and poor diet. I do not accept that this is a zero sum game, where every minute or every pound that is spent on tacking environmental justice concerns is subtracted from the effort and the resources put into other environmental and societal issues that may affect those same communities. Nor do I believe that communities forfeit their right to insist upon being protected from risks imposed on them by others because of any perceived deficiencies in their own lifestyle.

Foreman is particularly scathing of the environmental justice movement's inability to draw any boundaries around its list of concerns and then to prioritise among them. We exhibit a 'chronic and institutionally rooted inability to define and pursue a coherent set of environmental policy priorities'.[9] To his mind, therefore, environmental justice is no more than a bumper sticker attachable to all community claims for redress. He is disdainful of campaigns that he regards as being characterised by people's perceptions of the situation, instead of an orderly rational discussion based on the 'true facts' as revealed by professional and academic examination. Consequently, there is an appropriation of scarce resources, he suggests, as politicians succumb to outrageous demands bolstered by media hysteria.

It is a strain of thinking that is often articulated by those who are confronted with demands by local activists. The subtext is 'Why don't you make your case on our terms?' – where the authorities feel strongest and communities are at a disadvantage. Campaigns can be troublesome, adversarial and embarrassing for the authorities. They take place in pursuit of changes which some vested interests wish to oppose, or which authorities do not wish to accommodate. The fact that it is a concern not shared by the authorities does not mean the campaign is groundless. The lack of shared concern is often the reason for the campaign in the first place.

Opponents of activism invest belief in a wished-for land of compassionate consideration, knowledge of all available scientific facts, and the allocation of financial resources on the basis of urgency and fairness. These are all desirable outcomes but in the meantime we are operating within a system that is skewed against those concerned about local environmental issues. As we have seen already, there is still a de facto presumption in favour of the legal polluter. The knowledge of the impact upon the local community may be entirely absent because it has not been studied or even contemplated. Often resources are not available or are not applied on the basis of need but on the basis of past patterns of spending or political preferences. Where information is available it may be withheld as commercially confidential or simply because those in authority fear it may strengthen contrary views.

Allowing that rational decision-taking processes may still lead to strongly held differences of opinion and dispute, then the availability to all of mediation, independent adjudication and ultimately legal redress needs to be secure. But, as we have discussed already, this is not the case. Communities have no right to appeal decisions by planning authorities, they lack the resources and expertise to compete in the quasi-judicial public inquiries and the courts are either too expensive or the right to prosecute is withheld.

There is a palpable sullenness where communities feel that they have been neglected or unjustifiably imposed upon. Often they feel that they can secure redress or response only through effective campaigning. If we want to secure a better way of doing things than at present, it is no good insisting that

Protest – 'campaigns can be troublesome, adversarial and embarrassing for the authorities.'
Norman Armstrong

community activists should simply become more reasonable. It requires a change in attitude of those who are in authority and the ability for them to begin to see things through the eyes of those who believe they are facing environmental injustice. To that extent it is entirely correct to say that the environmental justice movement is characterised by 'a desire for transformed power relationships to be achieved on behalf of politically energised and engaged communities'.[10] This is somehow seen as a hidden agenda, whereby communities, which may only be interested in achieving compensation or removal of a nuisance, are being used as a battering ram for a wider political objective. Alternatively, it is portrayed as the manifest agenda of a loose coalition of otherwise disparate interests, the charge being that they have no inclination to sift through their grievances and establish what is valid and what is not, or what is a priority and what is of lesser consequence.

Environmental justice it is said, dismissively, is borne out of an 'eternal yearning for a more democratic and egalitarian society comprised of livable communities'.[11] Maybe in the US context such a language serves to be both scornful and revealing. Perhaps egalitarian is meant to signify an extreme agenda but has less baggage in Scotland, where it suggests an equitable, or fair, society. Here, it still represents a mainstream political and social goal. Indeed if we displace the mocking 'eternal yearning' and replace it with 'legitimate aspiration' or 'common societal goal' then such suggestions as to the roots of the environmental justice movement here in Scotland would be perfectly acceptable.

Those who reject environmental justice concerns, especially over recent controversies on GM crops, toxic-waste dumps or radioactive emissions, depict a fair and reasonable, politically neutral, expert authority structure. In their view, far from exercising power, it has in many instances surrendered its leadership responsibilities to appease a politicised, uncompromising activist movement with an ideological bent. This is not how many others see it. The alternative perception is of a process that can be authoritarian not authoritative, irritable rather than inquisitive when external influences intrude and dominated by elites that have created the systems which they claim to be neutral in applying.

Approaches such as cost–benefit analysis, revealed and expressed preferences, and so on are expected to establish a consensus based on the 'political ideological assumption that society is sufficiently cohesive and common goaled that problems can be resolved by reason and without confrontation'.[12] This is a mistaken assumption. There is no univocal, ideologically untainted statement of what is best for the individual or what is best for society, which somehow activism is disrupting. The reality is that decisions are shaped and influenced by competing norms and values.

There is still a powerful advocacy for a laissez-faire approach, which allows people to do as they wish with whatever they own. As this is based most often around property rights, it is the natural territory of those to the right of the political spectrum. It is tempered, as we have seen, by hard fought for societal checks against the potential harm to other individuals, the environment and indeed other people's private property from the activities carried on. In practice, such constraints have to be reasonable (that is, capable of being afforded and justified by science). The pursuit of an economic return from the utilisation of private property has consistently over the years fitted the commercial desire to externalise costs to the rest of society. The capacity of societal structures to constrain harmful or undesirable effects from such activities may be resisted or evaded. Traditionally the neo-liberal approach seeks to delay or prevent tougher safeguards from being implemented. 'At the state of policy implementation firms have an incentive to resist profit reduction . . . and then will exploit opportunities to weaken the impact of a regulatory regime.'[13]

Authorities, even whilst not benefiting directly from developments, may take a utilitarian view of them. They will permit activities, even where they pollute, on the basis that they maximise utility or welfare. The strong egalitarian nature of utilitarianism, which judges outcomes by their good or bad consequences for human welfare, means it is attractive to those on the left of the political spectrum. However, a utilitarian approach to policies and decision-making by authorities in Scotland can give rise to issues of social and environmental injustice. Decisions taken in the name of the people can impact adversely upon a section of the population, and may do so cumulatively. General commercial activities are often justified on the grounds of local economic benefit through job creation and localised input to the community from spending associated with the firm. This can even be enhanced where there is a direct planning gain arising from the development. This can be in the form of a community fund or infrastructural improvements associated with the development such as improved transport links. Furthermore, it may be argued that certain of these activities, whether carried out directly on behalf of a public authority or commercially pursued, produce a necessary societal benefit, for example, waste collection and disposal, waste incineration, power generation, or sewerage treatment.

As we have seen, however, some of these activities either naturally tend to cluster on poor-quality or degraded land or, because they are undesirable neighbours, are not located next to high-value sites, such as electronics manufacture or middle-class residential areas. They may compound previous polluting activities, so that generations of the same population are targeted for environmentally polluting activities.

Where people complain that they are being adversely affected, either by the utilisation of individual property rights or are perennially disadvantaged by measures which overall seek to maximise societal goods, they tend to be confronted by two options. They can be told that they have the choice to remove themselves from the problem. No one requires them to live where they do, as was suggested to the community living next to Paterson of Greenoakhills landfill site. Or they just have to put up with the development, compensated for the unattractive nature of their surroundings by lower land values and property costs and protected from harm by a robust regulatory framework. In the absence of evidence of actual harm, then, they will be told, there is no injustice.

A different approach has been adopted by writers on social justice, such as John Rawls, who seek to view things from another perspective. Not as the property holder who wishes to carry out activities as far as possible unfettered by any external interference. Nor by blind aggregation, which ignores the adverse consequences for individuals or groups as long as a greater societal benefit is achieved. A social justice approach is based, first, on a view that something is right in itself and is not merely dependent on good consequences. And, second, it starts from the premise of equality, but recognises that particular regard and special provision has to be made for not only safeguarding but also improving the lot of the poorest members of society. Under social justice the test would be 'does this set of institutions operate in such a way that the worst of the group – those who do least well out of them – could not do any better under any alternative set of arrangements?'[14]

As has been argued throughout this book, there are alternative ways of doing things, which would either improve or at least safeguard the position of the poorest in our society. But this requires us to consider the possibility of environmental injustice arising out of decisions and activities and to be prepared to contemplate the consequences of mitigating or avoiding such outcomes. This could mean stopping the proposed activity or it could mean it taking place somewhere else so as to share the burden of impacts more fairly across society. It could mean imposing conditions and constraints upon the activity, which may increase the costs associated with it. This in turn may lead to a reduction in the profit from those utilising their property. It may mean that the costs borne by us all are increased, for example for waste collection and disposal. Within a progressive society then these costs should be disproportionately borne by the better off.

In this respect it will be argued that there has been a consistent record of intervening to safeguard the environment, with associated higher costs for industry and society. Look at the forthcoming European Union directive that will bring an end to landfilling. But such interventions are often compromised. Can't dump in a landfill? Then let's build an incinerator to burn it instead. Because these improvements have not been driven or measured against their impact on environmental justice, then the solutions may be just as unfair and blind to environmental justice as the problem.

We should ask, are we aware of whether or not potentially polluting activities are equitably spread across society? Are we prepared to examine or re-examine the justification provided, where it is clear that the impacts are being borne directly, and in combination with other deleterious effects, upon a portion of society? Are we prepared to rigorously examine the efficacy of the measures that we claim will protect populations from the negative consequences of such siting? More fundamentally are we prepared to contemplate whether such activities can be justified in the first place? And finally given the advantages of wealth, education and contacts and the potential for the professional exclusion of the voices of those who may have a justified concern, will we take the necessary steps to ensure equal provision and treatment for such excluded groups?

These questions have also got to be considered in respect of our relationship with the poor outside of our own society. Peter Singer doubts whether the special provision called for by social justice extends beyond our shores (or to outsiders such as refugees within our borders). Rawls, he says, 'ignores all the hard questions about how the principles that ought to govern how wealthy societies respond to the claims of poor nations.'[15]

The ecocentric concepts of environmental space, ecological footprint or ecological debt are based around a requirement for rich nations to reduce substantially their appropriation of world resources and reduce their emissions. It is a challenge which Alfred Crosby says will need 'a flowering of ingenuity . . . or lacking that wisdom'.[16]

The core of environmental injustice set out in this book is largely about the deficiencies of the decision-making system. There is still an inadequate recognition that those who may be affected by a decision or who are expected to take a risk (however small or remote the authorities believe it to be) need to be prominently involved in the decision-taking process.

There is a chronic lack of prior information provided to communities and individuals who may be affected. What information is available is often not provided in a format that is useful or accessible but is passively held by authorities and regulatory bodies, who may regard those demanding its release as potential troublemakers.

Planning authorities determine applications in the knowledge that the developer has the potential to appeal against their decision but safe in the knowledge that communities have no such rights. Where a community is able to express its view at a public local inquiry, it finds these to be adversarial and legalistic. The costs are often outside the compass of poor communities to contemplate. If they seek to represent themselves then there is a complete absence of any infrastructure to support a community voice or information available in lay person's language.

Experts giving evidence on behalf of the authorities or the developer confront a lack of trust from communities. This often derives from first-hand or anecdotal experience of the deficiencies in reassurances issued in the past. Undertakings to avoid or mitigate the effects of potential environmental pollution either through regulatory requirements or managerial systems are also viewed sceptically. Local experience may be that such conditions are never sufficient to preclude loopholes being exploited. Inadequacies in the regulatory regime means that polluters are not held to account sufficiently.

There is an enormous frustration that the system discounts the lived experience of residents, as being ill-constructed, unscientific and partial, in favour of what is regarded as impartial, methodological and professionally robust evidence. But there can be an inverse relationship between what can be measured and what it actually tells us about the circumstances being studied. What communities look for is what has been described as trustworthiness and relevance. 'Trustworthiness is the quality of being believable as a representation of reality; the relevance refers to practical utility for learning and action.'[17] Instead, people see environmental assessments which construct a false reality designed specifically to secure permission for the development which has caused the assessment to be conducted in the first place. High-status professionals approach issues, it is said, with a tendency towards measurement, reductionism and precision. By contrast lower-status professionals tend to have greater regard to judgement, holism and fitness.[18]

It is not the purpose of this book to provide a litany of grievances, as if nothing can be done – or is being done – about them. We can do much to address the environmental justice agenda. And in recent times there is an evident willingness among some of those in the Scottish Parliament, and the Executive, to incorporate the agenda into the mainstream of political decision-making. The programme for ending the scourge of fuel poverty, the passage of the Freedom of Information Act, the publication of sustainability indicators, proposed changes to the planning inquiry system, all point to an intent to improve. There is a real opportunity now to develop a dynamic so that environmental concerns are not held at arm's length but are integral to social justice and economic development.

The agenda should encompass the following points below – some of which can be pragmatically implemented; others which require political leadership and popular pressure.

Securing Full Disclosure

The scope and manner of environmental information provision should be overhauled. SEPA and other public bodies should adopt a culture of proactive provision of environmental information through accessible, searchable, websites as well as prominent displays of summary information in the communities of our most polluting industries.

Companies should publish environmental information as part of their annual accounts. Legislating for an obligation to do so is a matter reserved to the Westminster Parliament (where legislation is being sought by groups such as Friends of the Earth, Amnesty International, World Development Movement and others). Companies should demonstrate a sense of corporate accountability by volunteering such information through an environmental and social audit of their activities.

Promoting Good Practice

Where community company relations warrant it, local agreements should be explored. The company should be asked to provide a regular supply of information, access to the site, permit independent inspection of operations, particularly following incidents of concern to the community. Efforts should be made to secure community benefit from the operation, for example through provision of local employment.

These are often called 'good neighbour agreements'. However, even those who advocate the benefit of them baulk at providing this tag to companies that may in any case prove neither to be good nor neighbourly. Sandford Lewis suggests that a more neutral term such as Community–Company Compact may be preferable, while adding that 'although these agreements are no panacea for the ills that corporations impose on local communities, they can represent significant advances in community empowerment'.[19]

Tightening Regulatory Control

There should be a review of all current polluting activities to ensure that companies are not able to walk off the site, leaving behind orphan contaminated sites. Landfills and others should all have in place a financial bond sufficient to ensure the restoration of the site at the conclusion of operations.

Even this is not enough – bonds may be difficult to access and site remediation may require specialist skills not available to the local authority. So operators of opencast mines, quarries and so on should have to pay for regular monitoring of their operations, by independent, local authority-appointed experts. (These have been termed 'compliance assessors'.)[20] Where practicable, sites should be restored as they go along.

Fair Deal in Planning

The planning system should be overhauled so that developers and communities are on a more equal footing. In particular third-party rights of appeal should be provided to communities and individuals in certain circumstances. It is reasonable to allow the public to appeal decisions where the planning authority has a direct interest in the outcome of the application (for example, due to a public–private partnership road development or waste incinerator). It should also apply where the proposed development is at variance with the development plan or is subject to a recommendation for refusal by the local authority planning officers. Any planning application that is of a scale requiring an environmental statement by the developer should also be capable of third-party right of appeal.

The adversarial, legalistic nature of the public local inquiry, which often rewards the developer who has the financial resources to outspend the opposition, should be diminished. This can be done by a greater investment on the part of reporters playing a more inquisitorial role in seeking to secure information required for their decision and to ensure that community concerns are being addressed.

However, this could be further amplified by the provision of a mediation service (such as performed by Advisory, Conciliation and Arbitration Service (ACAS) in the cases of disputes taken to employment tribunals) where key matters of contention and potential resolution are addressed in a forum facilitated by an impartial and experienced mediator.

Where issues do go to public local inquiry, provision has to be made for an advisory service that will assist communities in understanding the process and in presenting their case effectively. In Canada there is a Participants' Funding Programme, which supports public participation in review panels and mediations conducted under the Canadian Environmental Assessment Act. The funding can be used to review the Environmental Impact Statement submitted by the developer and to prepare for and participate in public hearings to consider the proposed project. Individuals as well as organisations are eligible, as long as they can demonstrate an interest in the project's potential environmental effects, which are widely drawn to include related effects on health, social, economic or cultural conditions. Applicants are expected to represent themselves at public hearings but funding may be used to pay for fees for expert advice, and the purchase of relevant information materials such as maps and technical documents.[21]

Holding Polluters to Account

We need to resolve the deficiencies in the regulatory system to hold polluters to account, recognising that far fewer cases are taken to court for pollution than for other offences. The remedies available seem to be either to increase and improve the capacity in the Procurator Fiscal (PF) service by having either specialist PFs or more PFs with compulsory training in environmental crimes.

If no improvement is charted then consideration needs to be given to removing the exclusive rights of Fiscals to decide on prosecution, and so permitting SEPA to take cases directly to court, as happens in England. SEPA should also be able to impose administrative fines (in the way that the Inland Revenue can determine liability) with the polluter able to choose to go to court. Capacity might also be expanded by having environmental courts, responsible for dealing with prosecution and public inquiries.

Assessing Alternatives

Some of these measures would be relatively simple to implement, others go against the grain. There is always a problem with introducing new concepts and ways of doing things. Commentators have remarked upon the preference of the bureaucracy to extend and adapt existing standard operating procedures, rather than undertake a wholesale readjustment of its activities when challenged by new legislation or policy approaches. But without substantial change it is not likely that environmental justice will be delivered and we can be certain that sustainable development will not. In addition to the pragmatically implementable, we need to contemplate radically different ways of doing things.

Certainly there should be a review of the planning system in Scotland. We need to be making better environmental decisions. Instead of deciding 'what' and 'where', we should be asking 'why?' and 'what instead'. The rational decision-making processes which we have introduced – cost benefit analysis, risk assessment, environmental impact assessment – have not produced the neutral information for decision-takers. They are subjective, value laden and above all influenced strongly by those who commission them. As one commentator has said, 'The most basic unstated goal of risk assessment . . . is to provide permission for undertaking some amount or form of the activity whose risks are being assessed.'[22]

Conventional development starts from the premise of presumed permission unless there is good reason – indeed proven reason – to withhold such permission. The vast majority of chemicals in use today have not been tested for impact on human health. The producers of genetically modified crops argued that they were substantially equivalent to conventional crops and should not be subject to more rigorous evaluation.

Environmental justice, indeed sustainable development, starts not from the premise of how we mitigate the harm which this activity will do, but why we need this activity in the first place. It asks whether there is another way to achieve similar outcomes without the same risks or costs to society and the environment. This is what is required by Rawls' insistence that we have to consider alternative arrangements.

There is currently scope for challenging proposed developments through the requirement of an environmental impact assessment (EIA) to consider alternatives or by invoking the precautionary principle where there is sufficient uncertainty. But the reality is that environmental statements by companies rarely fully consider alternatives and often authorities do not either. EIAs are weighty and expensive tomes (consequently difficult for the community to access) but still may not address issues which the community is concerned about.

We need a greater investment in alternatives assessment, which would approach behaviours that affect the environment (not just site-specific developments) by considering a range of reasonable alternatives, discussing the potential environmental, public health and social benefits of each and similarly the impacts of each. This would allow the introduction of issues which conventional EIAs and risk assessments ignore.[23] Furthermore, consideration should be given to those who bear the cost and those who profit from the different alternatives, and give weight to those alternatives which are more likely to be controlled and which can be sustained long into the future.[24] Assessing alternatives would give people a better say about what happens in their life.

Conclusion

This is a challenging time for the environmental movement. Pollution concerns need complex modelling and allow even more scope for claim and counter-claim. In any case, sustainable development means we should be concerned as much with the scale of consumption as with the impacts of production. The message that everyday life in the north is harmful to people in our own society and the majority in the south is a hard one. Green groups split into problemsolvers or agenda setters. Some years ago, the characteristics of a green social movement were described as 'its intimate relationship with science, its practical claims to international solidarity, and its ability to offer a critique of, and an alternative to, capitalist industrialism'.[25]

Strong southern groups are expanding the critique to encompass democracy, human rights and economic self-determination. Mutual solidarity is going to be required if the movement is to mature.[26] Northern groups cannot set an agenda and simply look for followers and case studies from the south. There should be a shared experience between those groups, north and south, who suffer exclusion and deprivation, and who are reacting to a sense of things being done to them, not for them.

In many respects southern groups have a vocalism and insistence that contrasts with the careless passivity and grumbling resignation of the north. These are failings that are all too apparent in Scotland, which is why we should not seek to silence those who are regarded as troublemakers.

The aspirations for the Scottish Parliament were not just to bring decision-making geographically north of the border, but to extend the range of voices being heard in the making of decisions.

According to Neal Ascherson, there is a dream at the heart of having a Scottish Parliament. 'The dream is to throw bridges across that historic gap, the chasm which separates those who are accustomed to be heard and those taught by centuries of uprooting that their lot is to survive change, not to plan it.'[27]

Environmental justice advocacy throws a span across that gap.

Notes

1. *The Independent*, 17 August 2001.
2. Foreman, *The Promise and Peril of Environmental Justice*, p. 39.
3. Fischhoff et al., 'Weighing the Risks: Which Risks are Acceptable?', in Slovic, *The Perception of Risk*, p. 132.
4. Beck, 'Risk Culture', in Adam et al. (eds), *The Risk Society and Beyond*, pp. 47–62.
5. See Lash, 'Risk Culture', in Adam et al. (eds), *The Risk Society and Beyond*, p. 51.
6. Steingraber, *Living Downstream*, p. 268.
7. Easterbrook, *A Moment on the Earth*, pp. 246–7.
8. Steingraber, *Living Downstream*, p. 269.
9. Foreman, *The Promise and Peril of Environmental Justice*, p. 4.
10. Ibid. p. 58.
11. Ibid. p. 4.
12. Fischhoff et al., 'Weighing the Risks: Which Risks are Acceptable?', in Slovic, *The Perception of Risk*, p. 133.
13. Weale, *The New Politics of Pollution*, p. 46.
14. Barry, quoted in Smith, *Geography and Social Justice*, p. 75.
15. Singer, *Practical Ethics*, p. 253.
16. Crosby, *Ecological Imperialism*, p. 308.
17. Chambers, *Whose Reality Counts? Putting the Last First*, p. 158.
18. Ibid. p. 35.
19. Lewis and Henkels, 'Good Neighbour Agreements: A Tool for Environmental and Social Justice', in Williams (ed.), *Environmental Victims*, pp. 138–9.
20. Chris Norman, 'Ensuring Compliance: Safeguarding the Community and the Environment when Things go Wrong'. Delivered at European Conference on Mineral Planning, 2002.
21. Canadian Environmental Assessment Agency (December 2000), Participant Funding programme – Guide for assessments by Review Panels, http://www.ceaa-acee.gc.ca.
22. O'Brien, *Making Better Environmental Decisions*, p. 6.
23. Ibid. p. 147.
24. Ibid. p. 172.

25. Yearley, 'Social Movements and Environmental Change', in Redclift and Benton (eds), *Social Theory and the Environment*, p. 167.
26. Dunion, *Living in the Real World*, p. 35.
27. Ascherson, *Stone Voices*, p. 298.

Bibliography

Adam, Barbara, Beck, Ulrich, and van Loon, Joost (eds) (2000), *The Risk Society and Beyond*, London: Sage.

Alinsky, Saul (1972), *Rules for Radicals*, New York: Bantam Press.

Allen, Robert, and Jones, Tara (1990), *Guests of the Nation: The People of Ireland versus the Multinationals*, London: Earthscan.

Anderson, Victor (1991), *Alternative Economic Indicators*, London: Routledge.

Andrews, M. Frank, and Withey, B. Steven (1976), *Social Indicators of Wellbeing*, New York: Plenum Press.

Ascherson, Neal (2002), *Stone Voices: The Search for Scotland*, London: Granta.

Athanasiou, Tom (1997), *Slow Reckoning: The Ecology of a Divided Planet*, London: Secker and Warburg.

Baarsachers, J. William (1996), *Eco Facts and Eco-fiction: Understanding the Environmental Debate*, London: Routledge.

Balchin, N. Paul (1990), *Regional Policy in Britain*, London: Paul Chapman Publishing.

Beck, Ulrich (1992) *Risk Society*, London: Sage.

Beck, Ulrich (2000), *What is Globalization?*, Cambridge: Polity.

Bell, Simon, and Morse, Steven (1999), *Sustainability Indicators*, London: Earthscan.

Beynon, Huw, Cox, Andrew, and Hudson, Ray (2000), *Digging Up Trouble: The Environment, Protest and Opencast Coal Mining*, London: Rivers Oram Press.

Black, Jeremy (2000), *Modern British History*, London: Macmillan.

Blake, George (1934), *The Heart of Scotland*, London: B. T. Batsford.

Boardman, Brenda, Bullock, Simon, and McLaren, Duncan (1999), *Equity and Environment*, London: Catalyst/Friends of the Earth.

British Medical Association (1991), *Hazardous Waste and Human Health*, Oxford: Oxford University Press

Brown, Gordon, and Cook, Robin (eds) (1983), *Scotland: The Real Divide*, Edinburgh: Mainstream.

Bibliography

Bullard, Robert (1995), 'Residential Segregation and Urban Quality of Life', in B. Bryant (ed.), *Environmental Justice*, Washington, DC: Island Press.

Butler, Mark, and Hallowes, David (2002), *Corporate Accountability in South Africa*, Pietermaritzburg: Groundwork.

Bryant, Bunyan (ed.) (1995), *Environmental Justice*, Washington, DC: Island Press.

Byrne, John, Glover, Leigh, and Martinez, Cecilia (eds) (2002), *Environmental Justice: Discourses in International Political Economy*, New Brunswick: Transaction Publishers.

Cahill, Michael, and Fitzpatrick, Tony (eds) (2002), *Environmental Issues and Social Welfare*, London: Blackwell.

Campbell, Angus, Converse, Philip E., Rodgers, Willard L. (1976), *The Quality of American Life*, New York: Russell Sage Foundation.

Carley, Michael, and Spapens, Philippe (1998), *Sharing the World*, London: Earthscan.

Cauldwell, Lynton (1990), *Between Two Worlds: Science, the Environmental Movement and Policy Choice*, Cambridge: Cambridge University Press.

Cave, Susan (1998), *Applying Psychology to the Environment*, London: Hodder and Stoughton.

Centre for Science and Environment (1982), *The State of India's Environment*, New Delhi: Centre for Science and Environment.

Chambers, Nicky, Simmons, Craig, and Wackernagel, Mathis (2000), *Sharing Nature's Interest*, London: Earthscan.

Chambers, Robert (1997), *Whose Reality Counts? Putting the Last First*, London: ITDG Publishing.

Clapp, B. W. (1994), *An Environmental History of Britain*, London: Longman.

Clapperton, Chalmers, M. (1983), *Scotland: A New Study*, Newton Abbot: David and Charles.

Colpi, Terri (1991), *The Italian Factor: The Italian Community in Scotland*, Edinburgh: Mainstream.

Commission on Social Justice (1994), *Social Justice: Strategies for National Renewal*, London: Vintage.

Cooper, David, E. and Palmer, Joy A. (eds) (1992), *The Environment in Question*, London: Routledge.

Cramb, Auslan (1998), *Fragile Land: Scotland's Environment*, Edinburgh: Polygon.

Crosby, Alfred W. (1986), *Ecological Imperialism: The Biological Expansion of Europe, 900–1900*, Cambridge: Cambridge University Press.

Daly, Herman E., and Cobb, John B. (1990), *For the Common Good*, London: Green Print.

Darling, F. Fraser, and Boyd, J. Morton (1969), *The Highlands and Islands*, London: Collins.

Davidson, Eric A. (2000), *You can't eat GNP*, Cambridge, MA: Perseus.

Dean, Hartley (2002), 'Green Citizenship', in M. Cahill and T. Fitzpatrick (eds), *Environmental Issues and Social Welfare*, London: Blackwell, pp. 22–37.

Deegan, Denise (2001), *Managing Activism*, London: Kogan Page.

Devine, T. M. (1999), *The Scottish Nation, 1700–2000*, London: Allen Lane.

Dunion, K. (1995), *Living in the Real World: The International Role for Scotland's Parliament*, Edinburgh: SEAD.

Dunion, K. (1999), 'Sustainable Development in a Small Country: The Global and European Agenda', in E. McDowell and J. McCormick (eds), *Environment Scotland: Prospects for Sustainability*, Aldershot: Ashgate.

Dunion, K. (2000), 'On the Scottish Road to Sustainability?', in A. Wright (ed.), *The Scottish Parliament: The Challenge of Devolution*, Aldershot: Ashgate.

Dunion, K. and Scandrett, E. (2003), 'The Campaign for Environmental Justice in Scotland as a Response to Poverty in a Northern Nation', in Julian Agyeman, Robert D. Bullard and Bob Evans (eds), *Just Sustainabilities*, London: Earthscan/ MIT Press.

Dunion, K., Holbrook, J., and Sargent, B. (2002), 'The Role of Indicators in Reporting on the State of Scotland and its Environment', in M. B. Usher, E. C. Mackey, and J. C. Curran (eds), *The State of Scotland's Environment and Natural Heritage*, London: The Stationery Office.

Durning, Alan (1992), *How Much is Enough?*, London: Earthscan.

Easterbrook, Gregg (1995), *A Moment on the Earth*, London: Penguin.

Edelstein, Michael, R. (2002), 'Contamination: The Invisible Built Environment', in R. Bechtel and A. Churchman (eds), *Handbook of Environmental Psychology*, New York: John Wiley and Sons, pp. 559–88.

Faber, Daniel (1998), *The Struggle for Ecological Democracy*, New York: Guilford Press.

Faber, Daniel, and Krieg, Eric, J. (2001), 'Unequal Exposure to Ecological Hazards: Environmental Injustices in the Commonwealth and Massachusetts', Report by the Philanthropy and Environmental Justice Research Project, North Eastern University.

Fagin, Dan, and Lavelle, Marian (1996), *Toxic Deception*, Secaucus, NJ: Birchland Press.

Farber, Daniel, A. (1999), *Eco-pragmatism*, Chicago: The University of Chicago Press.

Ferris, Deeohn, and Hahn-Baker, David (1995), 'Environmentalists and

Bibliography

Environmental Justice Policy', in B. Bryant (ed.), *Environmental Justice*, Washington, DC: Island Press.

Foreman, Christopher, H. (1998), *The Promise and Peril of Environmental Justice*, Washington, DC: Brookings Institution Press.

Franzen, Jonathan (2001), *The Corrections*, London: QPD.

Friends of the Earth Scotland (undated), *Opencast Mining in Scotland: The Hole Story*, Edinburgh: Friends of the Earth Scotland.

Friends of the Earth Scotland (1996), *Towards a Sustainable Scotland*, Edinburgh: Friends of the Earth Scotland.

Friends of the Earth Scotland (2001), *The One That Got Away: Marine Salmon Farming in Scotland*, Edinburgh: Friends of the Earth Scotland.

Gadgil, Madhav, and Guha, Ramachandra (1993), *This Fissured Land: An Ecological History of India*, Delhi: Oxford University Press.

Gerrard, Michael, B. (1995), *Whose Backyard, Whose Risk: Fear and Fairness in Toxic Nuclear Waste Siting*, London: MIT Press.

Gibbs, Marie Louise (1995), *Dying from Dioxin*, Boston: South End Press.

Glendinning, Miles (ed.) (1997), *Rebuilding Scotland: The Postwar Vision 1945–1975*, East Linton: Tuckwell Press.

Glendinning, Miles, and Page, David (1999), *Clone City: Crisis and Renewal in Contemporary Scottish Architecture*, Edinburgh: Polygon.

Glover, Leigh (2002), 'globalization.com vs. ecologicaljustice.org: Contesting the End of History', in J. Byrne, L. Glover and C. Martinez (eds), *Environmental Justice Discourses in International Political Economy*, New Brunswick: Transaction Publishers, pp. 231–60.

Gottlieb, Robert (2001), *Environmentalism Unbound*, London: MIT Press.

Green Balance, Leigh Day and Co. Solicitors, John Popham and Prof. Michael Purdue (2002), *Third Party Rights of Appeal*, London: CPRE.

Greider, William (1993), *Who Will Tell the People*, New York: Pocket Books.

Hawken, Paul (1993), *The Ecology of Commerce*, London: Weidenfeld and Nicolson.

Hertz, Noreena (2002), *The Silent Takeover: Global Capitalism and the Death of Democracy*, London: Arrow.

Hofrichter, Richard (ed.) (2000), *Reclaiming the Environmental Debate: The Politics of Health in a Toxic Culture*, Cambridge, MA: MIT Press.

Holmes, George, and Crofts, Roger (eds) (2000), *Scotland's Environment: The Future*, East Linton: Tuckwell Press.

Huber, Peter (1999), *Hard Green: Saving the Environment from Environmentalists*, New York: Basic Books.

Huxham, Mark (2000), 'Science and the Search for Truth', in Huxham and Sumner, *Science and Environmental Decision Making*, Harlow: Prentice Hall, pp. 1–32.

Bibliography

Huxham, Mark, and Sumner, David (2000), *Science and Environmental Decision Making*, Harlow: Prentice Hall.

Irwin, Alan (1995), *Citizen Science*, London: Routledge.

Jackson, Tim (1996), *Material Concerns*, London: Routledge.

Jacobs, Michael (1991), *The Green Economy*, London: Pluto Press.

Johnson, Samuel (1978) [1775], *A Journey to the Western Islands of Scotland*, Oxford: Oxford University Press.

Johnston, Ronald, and McIvor, Arthur (2000), *Lethal Work: A History of the Asbestos Tragedy in Scotland*, East Linton: Tuckwell Press.

Keay, John, and Keay, Julia (eds) (1994), *Collins Encyclopaedia of Scotland*, London: HarperCollins.

Klein, Naomi (2001), *No Logo*, London: Flamingo.

Korten, David, C. (1996), *When Corporations Rule the World*, West Hartford, CT: Kumarian Press.

Lash, Scott (2000), 'Risk Culture', in B. Adam, U. Beck and J. van Loon (eds), *The Risk Society and Beyond*, London: Sage, pp. 47–62.

Lewis, Sandford, and Henkels, Diane (1998), 'Good Neighbour Agreements: A Tool for Environmental and Social Justice', in Williams Christopher (ed.), *Environmental Victims*, London: Earthscan, pp. 125–41.

Lomborg, Bjorn (2001), *The Skeptikal Environmentalist*, Cambridge: Cambridge University Press.

MacEwen, Malcolm (1991), *The Greening of a Red*, London: Pluto Press.

McDowell, Eleanor, and McCormick, James (eds) (1999), *Environment Scotland: Prospects for Sustainability*, Aldershot: Ashgate.

McGrahahan, Gordon, Jacobi, Pedro, Songsore, Jacob, Surjadi, Charles, and Kjellen, Marianne (2001), *The Citizen at Risk: From Urban Sanitation to Sustainable Cities*, London: Earthscan.

McIntosh, Alastair (2002), *Soil and Soul*, London: Aurum Press.

Markham, Adam (1994), *A Brief History of Pollution*, London: Earthscan.

Marris, Claire, Wynne, Brian, Simmons, Peter, and Weldon, Sue (2002), *Public Perceptions of Agricultural Biotechnologies in Europe*. http//www.pabe.net

Matthews, Philip (1994), *Watered Down*, Edinburgh: Friends of the Earth Scotland.

Mazur, Allan (1998), *A Hazardous Inquiry: The Rashomon Effect at Love Canal*, Cambridge, MA: Harvard University Press.

Midwinter, Arthur, Keating, Michael, and Mitchell, James (1991), *Politics and Public Policy in Scotland*, London: Macmillan.

Muir, John (1987), *The Story of My Boyhood and Youth*, Edinburgh: Canongate.

North, Richard, D. (1995), *Life on a Modern Planet*, Manchester: Manchester University Press.

Bibliography

O'Brien, Mary (2000), *Making Better Environmental Decisions*, Cambridge, MA: MIT Press.

Office of National Statistics (2002), *Health Statistics Quarterly*, 13, London: The Stationery Office, p. 85.

Ohmae, Kenichi (1995), *The End of the Nation State*, New York: Free Press Paperbacks.

O'Neill, Kate (2000), *Waste Trading Amongst Rich Nations*, Cambridge MA: MIT Press.

Organisation for Economic Co-operation and Development (OECD) (2002), *Indicators to Measure Decoupling of Environmental Pressures from Economic Growth*, Paris: OECD.

Paehlke Robert C. (1991), *Environmentalism and the Future of Progressive Politics*, New Haven, CT: Yale University Press.

Paterson, Anna (2002), *Scotland's Landscape: Endangered Icon*, Edinburgh: Polygon.

Peat, Jeremy, and Boyle, Stephen (1999), *An Illustrated Guide to the Scottish Economy*, London: Duckworth.

Ponting, Clive (1991), *A Green History of the World*, London: Penguin.

Porritt, Jonathon (2000), *Playing Safe: Science and the Environment*, London: Thames and Hudson.

Power, Thomas Michael (1996), *Lost Landscapes and Failed Economies*, Washington, DC: Island Press.

Prugh, Thomas, Costanza, Robert, and Daly, Herman (2000), *The Local Politics of Global Sustainability*, Washington DC: Island Press.

Rathje, William, and Murphy, Cullen (2001), *Rubbish: The Archaeology of Garbage*, Tucson, AZ: The University of Arizona Press.

Rawls, John (1999), *A Theory of Justice*, Oxford: Oxford University Press.

Redclift, Michael, and Benton, Ted (eds) (1994), *Social Theory and the Environment*, London: Routledge

Reid, Colin (ed.) (1992), *Green's Guide to Environmental Law in Scotland*, Edinburgh: W. Green/Sweet and Maxwell.

Rosie, George (1982), 'The Cromarty Firth: The Tale of Multinational Business in Scotland', in Stephen Maxwell (ed.), *Scotland, Multinationals and the Third World*, Edinburgh: Mainstream.

Rowan-Robinson, Jeremy, Watchman, Paul, and Barker, Christine (1990), *Crime and Regulation: A Study of the Enforcement of Regulatory Codes*, Edinburgh: T. and T. Clark.

Royal Commission on Environmental Pollution (2002), *Environmental Planning* (twenty-third report, Cm 5459), London: The Stationery Office.

Russell, Michael (1998), *In Waiting*, Glasgow: Neil Wilson Publishing.

Sachs, Wolfgang (1999), *Planet Dialectics*, London: Zed Books.

Sachs, Wolfgang (ed.) (2002), *The Jo'burg Memo: Fairness in a Fragile World*, Berlin: Heinrich Böll Foundation.

Sachs, Wolfgang, Losske, Reinhard, Linz, Manfred (1998), *Greening the North*, London: Zed Books.

Scott, Alan (2000), 'Risk Society or Angst Society?', in Adam et al. (eds), *The Risk Society and Beyond*, London: Sage, pp. 34–43.

Scottish Executive (2001), *A Smart, Successful Scotland*, Edinburgh: The Scottish Executive.

Scottish Executive (2002), *Meeting the Needs*, Paper 2002/14, Edinburgh: The Scottish Executive.

Setterberg, Fred, and Shavelson, Lonny (1993), *Toxic Nation*, New York: John Wiley and Sons.

Shipman, Alan (2002), *The Globalization Myth*, Cambridge: Icon.

Singer, Peter (1993), *Practical Ethics*, Cambridge: Cambridge University Press.

Slesser, Malcolm, King, Jane, and Crane, David C. (1997), *The Management of Greed*, Dunblane: Resource Use Institute.

Slovic, Paul (2000), *The Perception of Risk*, London: Earthscan.

Smith, David (1994), *North and South*, London: Penguin.

Smith, David, M. (1973), *The Geography of Social Wellbeing in the United States*, New York: McGraw-Hill.

Smith, David, M. (1994), *Geography and Social Justice*, Oxford: Blackwell.

Smith, Joe (ed.) (2000), *The Daily Globe*, London: Earthscan.

Smout, T. C. (1987), *A Century of the Scottish People, 1830–1950*, London: Fontana.

Smout, T. C. (2000), *Nature Contested*, Edinburgh: Edinburgh University Press.

Stauber, John, and Rampton, Sheldon (1995), *Toxic Sludge is Good For You!*, Maine, CT: Common Courage Press.

Steingraber, Sandra (1997), *Living Downstream*, Reading, MA: Addison-Wesley.

Stiefel, Matthias, and Wolfe, Marshall (1994), *A Voice for the Excluded: Popular Participation in Development*, London: Zed Books.

Stiglitz, Joseph (2002), *Globalization and its Discontents*, London: Allen Lane.

Stone, Lawrence (1972), *The Causes of the English Revolution*, London: Routledge and Kegan Paul.

Stout, Linda (1996), *Bridging the Class Divide*, Boston: Beacon Press.

Szasz, Andrew (1995), *Ecopopulism*, Minneapolis, MN: University of Minnesota Press.

Tucker, Pamela (1995), *Report of the Expert Panel on the Psychological Responses to Hazardous Substances*. Agency for Toxic Substances and Disease Registry, USA.

Bibliography

United Nations Environment Programme (2002), *Global Environmental Outlook 3*, London: Earthscan.

Warner, Alan (2002), *The Man Who Walks*, London: Jonathan Cape.

Warren, Charles (2002), *Managing Scotland's Environment*, Edinburgh: Edinburgh University Press.

Weale, Albert (1992), *The New Politics of Pollution*, Manchester: Manchester University Press.

Weizsacker, Ernst von, Lovins, Amory B., and Lovins, L. Hunter (1997), *Factor Four*, London: Earthscan.

Welford, Richard (1997), *Hijacking Environmentalism*, London: Earthscan.

Williams, Christopher (ed.) (1998), *Environmental Victims*, London: Earthscan.

Wilson, Des (1986), *Citizen Action*, Harlow: Longman.

Woods, Emma (2002), *The Hydro Boys*, Edinburgh: Luath Press.

Wright, A. (1995), 'Environmental Equity Justice Centres', in B. Bryant (ed.), *Environmental Justice*, Washington, DC: Island Press.

Yearley, Steven (1994) 'Social Movements and Environmental Change', in Redclift and Benton (eds), *Social Theory and the Environment*, London: Routledge, pp. 150–68.

Zadek, Simon (2001), *The Civil Corporation*, London: Earthscan.

Index

Index

Index

Index

Index

social justice, 11
Steingraber, Sandra, 215
Stiglitz, Joseph, 166, 167
Stone, Lawrence, 31
Straid Farm landfill, 78
sustainable development, indicators, 176–81

Tetra Pak, 68
third party rights of appeal, 202–5
Tillietudlem, 2
Timberlands West Coast Ltd, 58
toxic waste, volunteer communities, 206–8
Transorganics, 94
transport policy inequity, 22
tree-huggers, 12, 13, 14
Trewavas, Anthony, 69
troublemakers, 12
Turner and Newall, 108, 158
Tyrone Waste Recycling Company, 79

UK, north–south divide, 151, 152
UN Commission on Sustainable Development, 165, 177

UNEP GEO 3 report, 183
Uruguay Agreement, 165
US Toxic Release Inventory, 144, 226

VisitScotland, 181

Warren County, North Carolina, 30–1
Warner, Alan, 76
waste recycling, 43
Welsh, Irvine, 16
Westfield, Fife, 6
William Forest and Sons (Paisley) Ltd, 101
Wilson, Des, 61
World Summit, Johannesburg, 161, 164, 167, 172
World Trade Organisation, 165, 166
WWF, 13, 21

Young, George, 4
Young's helleborine, 4

Zeneca, 5, 96